thai

WITHDRAWN

SCHAUMBURG TOWNSHIP DISTRICT LIBRARY
3 1257 01538 4497

Schaumburg Township District Library
130 South Roselle Road
Schaumburg, Illinois 60193

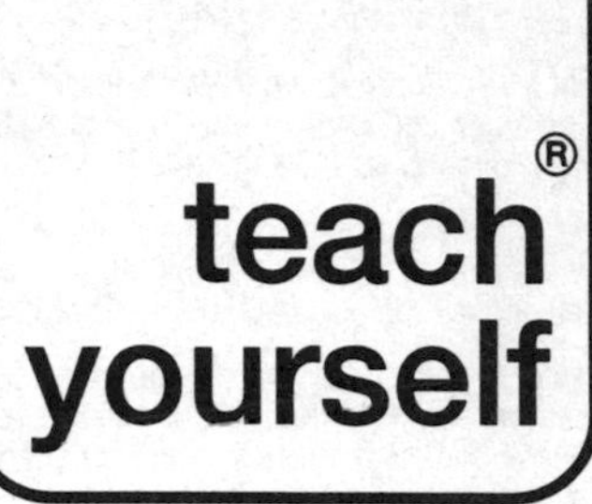

thai

david smyth

For over 60 years, more than 40 million people have learnt over 750 subjects the **teach yourself** way, with impressive results.

be where you want to be with **teach yourself**

SCHAUMBURG TOWNSHIP DISTRICT LIBRARY
130 SOUTH ROSELLE ROAD
SCHAUMBURG, ILLINOIS 60193

495.41 SMYTH, D
3 1257 01538 4497

For UK order enquiries: please contact Bookpoint Ltd., 130 Milton Park, Abingdon, Oxon OX14 4SB. Telephone: +44 (0) 1235 827720. Fax: +44 (0) 1235 400454. Lines are open 09.00–18.00, Monday to Saturday, with a 24-hour message answering service. You can also order through our website www.madaboutbooks.com.

For USA order enquiries: please contact McGraw-Hill Customer Services, PO Box 545, Blacklick, OH 43004-0545, USA. Telephone: 1-800-722-4726. Fax: 1-614-755-5645.

For Canada order enquiries: please contact McGraw-Hill Ryerson Ltd., 300 Water St, Whitby, Ontario L1N 9B6, Canada. Telephone: 905 430 5000. Fax: 905 430 5020.

Long renowned as the authoritative source for self-guided learning – with more than 30 million copies sold worldwide – the *Teach Yourself* series includes over 300 titles in the fields of languages, crafts, hobbies, business, computing and education.

British Library Cataloguing in Publication Data: a catalogue record for this title is available from The British Library

Library of Congress Catalog Card Number: On file

First published in UK 1995 by Hodder Headline Ltd., 338 Euston Road, London, NW1 3BH.

First published in US 1996 by Contemporary Books, a Division of The McGraw-Hill Companies, 1 Prudential Plaza, 130 East Randolph Street, Chicago, IL 60601 USA.

This edition published 2003.

The 'Teach Yourself' name is a registered trade mark of Hodder & Stoughton Ltd.

Copyright © 1995, 2003 David Smyth

In UK: All rights reserved. No part of this publication may be reproduced or transmitted in any form or by any means, electronic or mechanical, including photocopy, recording, or any information storage and retrieval system, without permission in writing from the publisher or under licence from the Copyright Licensing Agency Limited. Further details of such licences (for reprographic reproduction) may be obtained from the Copyright Licensing Agency Limited, of 90 Tottenham Court Road, London W1T 4LP.

In US: All rights reserved. Except as permitted under the United States Copyright Act of 1976, no part of this publication may be reproduced or distributed in any form or by any means, or stored in a database or retrieval system, without the prior written permission of Contemporary Books.

Typeset by Graphicraft Limited, Hong Kong

Printed in Great Britain for Hodder & Stoughton Educational, a division of Hodder Headline Ltd., 338 Euston Road, London NW1 3BH by Cox & Wyman Ltd., Reading, Berkshire.

Impression number 10 9 8 7 6 5 4 3 2 1
Year 2007 2006 2005 2004 2003

contents

About Thai

Thai is the national language of Thailand and is spoken by approximately 60 million people in that country. Lao, spoken in neighbouring Laos, is very closely related to Thai (although most Thais from Bangkok would have some difficulty understanding it), but the other neighbouring languages – Burmese, Cambodian and Malay – are completely different. Distinct dialects of Thai are spoken in the north, northeast and south of the country, but it is the language of the Central Region and Bangkok which is used throughout the country as the medium for education and mass media and which is taught in this course.

Thai is a *tonal* language. In tonal languages the meaning of a syllable is determined by the pitch at which it is pronounced. **kao**, for example, means 'news' when pronounced with a *low* tone, 'white' with a *rising* tone and 'rice' with a *falling* tone. If tones make pronunciation in Thai seem more complex than in more familiar European languages, the learner will probably find Thai grammar considerably easier to absorb, for there are no complex verb tenses and noun endings which seem to dominate many people's experience of trying to learn a foreign language.

Thai is written in its own unique alphabetic script which has developed from a script originally found in India. It is written across the page from left to right, with certain vowels appearing above the line of writing and others appearing below. There are no spaces between words; when spaces do occur, they act as a form of punctuation mark, similar to commas and full stops.

About the book

This book is intended for the complete beginner. It aims to equip the learner with the necessary vocabulary and grammar to cope with the day-to-day situations a foreigner is likely to encounter in Thailand. A further important aim of the course is to provide a solid introduction to the Thai writing system so that the learner will have the means to extend his or her knowledge of the language beyond this course.

Each unit is built around dialogues, followed by a brief cultural background note which draws out aspects of the linguistic or social context of the dialogues. Key phrases and expressions are highlighted, while the full vocabulary lists and explanatory language notes should enable you to understand conversations without too much difficulty. A variety of practice exercises help to reinforce the material covered in the dialogues and the key at the end of the book allows you to keep a close check that you are on the right track. A considerable part of each unit is devoted to reading and writing Thai. The script is presented in manageable chunks and tested in reading exercises.

Most of the material in each unit is reproduced in recorded form to accompany this book. You are strongly advised to purchase this to gain a clear idea of how Thai should sound.

How to use the book

Each individual will have their own preferred way of working through the course. If you have the recorded material, you might like to start each unit by listening to the dialogue a number of times with your book closed, simply to get your ear attuned to the language. Alternatively, you may prefer to work out what the dialogue means before you consider listening to it. It does not really matter what approach you adopt as long as you are happy with it and you are prepared to follow it regularly. Whatever approach you adopt, however, you are ultimately faced with the task of memorizing and accurately reproducing unfamiliar combinations of sounds. It is best to memorize words in meaningful phrases rather than in isolation and your pronunciation and intonation will obviously be greatly aided if you have the recording to use as a model. Frequent review of earlier lessons and exercises is essential if the language in them is to become almost second nature.

People learning a language which is written in an unfamiliar script may often say: 'Oh, I only want to learn to speak it, I'm not bothered about writing.' They usually imagine that learning a new script will be extremely difficult and time consuming and that they will be able to steam ahead much more quickly if they concentrate merely on the spoken language. You can, if you choose, work through this book in that fashion, simply ignoring the sections on script. But if you do, you won't be getting your money's worth from the course and you'll be adopting a short-sighted and self-limiting view. Just think how ridiculous you would think it was if a Thai told you he was studying English conversation from this dialogue because he couldn't read western script:

A กุดมอร์นิง ไมเนมอิสจอห์น

B กุดมอร์นิง มิสเตอร์จอห์น เฮาอาร์ยูทูเด?

(When you have reached unit 11 you will see how silly it is!)

The familiar Thai script would encourage him to pronounce these English words with a Thai accent and he certainly wouldn't be able to get English speakers to write down new words for him if he were trying to expand his vocabulary; in short, he would never progress beyond the one or two books in which English is written phonetically in Thai letters.

You may not ever plan to write letters in Thai or read newspapers and novels; but if you want to build on what you can learn from a book such as this, becoming literate in Thai is an absolute must! It will also, as anyone who has mastered the script will tell you, improve your pronunciation immeasurably.

Now that you have decided that you do want to learn to read Thai, here is the good news. The Thai script is presented in this course in such a way as to persuade you that it is neither extremely difficult nor time consuming and that even if you are one of the least gifted language learners, you can, with regular practice, learn to read and write Thai. All it really requires is the patience to copy out letters, words and then phrases a sufficient number of times until it becomes almost second nature. Eventually copying out whole passages will improve not only your reading and writing skills but will also reinforce everything else you have learned about the language, including pronunciation and grammar. Keep going back over earlier lessons, because by reading material that is familiar, you will begin to read more quickly and develop the ability to recognize words instantly without having to labour over individual letters each time.

Remember that when learning a foreign language, 'little and often' is much more effective than long but infrequent sessions. Ten to 15 minutes every day is far more productive than one long session once a week.

Romanization of Thai

For westerners learning the language it is convenient to use romanized Thai at the beginning, but it must be stressed that this is no more than a learning aid. It is not an acceptable alternative to the Thai script and most Thais would not be able to read Thai written in romanized form. There are a number of different systems of romanizing Thai, each with its advantages and disadvantages. Like all systems, the one used in this book can offer only an approximate representation of the Thai sound. The most effective strategy is to learn pronunciations from the recording and to memorize Thai script spellings rather than romanized spellings. You should treat the romanization system as a crutch and you should aim to discard it as quickly as possible.

There are a few sounds in Thai that do not exist in English and which can cause some problems. But the vast majority of Thai sounds have a reasonably close equivalent in English.

Consonants

At the beginning of a word, consonants are generally pronounced as in English. A few sounds, however, need further clarification:

g as in **get** (not **gin**)

ng a single sound which we are familiar with in English at the end of words like 'wrong' and 'song', but which also occurs at the beginning of words in Thai:

ngahn **ngâi** **ngahm** **ngoo**

bp a single sound which is somewhere between a **b** sound and a **p** sound in English. Many learners find it hard to both produce this sound accurately and to distinguish it from **b**. Don't be discouraged if you do have problems; you will probably find that over a period of time you will gradually master it:

bpai **bpen** **bpoo** **bplào**

dt a single sound which is somewhere between a **d** sound and a **t** sound in English. Again, many learners find it difficult to distinguish from **t** at first, although usually such problems are short lived:

dtàir **dtìt** **dtorn** **dtrong**

At the end of a word the sounds **k, p** and **t** are not 'released'. Examples of 'unreleased' final consonants in English include the **t** in 'rat' when 'rat trap' is said quickly and the **p** in the casual pronunciation of 'yep!' At first you may feel that words ending in **k**, **p** and **t** all sound the same, but within a very short time you will find that you can hear a distinct difference:

bpàhk	**bàhp**	**bàht**
yâhk	**yâhp**	**yâht**

Many Thais have difficulty pronouncing an **r** sound and will substitute a **l** sound instead. Thus, **a-rai?** (*what?*) becomes **a-lai?** In words that begin with two consonants, you might also hear some Thais omit the second consonant sound. **krai?** (*who?*) becomes **kai?** and **bplah** (*fish*) becomes **bpah.** An even more bewildering change, associated with Bangkok working-class speech, is when **kw** at the beginning of a word becomes **f**, so that **kwăh** (*right*) is pronounced **făh**!

Vowels

Most Thai vowels have near equivalents in English. In the romanization system used in this book, vowels are pronounced as follows:

a as in *ago*
e as in *pen*
i as in *bit*
o as in *cot*
u as in *fun*
ah as in *father*
ai as in *Thai*
air as in *fair*
ao as in *Lao*
ay as in *may*
ee as in *fee*
er as in *number*
ew as in *few*
oh as in *go*
OO as in *book*
oo as in *food*
oy as in *boy*

Other sounds, however, have no near equivalent in English and you need to listen to the recording to have a proper idea of how they should be pronounced:

eu	**meu**	**séu**	**keu**
eu-a	**mêu-a**	**sêu-a**	**nĕu-a**
air-o	**láir-o**	**gâir-o**	**tăir-o**
er-ee	**ler-ee**	**ker-ee**	**ner-ee**

Tones

There are five tones in Thai: mid tone, low tone, high tone, rising tone and falling tone. These are represented in the romanization system by the following accents: mid tone (*no mark*), low tone (`), high tone (´), rising tone (ˇ) and falling tone (ˆ). To help you attune your ears to the different tone sounds, listen to the recording of a Thai speaker saying the following words. Don't worry about the meanings at this stage – simply concentrate on listening:

mid tone	kOOn	krai	mah	bpai
	pairng	mee	dairng	bpen
low tone	jàhk	bpàirt	sìp	bàht
	yài	jòrt	èek	nèung
high tone	mái	káo	lót	lék
	róo	rót	náhm	púk
rising tone	sŏo-ay	pŏm	sŏrng	kŏr
	sĕe-a	kŏrng	năi	dĕe-o
falling tone	mâi	châi	dâi	têe
	gâo	mâhk	chôrp	pôot

It is obviously important to be able both to hear and to reproduce tones correctly if you are going to make yourself understood. But don't let a fear of getting a tone wrong inhibit you from practising. Surprisingly, wrong tones are very seldom the cause of misunderstandings and communication breakdowns. Indeed, many non-Thais operate confidently and effectively in the language with far from perfect accuracy in their tones.

kOOn chêu a-rai?

what's your name?

คุณชื่ออะไร

In this unit you will learn

- **how to state your name, nationality, place of origin and occupation**
- **what? questions**
- **yes/no questions: . . . châi mái?**
- **consonants: น ม ง ร ย ล ว**
- **vowels: -า -ำ -ั- -อ -าย -าว**
- **numbers 1–10**

Dialogues

Peter is spending some time working at his company's Bangkok branch. The first person he meets at the office is Malee.

Malee	สวัสดีค่ะ	sa-wùt dee kâ
	คุณชื่ออะไรคะ	kOOn chêu a-rai ká?
Peter	ชื่อ ปีเตอร์ ครับ	chêu Peter krúp.
Malee	คุณปีเตอร์เป็น	kOOn Peter bpen
	คนอเมริกันใช่ไหมคะ	kon a-may-ri-gun châi mái ká?
Peter	ไม่ใช่ครับ	mâi châi krúp
	เป็นคนอังกฤษครับ	bpen kon ung-grìt krúp.
	มาจากแมนเช็สเตอร์	mah jàhk Manchester.
	ขอโทษครับ	kŏr-tôht krúp,
	คุณชื่ออะไรครับ	kOOn chêu a-rai krúp?

sa-wùt dee	*good morning/afternoon /evening; hello; goodbye*	สวัสดี
kâ, ká, krúp	(polite particles)	ค่ะ, คะ, ครับ
kOOn	*you*; (polite title)	คุณ
chêu	*first name, to have the first name . . .*	ชื่อ
a-rai?	*what?*	อะไร
bpen	*to be*	เป็น
kon	*person*	คน
a-may-ri-gun	*American*	อเมริกัน
châi mái?	*isn't that so?*	ใช่ไหม
mâi châi	*no* (to **. . . châi mái?** questions)	ไม่ใช่
ung-grìt	*English*	อังกฤษ
mah	*to come*	มา
jàhk	*from*	จาก
kŏr-tôht	*excuse me*	ขอโทษ

Malee has taken Peter down to the Labour Department to sort out his work permit. An official is asking her for the information he needs to fill in his form.

Official	เขาชื่ออะไรครับ	káo chêu a-rai krúp?
Malee	ชื่อ ปีเตอร์ ค่ะ	chêu Peter kâ.
Official	นามสกุลอะไร	nahm sa-gOOn a-rai?
Malee	นามสกุล กรีน ค่ะ	nahm sa-gOOn Green kâ.
Official	เป็นคนชาติอะไรครับ	bpen kon châht a-rai krúp?
Malee	เป็นคนอังกฤษค่ะ	bpen kon ung-grìt kâ.
Official	คนอังกฤษใช่ไหม	kon ung-grìt, châi mái?
Malee	ใช่ค่ะ	châi kâ.
Official	ทำงานอะไร	tum ngahn a-rai?
Malee	เป็นนักธุรกิจค่ะ ทำงานกับบริษัท เอ ไอ จี	bpen núk tÓO-rá-gìt kâ. tum ngahn gùp bor-ri-sùt AIG.

káo	*he, she, they*	เขา
nahm sa-gOOn	*surname; to have the surname . . .*	นามสกุล
châht	*nation*	ชาติ
tum ngahn	*to work*	ทำงาน
núk tÓO-rá-gìt	*businessman*	นักธุรกิจ
gùp	*with*	กับ
bor-ri-sùt AIG	*AIG Company*	บริษัท เอ ไอ จี

1 What nationality does Malee assume Peter is?
2 What is Peter's real nationality and where does he come from?
3 What is Peter's occupation?
4 Who are his employers?

i First names are used in both formal and informal situations in Thailand. Thais, both male and female, should normally be addressed by their first name preceded by the title **kOOn** – usually spelt *khun* in romanized letters. Thus, Mrs Patcharee Saibua, Mr Sompong Tongkum and Miss Araya Jaroenwong should be addressed as *Khun* Patcharee, *Khun* Sompong and *Khun* Araya respectively. Thais dealing with westerners in a formal professional context will often prefer to use *khun* with the westerner's surname, Charles Phillips being addressed as *Khun Phillips* rather than *Khun Charles*. Surnames have only come into general usage in Thailand within the last 100 years and their usage is restricted to written documents.

Key phrases and expressions

How to:

1 greet someone

sa-wùt dee krúp (male speaking) สวัสดีครับ

sa-wùt dee kâ (female speaking) สวัสดีค่ะ

2 ask somebody's name and say your name

kOOn chêu a-rai? คุณชื่ออะไร

pŏm (di-chún) chêu . . . ผม (ดิฉัน)ชื่อ . . .

3 ask somebody's surname and say your surname

kOOn nahm sa-gOOn a-rai? คุณนามสกุลอะไร

pŏm (di-chún) nahm sa-gOOn . . . ผม (ดิฉัน)นามสกุล . . .

4 ask somebody's nationality and state your nationality

kOOn bpen kon châht a-rai? คุณเป็นคนชาติอะไร

pŏm (di-chún) ผม (ดิฉัน)
bpen kon ung-grìt เป็นคนอังกฤษ

5 ask somebody's occupation and state your occupation

kOOn tum ngahn a-rai? คุณทำงานอะไร

pŏm (di-chún) bpen . . . ผม (ดิฉัน) เป็น . . .

pŏm (di-chún) ผม (ดิฉัน)
tum ngahn gùp . . . ทำงานกับ . . .

Language notes

1 Greetings

sa-wùt dee is a general greeting which can be used regardless of the time of day. In informal spoken Thai it is often abbreviated to **'wùt dee**. The expression is also used when saying goodbye.

2 Polite particles

Particles are untranslatable words that occur at the end of utterances. There are three main types of particle – polite particles, question particles and mood particles.

Polite particles are added to the end of statements and questions to make the speaker's words sound more polite; they have no direct equivalent in English and therefore cannot be translated. The most common polite particles are **krúp, kâ** and **ká.** Male speakers use **krúp** at the end of both statements and questions, while females use **kâ** at the end of statements and **ká** after questions. It is not necessary to use these particles after every sentence in a conversation, although for the learner it is best to risk sounding too polite.

3 Pronouns

There are many more pronouns in Thai than in English; the correct choice will depend on such factors as the relative status and degree of intimacy between speakers. For the learner, however, it is quite possible to use Thai effectively with a limited number of pronouns, the most common of which are:

pŏm	*I* (male)
di-chún/chún	*I* (female)
kOOn	*you* (singular and plural)
káo	*he, she, they*
rao	*we*

Unlike western languages, the word for *I* varies according to the gender of the speaker; of the two female forms, **chún** is the less formal. However, Thais frequently omit pronouns altogether when it is clear from the context who is speaking, being addressed or being referred to. In many of the examples in this course, you will find that the pronoun has been omitted in Thai to make it sound more natural and that an arbitrary choice of pronoun has been included in the English translation:

chêu a-rai?	*What's your name?*
chêu Peter.	***His name is Peter.***

The first example could just as correctly have been translated as *What's his/her name?* and the second as *My name is Peter*. If you look at the dialogues at the beginning of this lesson, you will notice that **bpen kon ung-grìt** in the first dialogue means ***I'm** English* and, in the second, *He's English*.

4 Noun (singular/plural) + adjective

Nouns in Thai, unlike in many European languages, have a single fixed form, which does not distinguish between singular and plural. Thus **kon** can mean either *person* or *people*, depending on the context. Adjectives follow the noun they modify:

kon ung-grìt	*British person/people*
káo bpen kon tai.	*He/they is/are Thai.*

5 The verb 'to be': bpen + noun

bpen is one of several different Thai verbs that are used to translate *is/are*, *was/were* etc. **bpen** does have other meanings (see unit 7), but when it means *to be*, it is always followed by a noun:

pǒm bpen kon ung-grìt.	*I am British.* (I-am-person-British)
káo bpen núk tÓO-rá-gìt.	*He is a businessman.*

In negative sentences like, *I am not a . . .*, **bpen** is replaced by **mâi châi**; it is important to understand that the negative word **mâi** (*not*) cannot be used before **bpen** to mean *is not*:

pǒm mâi châi kon a-may-ri-gun.	*I am not American.*
káo mâi châi núk sèuk-sǎh.	*He is not a student.*

6 'Yes/no' questions: . . . châi mái?

Yes and *no* answers to questions in Thai are determined by the form of the question; there is no single word for *yes* and *no*, so the learner has to listen carefully to the *question particle* in order to be able to answer correctly.

The question particle . . . **châi mái?** is tagged onto the end of a statement to transform it into a confirmation-seeking question, rather like . . . *isn't it*, . . . *don't they?* etc. in English; it can be used for checking that you have heard or understood correctly what has just been said. . . . **châi mái?** questions are answered either **châi** *yes* or **mâi châi** *no*:

káo chêu Peter châi mái?	*His name is Peter, isn't it?*
– châi.	*– Yes.*
káo bpen kon a-may-ri-gun châi mái?	*He's American, isn't he?*
– mâi châi.	*– No.*

7 'What?' questions

The Thai word for *what?* is **a-rai**. It normally occurs at the end of a sentence:

káo chêu a-rai?	*What is his name?*
káo nahm sa-gOOn a-rai?	*What is his surname?*
káo bpen kon châht a-rai?	*What nationality is he?*
káo tum ngahn a-rai?	*What (job) does he do?*

To answer such questions, substitute **a-rai** with the appropriate word; an exception is the question **káo tum ngahn a-rai?** to which the normal response is **káo bpen . . .** (*He is a . . .*) followed by the name of the occupation:

káo chêu a-rai?	*What is his name?*
– káo chêu sŏm-chai.	*– His name is Somchai.*
káo bpen kon châht a-rai?	*What nationality is he?*
– káo bpen kon tai.	*– He is Thai.*

but

káo tum ngahn a-rai?	*What (job) does he do?*
– káo bpen mŏr.	*– He is a doctor.*

Exercises

1 How would you respond if a Thai asked you these questions?

(a) kOOn chêu a-rai?
(b) kOOn nahm sa-gOOn a-rai?
(c) kOOn bpen kon châht a-rai?
(d) kOOn tum ngahn a-rai?

2 How would you respond if Malee asked you these questions about Peter?

(a) káo chêu Peter châi mái ká?
(b) káo nahm sa-gOOn a-rai ká?
(c) káo bpen kon a-may-ri-gun châi mái ká?
(d) káo bpen kon châht a-rai ká?
(e) káo tum ngahn gùp bor-ri-sùt AIG, châi mái ká?
(f) káo tum-ngahn a-rai ká?

3 Chantana, a Thai student (*student* **núk sèuk-săh**), is applying for a visa to study in England. Match the questions she was asked when she went to the British Embassy with the answers she gave.

Questions
(a) bpen kon tai, châi mái krúp?
(b) tum-ngahn a-rai krúp?
(c) nahm sa-gOOn a-rai krúp?
(d) kOOn chêu a-rai krúp?

Answers
(i) nahm sa-gOOn bOOn-dee kâ.
(ii) châi kâ.
(iii) di-chún chêu chŭn-ta-nah kâ.
(iv) bpen núk sèuk-săh kâ.

4 How would you introduce these people?

	1	2	3	4
name	Somsak	John	Makoto	Paula
surname	Torngkum	Stevens	Iwasaki	Besson
nationality	Thai (tai)	American (a-may-ri-gun)	Japanese (yêe-bpÒOn)	French (fa-rùng-sàyt)
home town	Chiangmai (chee-ung mài)	New York (new yórk)	Tokyo (dtoh-gee-o)	Paris (bpah-rít)
occupation	doctor (mŏr)	student (núk sèuk-săh)	businessman (núk tÓO-rá-gìt)	teacher (ah-jahn)

Example
káo chêu sŏm-sùk
nahm sa-gOOn torng-kum
bpen kon tai
mah jàhk chee-ung-mài
bpen mŏr

5 Using the information in exercise 4, complete the following sentences using **bpen** and **mâi châi:**

(a) sŏm-sùk . . . kon tai . . . kon yêe-bpÒOn
(b) John . . . kon ung-grìt . . . kon a-may-ri-gun
(c) Makoto . . . núk sèuk-săh . . . núk tÓO-rá-gìt
(d) Paula . . . ah-jahn . . . mŏr

6 How would you ask the following questions?

(a) Excuse me, what's your name?
(b) His name is Somsak, isn't it?
(c) What is his surname?
(d) What nationality is he?
(e) He's Thai, isn't he?
(f) She's a teacher, isn't she?
(g) She is not Thai; she is Japanese.
(h) He is not English; he is French.

Reading and writing

1 Consonants

Consonants in Thai are divided into three groups or 'classes' called low class, mid class and high class. It is important to remember which class a consonant belongs to as the class of the initial consonant in a word will partly determine the tone of that word. The consonants in this unit are all *low-class* consonants.

Thai consonants are all pronounced with an inherent **'-or'** sound; thus we can say at the end of this lesson that we know the letters **'nor'**, **'mor'**, **'ngor'**, **'ror'** and so on. Each Thai consonant also has a 'name' – **'nor'** is known as **nor nŏo** (**nŏo** means *rat*) and then there is **mor máh** (**máh** means *horse*), **ngor ngoo** (**ngoo** means *snake*) and so on. When Thais learn their alphabet at school, they always learn the name of the letter, but it is not necessary for the foreigner to know these names in order to be able to read.

Look carefully at the following letters. They are all written with a single stroke starting from the inside of the loop and moving outwards. In letters where there are two loops, the starting point is the top loop on the left-hand side. Copy out each letter a number of times until you can reproduce it accurately and naturally; say the name of the letter (e.g. **mor**) each time you write it to help you memorize it:

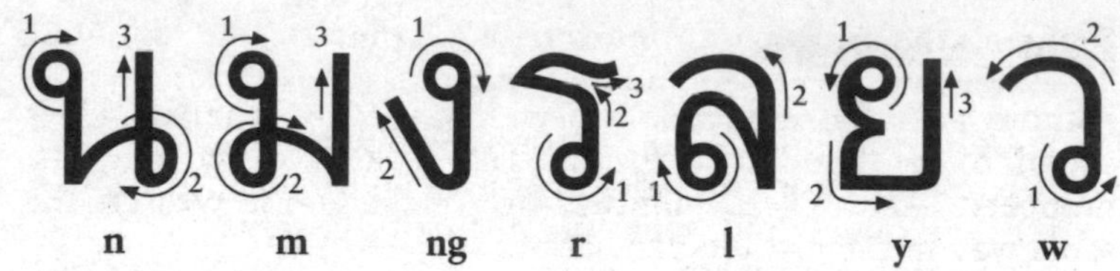

n	m	ng	r	l	y	w

2 Vowels

Vowels are classified as either long or short. In English, an example of a short vowel sound is the *i* in 'bin', while the vowel sound in 'seen' is long. As each vowel symbol is introduced you will need to remember whether it is a long or short vowel, as vowel length plays a part in determining the tone of a word. A full list of long and short vowels appears in an appendix.

The vowels symbols in this unit, with the exception of **-u-**, are written after a consonant symbol, the dash representing the position of a consonant; in subsequent units, however, you will see that certain vowel symbols are written above the consonant, others below and some in front.

-า	-ำ	-ั-	-อ	-าย	-าว
-ah (long)	**-um** (short + 'm')	**-u-** (short)	**-or** (long)	**-ai** (long)	**-ao** (long)

3 Words

Here are some simple words combining the consonants and vowels you have met in this unit. If you have the recording that accompanies the course listen to them and then copy each word out a few times. The first two words occurred at the beginning of the unit in the conversation. Go back to this section and see if you can identify them in the Thai script.

มา	งาน	นาน	นาย	ลาว
mah	**ngahn**	**nahn**	**nai**	**lao**
to come	*work*	*a long time*	*Mr*	*Lao*

นำ	มัน	รอ	ยอม
num	**mun**	**ror**	**yorm**
to lead	*it*	*to wait*	*to agree*

4 Numbers

Although Arabic numerals are widely used in Thailand it is useful to be familiar with the Thai system of writing the numbers 1–10. These numbers are, incidentally, written the same way in the Cambodian script.

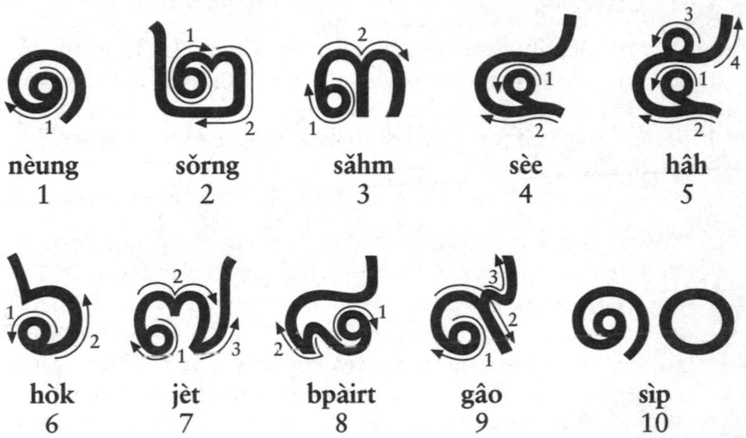

Reading practice

1 Letters

How many letters can you identify in this sample of Thai? Put a faint pencil stroke through every letter you can recognize.

ตลาดทางด้านยุโรปของเราในตอนนี้พูดได้ว่าไปได้สวย โดยเฉพาะที่อังกฤษ ตอนนี้การไปเที่ยวเมืองไทยป็นที่นิยม กันมากเหมือนกับเป็นแฟชั่นอีกอย่างหนึ่ง เดิมเขาจะไป ฮ่องกงกันมากกว่าเพราะฮ่องกงเป็นเมืองขึ้นของเขาและ คนพูดภาษาอังกฤษกันได้เป็นส่วนมาก

Perhaps learning to read Thai isn't quite as daunting as you thought! You probably found, however, that it required quite an effort of concentration to scan through these few lines. As you become more accustomed to the Thai script, you will find that you can pick out letters and words quickly and effortlessly.

2 Words

Read the words in the table several times until you can read both rows and columns quickly and accurately. When you can do this, pick words at random and see how quickly you can read them. As a further test, listen to the exercise on the recording and write down the words as dictation. Don't worry about what the words mean at this stage.

มา	นา	นาม	นาน	นาง	งาน
นำ	รำ	ลำ	วัน	ยัง	มัน
ลัง	รัง	รอ	รอง	มอง	นอน
ราย	นาย	ยาย	ลาว	ยาว	ราว

3 Sentences

In Thai writing there are no spaces between words. Spaces are used rather for punctuation purposes and tend to occur where there would be a full stop or comma in English. For the western learner, this means that there is the added complication of having to recognize where one word ends and another begins. Start reading each line from the left, adding a word in each column until you have the full three-word sentence on the right-hand side. Check in the key how well you read the sentences. And yes, the sentences are not terribly useful, but if you have read them correctly, you have cleared your first big hurdle in reading Thai!

ยาม *watchman*	ยามลาว *Lao watchman*	ยามลาวมา *The Lao watchman comes.*
นาย *boss*	นายรอ *the boss waits*	นายรอนาน *The boss waits for a long time.*
นาง *Mrs*	นางลา *Mrs leaves*	นางลางาน *Mrs leaves work.*
ยาย *Granny*	ยายรำ *Granny dances*	ยายรำนาน *Granny dances for a long time.*

4 Numbers

How would you dial these Bangkok telephone numbers?

1 ๒๓๖-๔๘๙๐

2 ๕๘๐-๗๓๕๙

3 ๒๒๕-๗๓๘๑

4 ๖๙๓-๒๑๔๕

5 ๓๗๑-๙๕๔๘

Learning a new script

You can only learn to read and write Thai by regular practice. Ten to 15 minutes practice each day is much more effective than one hour twice a week and as long as you stick to daily practice you should find that you make rapid progress. You might, for example, try some of the following 'learning strategies': copy each letter and each word a dozen or so times until you can write it quickly and accurately; look at the dialogues in Thai script and see how many letters and how many parts of words you can recognize; and get into the habit of doodling in Thai so as to improve your handwriting or making up sentences with the Thai words you can spell.

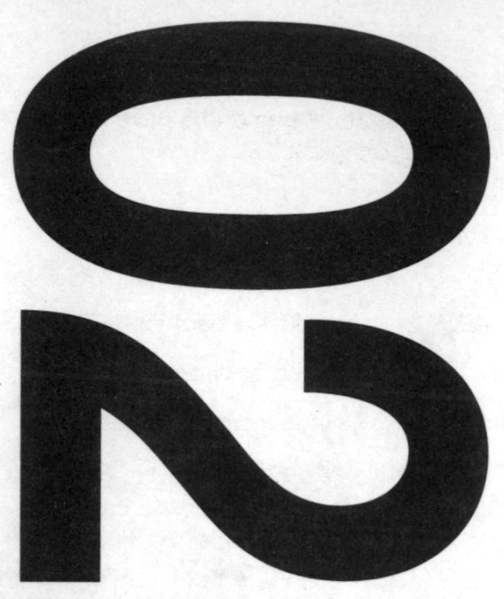

02

nêe tâo-rài ká?

how much is this?

นี่เท่าไรคะ

In this unit you will learn

- **the language of shopping and bargaining**
- **how much? questions**
- **yes/no questions: . . . mái?; . . . lĕr?; . . . ná?**
- **can: verb + dâi**
- **some more numbers: 20, 30, 40 . . . 100**
- **consonants: ก จ ด ต บ ป อ**
- **vowels: ไ- ใ- โ- -ิ -ี -ุ -ู**

Dialogues

Peter's wife, Sue, is admiring the shirts at one of the pavement stalls along Sukhumwit Road in central Bangkok.

Sue	นี่เท่าไรคะ	nêe tâo-rài ká?
Vendor	แปดสิบบาทค่ะ	bpàirt-sìp bàht kâ.
Sue	แปดสิบบาทหรือคะ	bpàirt-sìp bàht lĕr ká?
	แพงไปหน่อย	pairng bpai nòy.
	หกสิบบาทได้ไหม	hòk-sìp bàht dâi mái?
Vendor	ไม่ได้ค่ะ	mâi dâi kâ.
	ไม่แพง	mâi pairng.
	สวยนะ	sŏo-ay ná.
Sue	สีแดงมีไหม	sĕe dairng mee mái?
Vendor	มีค่ะ	mee kâ.
	สีแดงสวยมากนะคะ	sĕe dairng sŏo-ay mâhk ná ká.
	คิดเจ็ดสิบบาทก็แล้วกัน	kít jèt-sìp bàht gôr láir-o gun.
	ไม่แพงนะ	mâi pairng ná.
Sue	โอ เค	oh kay.
	ตกลงเจ็ดสิบบาท	dtòk long jèt-sìp bàht.

nêe	*this*	นี่
tâo-rài?	*how much?*	เท่าไร
bpàirt-sìp	*eighty*	แปดสิบ
bàht	*baht* (unit of currency)	บาท
lĕr? (spelt **rĕu**)	(question particle)	หรือ
pairng	*expensive*	แพง
. . . bpai nòy	*a little too . . .*	. . . ไปหน่อย
hòk-sìp	*sixty*	หกสิบ
dâi	*can*	ได้

. . . dâi mái?	*can you . . . ?*	ได้ไหม
mâi	*not*	ไม่
mâi dâi	*can't; no* (in **. . . dâi mái?** questions)	ไม่ได้
sŏo-ay	*beautiful, pretty*	สวย
ná	(question particle)	นะ
sĕe dairng	*red*	สีแดง
mee	*to have*	มี
. . . mái?	(question particle)	ไหม
mâhk	*very, much*	มาก
kít	*to think, calculate, charge*	คิด
jèt-sìp	*seventy*	เจ็ดสิบ
. . . gôr láir-o gun	*let's settle for . . .*	. . . ก็แล้วกัน
oh kay	*OK*	โอ เค
dtòk long	*agree(d)*	ตกลง

Peter, meanwhile, has gone to a market, where he spots some unfamiliar fruits.

Peter	นี่อะไรครับ	nêe a-rai krúp?
Vendor	น้อยหน่าค่ะ	nóy-nàh kâ.
Peter	อะไรนะครับ	a-rai ná krúp?
Vendor	เรียกว่าน้อยหน่าค่ะ	rêe-uk wâh nóy-nàh kâ.
Peter	น้อยหน่าใช่ไหม	nóy-nàh, châi mái?
Vendor	ใช่ค่ะ	châi kâ.
	อร่อยนะ หวาน	a-ròy ná. wăhn.
	ลองชิมไหม	lorng chim mái?
	. . . อร่อยไหม	. . . a-ròy mái?
Peter	อร่อยครับ โลละเท่าไร	a-ròy krúp. loh la tâo-rài?
Vendor	โลละสี่สิบบาทค่ะ	loh la sèe-sìp bàht kâ.

Peter	ลดหน่อยได้ไหมครับ	lót nòy, dâi mái krúp.
Vendor	สี่สิบไม่แพงค่ะ	sèe-sìp mâi pairng kâ.
	คิดสองโลเจ็ดสิบห้า	kít sŏrng loh jèt-sìp-hâh
	ก็แล้วกัน	gôr láir-o gun.
Peter	ครับ . . .	krúp . . .
	แล้วกล้วยหวีละเท่าไร	láir-o glôo-ay wĕe la tâo-rài?
Vendor	หวีละยี่สิบค่ะ	wĕe la yêe-sìp kâ.

nóy-nàh	*custard apple*	น้อยหน่า
a-rai ná?	*pardon?*	อะไรนะ
rêe-uk wâh . . .	*(it's) called . . .*	เรียกว่า . . .
a-ròy	*to be tasty*	อร่อย
wăhn	*to be sweet*	หวาน
lorng	*to try out*	ลอง
chim	*to taste*	ชิม
loh	*kilo*	โล
la	*per*	ละ
tâo-rài?	*how much?*	เท่าไร
lót	*to reduce*	ลด
nòy	*a bit*	หน่อย
glôo-ay	*banana*	กล้วย
wĕe	*bunch*	หวี

1 What colour shirt does Sue want?
2 What price does the vendor say at first?
3 What price do they finally agree on?
4 Does Peter like the custard apple he tries?
5 How many kilos does he buy and how much does he pay?
6 How much are the bananas?

i Most financial transactions in Thailand, whether shopping, booking hotel rooms or taking a taxi, have traditionally been open to bargaining. While there are now areas of Bangkok life where this practice has disappeared (e.g. fixed prices in department stores, supermarkets and meter taxis), the ability to haggle *politely* over prices can still be useful for the foreigner in Thailand. You need some idea in advance of a reasonable price for the goods or services you are trying to purchase if your bargaining is to carry credibility: to assume that all prices have been marked up by a certain percentage is too simplistic. Above all else, the bargaining should be carried out in a relaxed and easy-going manner; a smile and a sense of humour are far more likely to secure a satisfactory deal than an angry and aggressive approach.

Early morning markets were, until recently, a good place to watch Thais haggling over prices and to practise bargaining. But while prices may now be less open to negotiation, markets can still provide a venue to try out some simple language skills. When business is slack, you can, like Peter, in the second dialogue, ask what unfamiliar (and familiar) fruits are called in Thai (**nêe a-rai?** or **nêe rêe-uk wâh a-rai?**), ask the vendor to repeat what she said (**a-rai ná?**), confirm that you have heard it correctly (**rêe-uk wâh . . . châi mái?**), ask her the price of her produce and even try to knock the price down a little. If you have the same conversation with half a dozen different vendors, you will find that within a matter of days your confidence will begin to soar.

Key phrases and expressions

How to:

1 ask the price of something

nêe tâo-rài? นี่เท่าไร

2 say something is too expensive

pairng bpai nòy แพงไปหน่อย

3 suggest a price

jèt-sìp bàht dâi mái? เจ็ดสิบบาทได้ไหม

4 ask for a discount

lót nòy dâi mái? ลดหน่อยได้ไหม

5 ask what something is called

nêe a-rai? นี่อะไร

nêe rêe-uk wâh a-rai? นี่เรียกว่าอะไร

6 ask how much something costs per kilo

X loh la tâo-rài? X โลละเท่าไร

Language notes

1 'How much?' questions

The Thai word for *how much?* is **tâo-rài?** It always occurs at the end of a sentence:

nûn (*that*) **tâo-rài?**	*How much is that?*
séu (*buy*) **tâo-rài?**	*How much did you buy it for?*
séu rót (*car*) **tâo-rài?**	*How much did you buy the car for?*

2 Numbers

In the first unit you learned the numbers 1–10. This unit adds the multiples of ten up to 100. These are formed in a regular way with the exception of 20:

twenty	**yêe-sìp**	๒๐
thirty	**săhm-sìp**	๓๐
forty	**sèe-sìp**	๔๐
fifty	**hâh-sìp**	๕๐
sixty	**hòk-sìp**	๖๐
seventy	**jèt-sìp**	๗๐
eighty	**bpàirt-sìp**	๘๐
ninety	**gâo-sìp**	๙๐
one hundred	**(nèung) róy**	๑๐๐

3 'Yes/no' questions: . . . lĕr?

The question particle **lĕr?**, like **châi mái?** (unit 1), is used in confirmation-seeking questions; but while **châi mái?** tends to be neutral, **lĕr?** often conveys a sense of surprise or disappointment about the confirmation it seeks. In the first dialogue, Sue does not give the vendor time to respond (*Eighty baht, eh? That's a bit expensive*). The polite particles **krúp** (male speakers) or **kâ** (female speakers) (unit 1) can be used as *yes* answers to **lĕr?** questions and **bplào krúp** or **bplào kâ** for *no* answers:

bpàirt-sìp bàht lĕr ká?	*Eighty baht, eh?*
– kâ. / bplào krúp (kâ). gâo sìp.	*– Yes. / No. Ninety.*

4 Verb + dâi

The meaning of the verb **dâi** depends on its position in a sentence. As an auxiliary verb (as it is in this unit), it means *can, able to* and occurs in the pattern verb + **dâi**:

pŏm tum dâi.	*I can do (it)*. (I-do-can)
kOOn bpai (*go*) **dâi.**	*You can go*. (I-go-can)
káo lót dâi.	*He can lower the price.* (He-lower-can)

5 Yes/no questions: . . . mái?

The question particle **mái?** occurs at the end of a sentence and is used in neutral questions requiring a *yes/no* answer. To answer *yes* to a **mái?** question, the verb in the question is repeated; to answer *no*, the pattern **mâi** + verb is used. Be careful not to confuse question word **mái?**, pronounced with a high tone, and negative **mâi**, pronounced with a falling tone:

hòk-sìp bàht dâi mái?	*How about sixty baht?*
– dâi kâ/mâi dâi kâ.	*– Yes/no.*
sŏo-ay mái?	*Is it pretty?*
– sŏo-ay/mâi sŏo-ay.	*– Yes/no.*
nóy-nàh a-ròy mái?	*Is the custard apple tasty?*
– a-ròy/mâi a-ròy.	*– Yes/no.*
sĕe dairng mee mái?	*Do you have (it in) red?*
– mee/mâi mee.	*– Yes/no.*

Notice the difference between the neutral **mái?** question and the confirmation-seeking **châi mái?** question:

sŏo-ay mái?	*Is it pretty?*
sŏo-ay châi mái?	*It's pretty, isn't it?*
sĕe dairng mee mái?	*Do you have a red one?*
sĕe dairng mee châi mái?	*You have a red, one don't you?*

6 Negatives

The negative is formed by the pattern **mâi** + verb/adjective:

mâi pairng.	*It's not expensive.*
mâi sŏo-ay.	*It's not beautiful.*
mâi mee.	*I don't have (any)/there aren't (any).*

Sentences involving the auxiliary verb **dâi** are negated by the pattern verb + **mâi dâi**:

pŏm tum mâi dâi.	*I can't do (it).* (I-do-not-can)
kOOn bpai mâi dâi.	*You can't go.* (You-go-not-can)
káo lót mâi dâi.	*He can't lower the price.* (He-lower-not-can)

7 Adjectives

Adjectives in Thai do not occur with the verb **bpen** (*to be*); a word like **pairng** can mean both *expensive* and *it is expensive*.

8 Yes/no questions: . . . ná?

ná? is a question particle which invites agreement with the preceding statement (e.g. *The traffic is terrible today, isn't it?*). It is used commonly when initiating a conversation. The polite particles **krúp** (male speakers) or **kâ** (female speakers) can be used as *yes* answers to **ná?** questions and **mâi** + verb + **krúp** (**kâ**) for *no* answers:

a-ròy ná?	*It's tasty, isn't it?*
– krúp / mâi a-ròy kâ.	*– Yes. / No it isn't.*
pairng ná?	*It's expensive, isn't it?*
– kâ / mâi pairng krúp.	*– Yes. / No it isn't.*

In the second dialogue **ná?** occurs in the expression **arai ná?** (*pardon?*):

Peter	**née a-rai krúp?**	*What's this?*
Vendor	**nóy-nàh kâ.**	*A custard apple.*
Peter	**a-rai ná krúp?**	*Pardon?*

Here **ná?** is used with the question word **arai?** (*what?*) to request that a piece of information be repeated; it can also occur with the question words *when?*, *who?*, *where?*, *why?* and *how?* (which you will meet in later units), to convey the meaning *When was that again?*, *Who was that you saw?* and so on.

9 Colours

The word sěe is both the noun *colour* and the verb *to be the colour X*. sěe occurs before a specific colour word when describing the colour of something:

sěe a-rai?	*What colour is it?*
sěe dairng.	*Red. / It is red.*
sêu-a (*shirt*) **sěe a-rai?**	*What colour is the shirt?*
sêu-a sěe dairng mee mái?	*Do you have a red shirt?*

The most common colour words are:

sěe dairng	*red*
sěe kěe-o	*green*
sěe lěu-ung	*yellow*
sěe núm ngern	*blue*
sěe dum	*black*
sěe núm dtahn	*brown*
sěe kǎo	*white*

10 Word order

Normal word order in Thai is subject + verb + object. Notice how Sue puts **sěe dairng** at the beginning of the sentence when she is asking if the vendor has any red t-shirts. This strategy of putting the topic at the beginning of the sentence is very common in Thai. It would also have been perfectly correct for her to have said **mee sěe dairng mái?**

11 per kilo/fruit/bunch

The Thai word for *per* (as in *per kilo*) is **la**. When asking and stating the price of things per kilo, per fruit, per bunch and so on, the word order in Thai is quite different from English:

nóy-nàh loh la tâo-rài?	custard apple – kilo – per – how much?
sôm loh la sèe-sìp bàht	orange – kilo – per – forty baht

However, not all fruits are bought by the kilo. Bananas are bought by the bunch (**wěe** – which literally means *comb*), while large fruit, such as water melons (**dtairng moh**), papayas (**ma-la-gor**), pineapples (**sùp-bpa-rót**) and mangoes (**ma-môo-ung**) are bought by the individual fruit (**bai**):

glôo-ay wěe la tâo-rài?	*How much are bananas per bunch?*
ma-la-gor bai la tâo-rài?	*How much are papayas per fruit?*
ma-môo-ung bai la tâo-rài?	*How much are mangoes per fruit?*

Exercises

1 How well can you bargain? Imagine that you have been quoted the following prices. Remark that it is a little too expensive and suggest a price 20 baht cheaper. The first one has been done for you:

(a) gâo-sìp bàht
– pairng bpai nòy krúp/kâ.
jèt-sìp bàht dâi mái?
(b) jèt-sìp bàht
(c) bpàirt-sìp bàht
(d) sèe-sìp bàht
(e) hâh-sìp bàht

2 How would you say:

(a) How much is this?
(b) That's a bit expensive.
(c) Can you lower the price a little?
(d) How about 50 baht?
(e) The red (one) isn't pretty.
(f) Do you have green?

3 How would you ask the price of these different kinds of fruit? Use the word given in brackets to help.

(a) sùp-bpa-rót (**bai**)
(b) sôm (**loh**)
(c) glôo-ay (**wěe**)
(d) ma-la-gor (**bai**)
(e) ma-môo-ung (**bai**)
(f) nóy-nàh (**loh**)
(g) dtairng-moh (**bai**)

4 Translate the following pairs of questions into Thai:

(a) Is it tasty? / It's tasty, isn't it?
(b) Is it expensive? / It's expensive, isn't it?
(c) Is it pretty? / It's pretty, isn't it?
(d) Do you have a red one? / You have a red one, don't you?

5 Peter is trying to find out the Thai word for *mango*. This is what the vendor said to him. What were his questions?

Peter _____ ?
Vendor rêe-uk wâh ma-môo-ung kâ.
Peter _____ ?
Vendor ma-môo-ung kâ.
Peter _____ ?
Vendor châi kâ.
Peter _____ ?
Vendor bai la yêe-sìp bàht kâ.
Peter: _____ ?
Vendor lót mâi dâi kâ.

Reading and writing

1 Consonants

In unit 1 you learned the most common low-class consonants. In this unit you meet the main *mid-class* consonants:

g j d dt b bp ('zero')

2 'Zero' consonant

Notice that the final symbol of this group is identical in appearance to the vowel **-or** you learned in unit 1. When the symbol occurs at the beginning of a word, however, it is a consonant, which we can call 'zero consonant' because it has no sound of its own. It is used when writing words which begin with a vowel *sound*:

อาง	อาว	อำ	อาย	อัน
ahng	**ao**	**um**	**ai**	**un**

3 Vowels

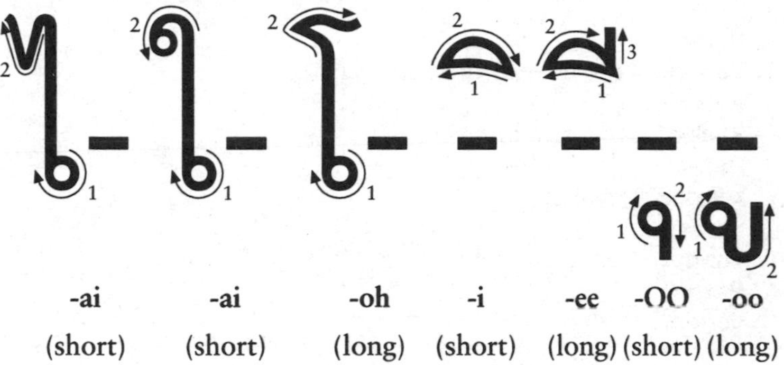

The first three vowels are written in front of the consonant, even though the consonant is pronounced first. Although the first two vowels are pronounced exactly the same, when it comes to writing, they are not interchangeable and you should memorize the correct spelling of a word.

Reading practice

1 Letters

Here is the same sample of Thai script that you met in unit 1. Again, put a faint pencil stroke through all the letters you can now recognize:

ตลาดทางด้านยุโรปของเราในตอนนี้พูดได้ว่าไปได้สวย โดยเฉพาะที่อังกฤษ ตอนนี้การไปเที่ยวเมืองไทยเป็นที่นิยมกันมากเหมือนกับเป็นแฟชั่นอีกอย่างหนึ่ง เดิมเขาจะไปฮ่องกงกันมากกว่าเพราะฮ่องกงเป็นเมืองขึ้นของเขาและคนพูดภาษาอังกฤษกันได้เป็นส่วนมาก

2 Words

Try to read these words before listening to them on the recording. Don't worry if you find it difficult to hear the difference between ด and ต at this stage. It will come with practice:

กิน	กัน	ใจ	ดู	ดี
ตา	ตี	บิน	ใบ	ไป
ปี	โมง	ปู	โรง	ยุง
อัน	มี	กัน	ลอง	โล

3 Sentences

The sentences in the right-hand column all have five words. Read aloud across the page from left to right, gradually building up the sentence. Don't worry about meanings. If you are having difficulty, it may help to draw a faint pencil line to mark word boundaries, but beware of being too dependent on this strategy. Note that all the words that you are reading at the moment are pronounced with a mid tone:

บินมา	บินไปบินมา	ยุงบินไปบินมา
มาดู	ยินดีมาดู	ลุงยินดีมาดู
ปูดำ	มีปูดำ	ในนามีปูดำ
งูตาย	ตีงูตาย	ยามลาวตีงูตาย
นางงามดัง	ดูนางงามดัง	รอดูนางงามดัง

4 Match the dates

In Thailand, the year is normally counted according to BE (Buddhist era) which is 543 years ahead of the AD year. 2500 BE is thus 1957 AD, while 2000 AD is 2543 BE:

(i) ๕/๑/๒๔๙๗	(a) 19 July 1981
(ii) ๒๕/๑๒/๒๕๓๙	(b) 8 November 1948
(iii) ๑๙/๖/๒๕๒๔	(c) 5 January 1954
(iv) ๓/๙/๒๕๓๗	(d) 25 December 1996
(v) ๘/๑๑/๒๔๙๑	(e) 3 September 1994

bpai sa-yăhm sa-kwair mái?

will you go to Siam Square?

ไปสยามสแควร์ไหม

In this unit you will learn

- **the language of taxi transactions**
- **completed actions: verb + láir-o**
- **reduplication of adjectives and adverbs**
- **mâi . . . ròrk in simple contradictions**
- **numbers 21–99**
- **'live' syllables and 'dead' syllables**

Dialogues

Sue has flagged down a taxi and before stepping into the vehicle she checks that the driver is willing to take her to Siam Square.

Sue	ไปสยามสแควร์ไหมคะ	bpai sa-yăhm sa-kwair mái ká?
Taxi	ไปครับ . . .	bpai krúp . . .

Sue tells the driver where to pull up . . .

Sue	จอดใกล้ ๆ สี่แยก	jòrt glâi glâi sèe yâirk
	ได้ไหมคะ	dâi mái ká?
Taxi	ได้ครับ	dâi krúp.
	ตรงนี้ใช่ไหมครับ	dtrong-née châi mái krúp?
Sue	ใช่ค่ะ เท่าไรคะ	châi kâ. tâo-rài ká?
Taxi	เก้าสิบเอ็ดบาทครับ	gâo-sìp-èt bàht krúp.
Sue	ร้อยบาทก็แล้วกัน	róy bàht gôr láir-o gun.
Taxi	ขอบคุณมากครับ	kòrp-kOOn mâhk krúp.
	โชคดีครับ	chôhk dee krúp.
Sue	โชคดีค่ะ	chôhk dee kâ.

Sue has called a taxi to take her back to her home in Soi 23 on Sukhumwit Road.

Sue	ไปถนนสุขุมวิท	bpai ta-nŏn sÒO-kŎOm-wít
	ซอยยี่สิบสามไหมคะ	soy yêe-sìp săhm mái ká?
Taxi	ไปครับ . . .	bpai krúp . . .

As they approach their destination, the taxi driver asks Sue if she wants him to drive into the **soi** (*lane*).

Taxi	เข้าซอยไหมครับ	kâo soy mái krúp?
Sue	เข้าค่ะ	kâo kâ.
	ไปสุดซอย . . .	bpai sÒOt soy . . .
	จอดใกล้ ๆ รถสีแดงค่ะ	jòrt glâi glâi rót sěe dairng kâ.
Taxi	ครับ ตรงนี้ใช่ไหมครับ	krúp. dtrong-née châi mái krúp?
Sue	ใช่ค่ะ เท่าไรคะ	châi kâ. tâo-rài ká?

bpai	*to go*	ไป
sa-yăhm sa-kwair	*Siam Square*	สยามสแควร์
jòrt	*park* (v)	จอด
glâi	*near*	ใกล้
sèe-yâirk	*crossroads*	สี่แยก
dtrong-née	*right here*	ตรงนี้
gâo-sìp-èt	*ninety one*	เก้าสิบเอ็ด
kòrp-kOOn (mâhk)	*thank you (very much)*	ขอบคุณ(มาก)
chôhk dee	*good luck*	โชคดี
ta-nŏn	*road*	ถนน
ta-nŏn sÒO-kŎOm-wít	*Sukhumwit Road*	ถนนสุขุมวิท
soy	*soi, lane*	ซอย
yêe-sìp-săhm	*twenty three*	ยี่สิบสาม
kâo	*to enter*	เข้า
sÒOt soy	*end of the soi*	สุดซอย
rót	*car*	รถ

Peter, meanwhile, is taking a *tuk-tuk* to meet a friend at a small hotel in central Bangkok. Before stepping into the vehicle, he checks that the driver knows where it is.

Peter	รู้จักโรงแรมรีโนไหม	róo-jùk rohng rairm ree-noh mái?
Tuk-tuk	โรงแรมรีโนหรือ	rohng rairm ree-noh lĕr?
Peter	ครับ อยู่	krúp. yòo
	ซอยเกษมสันต์	soy ga-săym-sŭn
	ใกล้ ๆ	glâi glâi
	สนามกีฬา	sa-năhm gee-lah
	แห่งชาติ	hàirng châht.
Tuk-tuk	อ้อ สนามกีฬา	ôr . . . sa-năhm gee-lah
	แห่งชาติ ใช่ไหม	hàirng châht châi mái?
	รู้จัก	róo-jùk.

Peter	ไปเท่าไรครับ	bpai tâo-rài krúp?
Tuk-tuk	เก้าสิบบาทครับ	gâo-sìp bàht krúp.
Peter	แพงไปหน่อยครับ	pairng bpai nòy krúp.
Tuk-tuk	ไม่แพงหรอกครับ	mâi pairng ròrk krúp.
	รถติดมากนะ	rót dtìt mâhk ná.
Peter	เจ็ดสิบได้ไหม	jèt-sìp dâi mái?
Tuk-tuk	ไม่ได้ครับ	mâi dâi krúp.
	คิดแปดสิบก็แล้วกัน	kít bpàirt-sìp gôr láir-o gun.
Peter	โอ เค ไป	oh kay. bpai.

As they approach a crossroads, Peter gives the tuk-tuk driver further directions.

Peter	ถึงสี่แยกแล้ว	tĕung sèe yâirk láir-o
	เลี้ยวซ้ายครับ . . .	lée-o sái krúp . . .
Tuk-tuk	ครับ	krúp.
Peter	. . . แล้วเลี้ยวขวา	. . . láir-o lée-o kwăh
	เข้าซอยเกษมสันต์	kâo soy ga-săym-sŭn.
Tuk-tuk	เลี้ยวขวาที่นี่	lée-o kwăh têe-nêe
	ใช่ไหมครับ	châi mái krúp?
Peter	ใช่ครับ . . .	châi krúp . . .
	แล้วจอดที่โน่น	láir-o jòrt têe-nôhn
	ใกล้ ๆ รถสีขาว	glâi glâi rót sĕe kăo.
	นี่แปดสิบบาทครับ	nêe bpàirt-sìp bàht krúp.
Tuk-tuk	ขอบคุณครับ	kòrp-kOOn krúp.

róo-jùk	*to know*	รู้จัก
rohng rairm	*hotel*	โรงแรม
rohng rairm ree-noh	*Reno Hotel*	โรงแรมรีโน
yòo	*to be situated at*	อยู่
soy ga-săym-sŭn	*Soi Kasemsan*	ซอยเกษมสันต์

sa-năhm gee-lah	*stadium*	สนามกีฬา
. . . hàirng châht	*national . . .*	. . . แห่งชาติ
sa-năhm gee-lah hàirng châht	*National Stadium*	สนามกีฬาแห่งชาติ
ôr . . .	*ah!* (exclamation of realisation)	อ้อ
mâi . . . ròrk	*not . . . at all*	ไม่ . . . หรอก
rót dtìt	*traffic jam*	รถติด
jèt-sìp	*seventy*	เจ็ดสิบ
bpàirt-sìp	*eighty*	แปดสิบ
tĕung	*to reach*	ถึง
láir-o	*already; and then*	แล้ว
lée-o	*to turn*	เลี้ยว
sái	*left*	ซ้าย
krúp (kâ)	*yes*	ครับ (ค่ะ)
kwăh	*right*	ขวา
têe-nêe	*here*	ที่นี่
têe-nôhn	*over there*	ที่โน่น
sĕe kăo	*white*	สีขาว

1 On her trip to Siam Square, where does Sue ask the taxi to pull up?
2 How much does her journey cost?
3 How much does she give the taxi driver?
4 What part of Soi 23 does Sue live in?
5 In Soi 23, where does Sue ask the taxi to pull up?
6 What soi is the Reno Hotel situated on?
7 What is the nearest major landmark?
6 How much does the tuk-tuk driver want to charge?
7 What fare does Peter finally negotiate?
8 Does the tuk-tuk make a right turn or a left turn into the soi where the Reno Hotel is?
9 Where does the tuk-tuk pull up?

i You can travel around Bangkok by ordinary bus, air-conditioned bus, taxi, or **samlor (sǎhm lór)** – the three-wheeled motorized pedicab – popularly known as tuk-tuk (**dtÓOk dtÓOk**) after the unique spluttering sound of its engine. Parts of Bangkok are now linked by the overhead 'sky train', while plans are now underway to build an underground rail system.

On ordinary buses there is a fixed fare within the city centre, while on air-conditioned buses fares are calculated according to the distance travelled. Street maps with full details of all the bus routes are readily available from book shops and hotels in Bangkok, while route maps in English are also now posted at many bus stops. Buses are frequent, although often overcrowded, fares are cheap and, with exclusive bus lanes on some busy roads, the public transport system somehow manages to run reasonably efficiently amid the general chaos of Bangkok traffic.

Taxis offer a less stressful way of travelling around. To hail a taxi you should raise your hand and signal to the driver with a beckoning motion with the fingers pointing *downwards*. All taxis in central Bangkok are air conditioned and have meters, thus making it unnecessary to haggle over the price. Before getting into a vehicle, you do, however, need to enquire whether the driver is prepared to take you to your destination (he may decide that the traffic is just too bad to go that way). It is not a bad idea to check, also, that he knows the place you want to go to. Although tipping is not customary, many passengers round up the meter price. As your Thai improves, you may find that a taxi journey offers an excellent opportunity for a spot of conversation practice. Polite conversation is out of the question if you go by **samlor** (literally, 'three wheels'); you will also have to negotiate the price with the driver *before* stepping into the vehicle. Beware of causing offence by placing your feet against the rail behind the driver's seat; to do so is extremely bad manners and is likely to disturb your driver's concentration – with potentially disastrous consequences.

Many of the major roads in Bangkok have small roads or lanes – called **soy** (spelt *soi* in English) – leading off them. These are usually residential areas with a few small shops and vary in length from a couple of hundred metres to a kilometre or more. If you are negotiating a price with a tuk-tuk driver it can obviously make some difference as to whether you intend to get off at the entrance to the soi (**bpàhk soy**), the middle (**glahng soy**) or the end (**sÒOt soy**).

Key phrases and expressions

How to ask a taxi or tuk-tuk driver:

1 if he knows X

róo-jùk X mái? รู้จัก X ไหม

2 if he will take you to X

bpai X mái? ไป X ไหม

3 how much he will charge to go to X

bpai X tâo-rài? ไป X เท่าไร

X bpai tâo-rài? X ไป เท่าไร

How to tell a taxi or tuk-tuk driver:

4 the fare is too expensive and suggest an alternative

pairng bpai nòy แพงไปหน่อย

X (bàht) dâi mái? X(บาท)ได้ไหม

5 to go into the soi

kâo soy krúp (kâ) เข้าซอยครับ (ค่ะ)

6 to go to the entrance/middle/end of the soi

bpai bpàhk/glahng/ ไปปาก/กลาง/

sÒOt soy krúp (kâ) สุดซอยครับ (ค่ะ)

7 to turn left/right

lée-o sái/kwăh krúp (kâ) เลี้ยวซ้าย/ขวาครับ (ค่ะ)

8 to stop here/over there

jòrt têe-nêe/têe-nôhn จอดที่นี่/ที่โน่น

9 to go straight on

ler-ee bpai èek เลยไปอีก

Language notes

1 Reduplication of adjectives

In the first dialogue, Sue tells the taxi driver to park **glâi glâi** (*near near*) the crossroads. This repetition, or *reduplication*, of an adjective or adverb is a common feature of spoken Thai. It makes the meaning less precise and often corresponds to the English use of *-ish* in *nearish*, *whitish*, *sweetish* and so on:

jòrt glâi glâi sèe yâirk.	*Park closish to the crossroads.*
rót sĕe kăo kăo	*a whitish car*
sôm wăhn wăhn	*sweetish oranges*

You will sometimes find street vendors in tourist areas using reduplication in English to assure prospective customers that two items are 'same same' in either quality or price.

2 Numbers

The remaining numbers between ten and 100 are formed in a regular way with the exception of 21, 31, 41 etc., where the word for 'one' is **èt** and not **nèung**. (Remember that 20 is ***yêe*-sìp**.):

21 **yêe-sìp-èt**	41 **sèe-sìp-èt**
22 **yêe-sìp-sŏrng**	42 **sèe-sìp-sŏrng**
23 **yêe-sìp-săhm**	51 **hâh-sìp-èt**
24 **yêe-sìp-sèe**	52 **hâh-sìp-sŏrng**
25 **yêe-sìp-hâh**	61 **hòk-sìp-èt**
26 **yêe-sìp-hòk**	62 **hòk-sìp-sŏrng**
27 **yêe-sìp-jèt**	71 **jèt-sìp-èt**
28 **yêe-sìp-bpàirt**	72 **jèt-sìp-sŏrng**
29 **yêe-sìp-gâo**	81 **bpàirt-sìp-èt**
31 **săhm-sìp-èt**	82 **bpàirt-sìp-sŏrng**
32 **săhm-sìp-sŏrng**	91 **gâo-sìp-èt**
33 **săhm-sìp-săhm**	92 **gâo-sìp-sŏrng**

3 Location words: 'here' and 'there'

The basic words for 'here' and 'there' are **têe-nêe** and **têe-nûn** respectively. **têe-nôhn** suggests something further away – 'over there' – while **dtrong-née** is a more immediate 'right here'.

4 Place names

Individual place names follow the noun identifying the type of place:

ta-nŏn sÒO-kŎOm-wít	*Sukhumwit Road* (road-Sukhumwit)
soy ga-săym-sŭn	*Soi Kasemsan* (soi-Kasemsan)
rohng rairm ree-noh	*Reno Hotel* (hotel-Reno)
sa-năhm gee-lah hàirng châht	*National Stadium* (stadium-national)
sa-năhm bin dorn meu-ung	*Don Muang Airport* (airport-Don Muang)
jung-wùt (*province*) **dtràht**	*Trat Province* (province-Trat)

5 'Know'

róo-jùk means *know* in the sense of being acquainted with people, places or things. A different word, **róo,** or the more formal **sâhp**, is used for knowing facts:

róo-jùk mái? — *Do you know him?*
– mâi róo-jùk. — *– No.*

bpai mái? — *Are you going?*
– mâi sâhp / mâi róo. — *– I don't know.*

6 mâi . . . ròrk

The pattern **mâi** + verb/adjective + **ròrk** is used to contradict another person's stated opinion or assumption:

pairng — *It's expensive.*
– mâi pairng ròrk — *– No it isn't.*

sŏo-ay ná? — *It's pretty, isn't it?*
– mâi sŏo-ay ròrk — *– No it isn't.*

bpai mái? — *Shall we go?*
– chún mâi bpai ròrk — *– I'm not going.*

7 Verb + láir-o

láir-o has already occurred in the idiomatic expression . . . **gôr láir-o gun** (*let's settle for . . .*) used when negotiating prices. Its most common use, however, is in the pattern verb/adjective + **láir-o** to indicate that the action of the verb has been completed or the state of the adjective achieved. Often it can be translated as *already*:

káo bpai láir-o.	*He has gone (already).*
rao séu láir-o.	*We've bought some already.*
pŏm tum láir-o.	*I've done it alredy.*
por (*enough*) **láir-o.**	*That's enough.*
ìm (*full up*) **láir-o.**	*I'm full up.*
tòok (*correct*) **láir-o.**	*That's correct.*

láir-o is also used to link sequences of actions where it might be translated as *and then*:

tĕung sèe yâirk láir-o lée-o sái.	*Reach the crossroads and then turn left.*
lée-o sái láir-o lée-o kwăh.	*Turn left and then turn right.*
lée-o kwăh láir-o jòrt têe-nôhn.	*Turn right and then park over there.*

8 Yes: krúp and kâ

You have already met the polite particles **krúp** and **kâ** being used as *yes* answers (unit 2); they are also used as a *yes / right / OK* response to instructions:

lée-o sái krúp.	*Turn left.*
– krúp.	*– OK.*
pŏm bpai krúp.	*I'm going.*
– kâ.	*– OK.*

If you listen to a Thai man on a telephone you may hear him saying little more than **krúp . . . krúp . . . krúp . . . krúp**.

Exercises

1 How would you ask a taxi driver if he would take you to the following places:

(a) Siam Square
(b) the Reno Hotel
(c) Sukhumwit Road, Soi 39
(d) Don Muang Airport (**sa-năhm bin dorn meu-ung**)

2 Link the following pairs of sentences with **láir-o**:

(a) Reach the crossroads. Turn right.
(b) Turn left. Go into the soi.
(c) Turn right. Park over there.
(d) Go to the end of the soi. Park near the red car.

3 Match the numbers in the three columns:

(a) 56	(i) jèt-sìp-sèe	A ๓๘
(b) 97	(ii) sèe-sìp-sŏrng	B ๕๖
(c) 38	(iii) gâo-sìp-jèt	C ๗๔
(d) 74	(iv) săhm-sìp-bpàirt	D ๔๒
(e) 42	(v) hâh-sìp-hòk	E ๙๗

4 Peter is taking a taxi to a friend's house at the end of Sukhumwit Road, Soi 53. The tuk-tuk driver's words are given. What did Peter say?

Peter ________________ .
Tuk-tuk kâo soy mái krúp?
Peter ________________ .
Tuk-tuk bpai sÒOt soy châi mái krúp?
Peter ________________ .
Tuk-tuk gâo-sìp bàht krúp.
Peter ________________ .
Tuk-tuk mâi pairng ròrk krúp.
Peter ________________ .
Tuk-tuk kít bpàirt-sip bàht gôr láir-o gun.

5 Translate the following directions into Thai, using a polite particle to convey *please*:

(a) Park near the crossroads, please.
(b) Go to the end of the soi, please.
(c) When you reach the crossroads, turn left, please.
(d) Park over there near the reddish car, please.

Reading and writing

The words that you learned to read in the first two units were all pronounced with a mid tone. Now it is time to start learning how to read words pronounced with some other tones. By the end of this section you will have begun to read words with high tones, falling tones and low tones. In order to do this, you will have to bear three things in mind when reading a Thai word or syllable: (1) whether the initial consonant is a low-class, mid-class or high-class consonant; (2) whether the vowel is a long vowel or a short vowel; and (3) whether the syllable is a 'dead' syllable or a 'live' syllable.

1 Live syllables and dead syllables

The terms 'live' and 'dead' refer to the way a syllable ends. A 'live' syllable can be prolonged in a droning voice, whereas it is physically impossible to do this with a 'dead' syllable.

Live syllables end either with long vowels (e.g. **ah, ai, ao, ee, oo** etc.) or a **m, n** or **ng** sound, or the short vowels **ai** and **ao.** All the words in the script exercises in units 1 and 2 are live syllables. Here are some examples to remind you:

มา	นาย	ลาว	มี	ดู	นาม	งาน	ยัง	ไป
mah	**nai**	**lao**	**mee**	**duu**	**nahm**	**ngahn**	**yung**	**bpai**

Notice that they are all pronounced with a mid tone.

Dead syllables end with either a short vowel (e.g. **i, OO**) or a **p, t** or **k** sound. Here are some examples:

ติ	ดุ	รีบ	นิด	มาก
dtì	**dÒO**	**rêep**	**nít**	**mâhk**

First, you will see that these words are pronounced with different tones; the remainder of this section on the script will explain how the tone of a dead syllable is determined by the class of the initial consonant and the length of the vowel.

Second, notice that in our transcription, บ (**b**) and ด (**d**) have been written as **p** and **t**. This is because the sounds that can occur at the end of Thai words are quite limited and so certain letters change their pronunciation when they occur at the end of a word.

Here are the consonants you learned in unit 2 once more, indicating how they are pronounced when they occur as an initial consonant and as a final consonant:

	ก	จ	ด	ต	บ	ป	อ
initial	**g**	**j**	**d**	**dt**	**b**	**bp**	(zero)
final	**k**	**t**	**t**	**t**	**p**	**p**	—

A full list of initial and final consonant sounds appears in an appendix.

2 Dead syllables with low-class initial consonants

If the initial consonant in a dead syllable is low class, the tone will be either high or falling; if the vowel is short (e.g. -ิ, -ั, -ุ) the tone is high:

นิด　　รับ　　ลุก

nít　　rúp　　lÓOk

If the vowel is long (e.g. -อ, -า, -ี, -ู) the tone is falling:

มาก　　ยอด　　รีบ　　ลูบ

mâhk　　yôrt　　rêep　　lôop

3 Dead syllables with mid-class initial consonants

If the initial consonant in a dead syllable is mid class, the tone will always be low, regardless of whether the vowel is long or short:

กับ　　จาก　　ติด　　ดีด　　จุด　　จอด

gùp　　jàhk　　dtìt　　dèet　　jÒOt　　jòrt

4 Summary of tone rules

The tone rules you have just met are summarized in the following chart. You may find it helpful to make a copy of it to use for reference and checking until you feel completely confident about the rules.

Consonant class	Live syllable	Dead syllable	
		Short vowel	Long vowel
Low class	**Mid tone**	**High tone**	**Falling tone**
Mid class	**Mid tone**	**Low tone**	**Low tone**

Reading practice

Use the summary chart to help you work through these exercises. Don't worry if it takes you some time; if you understand the principles at this stage, you will find that your reading speed will quickly improve. It is well worth taking the time to work through this unit two or three times, rather than to push on to the next with a rather wobbly grasp of how tone rules operate.

1 Dead or live?

The words following occur in the dialogues. Which of these are live syllables? When you can read all these words, turn back to the dialogues and try to pick them out in the Thai script:

ไป จอด มาก กัน ดี รีโน ติด โรง

2 What tone?

The tone mark has been deliberately omitted in the transcription of these Thai words. What tone should they be pronounced with? (Remember, romanized words pronounced with a mid tone have no tone mark.)

บีบ	นาง	กัด	จุด	นัด
beep	**nahng**	**gut**	**jOOt**	**nut**
ปี	ดาบ	จาน	จาก	ตาย
bpee	**dahp**	**jahn**	**jahk**	**dtai**
ลาบ	ราว	มีด	รอบ	ปาก
lahp	**rao**	**meet**	**rorp**	**bpahk**

3 Words

Practise reading the following words, taking your time to make sure you get the tone correct. Do the exercise several times until you can read through from right to left and top to bottom at a reasonable speed. If you really want to challenge yourself, you can use the recording of this exercise to give yourself dictation practice:

ยาก	มี	นัด	กับ	งาน
ยุง	กัด	มาก	จาก	รีบ
อาย	นอน	ยอม	ลูก	จอด

ao kâo pùt gài

I'll have chicken fried rice

เอาข้าวผัดไก่

In this unit you will learn

- **how to order drinks and simple meals**
- **polite requests: kŏr + noun + nòy; kŏr + verb + nòy**
- **container words and numbers**
- **where? questions**
- **location words and prepositions**
- **consonants: ค ช ซ ท พ ฟ**
- **vowels: -ี -ื เ- แ-**

Dialogues

Peter is taking his two children out for lunch in a coffee shop.

Waitress	เอาอะไรคะ	ao a-rai ká?
Peter	ขอดูเมนูหน่อยครับ	kŏr doo may-noo nòy krúp.
Waitress	นี่ค่ะ	nêe kâ.
Peter	เอาข้าวผัดไก่สอง จานแล้วก็ . . . บะหมี่น้ำชามหนึ่ง	ao kâo pùt gài sŏrng jahn láir-o gôr . . . ba-mèe náhm chahm nèung.
Waitress	แล้วเอาน้ำอะไรคะ	láir-o ao náhm a-rai ká?
Peter	ขอเป๊ปซี่สองแก้ว แล้วเบียร์สิงห์ขวด หนึ่ง	kŏr bpép-sêe sŏrng gâir-o láir-o bee-a sĭng kòo-ut nèung.
Waitress	เป๊ปซี่ไม่มีค่ะ โคล่าได้ไหม	bpép-sêe mai mee kâ. koh-lah dâi mái?
Peter	ได้ครับ	dâi krúp.
Waitress	เอาเบียร์ขวดใหญ่ หรือขวดเล็ก	ao bee-a kòo-ut yài réu kòo-ut lék?
Peter	ขวดใหญ่ครับ เอาน้ำแข็งเปล่า แก้วหนึ่งด้วย	kòo-ut yài krúp. ao núm kăirng bplào gâir-o nèung dôo-ay.

ao	*to want (something)*	เอา
kŏr . . . (nòy)	*I'd like . . .*	ขอ
doo	*to look at*	ดู
may-noo	*menu*	เมนู
nêe kâ	*here you are*	นี่ค่ะ
kâo	*rice*	ข้าว
pùt	*to fry; fried*	ผัด
gài	*chicken*	ไก่
sŏrng	*two*	สอง

jahn	*plate*	จาน
nèung	*one*	หนึ่ง
láir-o gôr	*and*	แล้วก็
ba-mèe	*egg noodles*	บะหมี่
náhm	*water*	น้ำ
ba-mèe náhm	*egg noodle soup*	บะหมี่น้ำ
chahm	*bowl*	ชาม
bpép-sêe	*Pepsi*	เป๊ปซี่
gâir-o	*glass*	แก้ว
kòo-ut	*bottle*	ขวด
bee-a sĭng	*Singha beer*	เบียร์สิงห์
dôo-ay	*too, also*	ด้วย
koh-lâh	*Coca-Cola*	โคล่า
yài	*large*	ใหญ่
réu	*or*	หรือ
lék	*small*	เล็ก
núm kăirng	*ice*	น้ำแข็ง
núm kăirng bplào	*iced water*	น้ำแข็งเปล่า

▶ Their meal finished, Peter asks for the bill.

Peter	หนู หนู เก็บสตางค์	nŏo, nŏo gèp dtung.
Waitress	สองร้อยห้าสิบบาทค่ะ	sŏrng róy hâh sìp bàht kâ.
Peter	ขอโทษครับ	kŏr-tôht krúp
	ห้องน้ำอยู่ที่ไหน	hôrng náhm yòo têe năi?
Waitress	อยู่ข้างบนค่ะ	yòo kûng bon kâ.
	ห้องน้ำผู้ชาย	hôrng náhm pôo-chai
	อยู่ทางซ้าย	yòo tahng sái
	ห้องน้ำผู้หญิง	hôrng náhm pôo-yĭng
	อยู่ทางขวา	yòo tahng kwăh.
Peter	ขอบคุณครับ	kòrp-kOOn krúp.

nŏo	(way of addressing young waitresses)	หนู
gèp	*to collect, keep*	เก็บ
dtung, sa-dtahng	*money, satang*	สตางค์
hôrng	*room*	ห้อง
hôrng náhm	*toilet, bathroom*	ห้องน้ำ
. . . têe năi?	*where?*	...ที่ไหน
kûng bon	*upstairs; on top*	ข้างบน
pôo-chai	*man*	ผู้ชาย
pôo-yĭng	*woman*	ผู้หญิง
tahng	*way*	ทาง
tahng kwăh/sái	*to the right/left*	ทางขวา/ซ้าย

1 How many plates of fried rice did Peter order?
2 Did he order his children's drinks by the bottle or by the glass?
3 Why didn't his children have Pepsi to drink?
4 What did Peter have to drink?
5 How much did the meal come to?
6 Where are the toilets?

i Most Thais eat three meals a day although many will supplement this with snacks throughout the day. Traditionally, rice formed the basis of all three meals and would be accompanied by various side dishes such as fried or pickled vegetables, curry, soup and meat and fish dishes.

Thais living in towns and cities tend to eat out a lot. There are eating places to suit nearly every pocket, ranging from roadside stalls and noodle shops to air-conditioned coffee shops and restaurants. In recent years western fast food restaurants have become increasingly popular in Bangkok.

When you go into a restaurant you will usually find someone waiting attentively to serve you. But if you do need to attract a waiter's attention beckon with your palm uppermost and fingers pointing *downwards* (as when calling a taxi). If the waiter or waitress is a child, then you can call out **nŏo, nŏo** (literally 'rat, rat' – but also an affectionate way of addressing children!); otherwise it is more appropriate to say **kOOn krúp (ká)**. When you want to pay, you can say either **chék bin** or **gèp dtung**; although there are no strict rules, the former is more appropriate in air-conditioned restaurants – where tipping is customary – and the latter in noodle shops, where it is unnecessary to tip.

Key phrases and expressions

How to:

1 attract a waiter's or waitress's attention

kOOn krúp (ká) คุณครับ (คะ)

2 ask for the menu

kŏr doo may-noo nòy ขอดูเมนูหน่อย

3 ask for a glass of iced water

kŏr núm kăirng bplào gâir-o nèung ขอน้ำแข็งเปล่าแก้วหนึ่ง

4 ask for the bill

gèp dtung krúp (kâ) เก็บสตางค์ครับ (ค่ะ)

or

chéck bin krúp (kâ) เช็คบิลครับ (ค่ะ)

Language notes

1 Polite requests: asking for something

When asking for something, the pattern **kŏr** + noun + **nòy** (*a little*) is used. However, if the amount of the item requested is specified (e.g. two plates of fried rice, one bottle of beer), **nòy** is replaced by the number expression:

kŏr náhm nòy?	*Can I have some water?*
kŏr náhm sŏrng gâir-o?	*Can I have two glasses of water?*

In both cases, **dâi mái?** can be added at the end of the request for additional politeness:

kŏr náhm nòy dâi mái?	*Could I have some water?*
kŏr náhm sŏrng gâir-o dâi mái?	*Could I have two glasses of water?*

Note that in restaurants it is perfectly acceptable to use **ao** (*I want*) instead of **kŏr** when ordering.

2 Polite requests: asking to do something yourself

When asking to do something oneself, the pattern **kŏr** + verb + **nòy** is used:

kŏr doo nòy?	*Can I see it?*
kŏr chim nòy?	*Can I taste it?*

dâi mái? can be added at the end of the request for additional politeness:

kŏr doo nòy dâi mái?	*Could I see it?*
kŏr chim nòy dâi mái?	*Could I taste it?*
kŏr jòrt têe nêe nòy dâi mái?	*Could I park here?*

Remember that **kŏr** + verb + **nòy** is only used when asking to do something *yourself*. You cannot use it when asking a waitress to bring the bill or a taxi driver to pull up.

3 Container words

'Uncountable' nouns, such as Coke, rice, coffee and noodles can be counted by the container in which they are purchased or from which they are consumed. The order of words in Thai is noun + number + container word:

koh-lâh sŏrng kòo-ut	*two bottles of Coke*
kâo pùt gài săhm jahn	*three plates of fried rice*
gah-fair sèe tôo-ay	*four cups of coffee*
ba-mèe náhm hâh chahm	*five bowls of noodle soup*

However, if the number is **nèung** (*one*), it can occur either before the container word (see above) or after, in the pattern noun + container word + **nèung**; when it occurs after the container word it can be translated by the indefinite article *a/an*:

koh-lâh kòo-ut nèung	*a bottle of Coke*
kâo pùt gài jahn nèung	*a plate of fried rice*
gah-fair tôo-ay nèung	*a cup of coffee*
ba-mèe náhm chahm nèung	*a bowl of noodle soup*

When specifying the size of the container, the word order is noun + container word + adjective:

kâo pùt gài jahn yài	*a large plate of chicken fried rice*
bia sĭng kòo-ut lék	*a small bottle of Singha beer*

In unit 2 you learned how to ask how much various fruits cost per kilo, using the pattern noun + **loh** + **la** + **tâo-rài?** The same basic pattern can be used for asking the price of uncountable nouns, substituting a container word for **loh**:

koh-lâh kòo-ut la tâo-rài?	*How much is a bottle of Coke?*
kâo pùt gài jahn la tâo-rài?	*How much is a plate of fried rice?*
gah-fair tôo-ay la tâo-rài?	*How much is a cup of coffee?*

4 Alternative questions: . . . or . . . ?

The Thai word for *or* is **réu**:

ao bpép-sêe réu núm sôm?	*Do you want Pepsi or orange juice?*
ao sěe dairng réu sěe kǎo?	*Do you want red or white?*
yòo tahng sái réu tahng kwǎh?	*Is it on the left or the right?*

In Thai script **réu** is spelt exactly the same as the question particle . . . **lěr?** (unit 2), but in normal speech it is pronounced with a short vowel and a high tone. Many speakers will pronounce the word with an initial **l** rather than **r**.

5 'Water'

The long vowel in **náhm** (*water*) changes to a short vowel when it occurs as the first word in compound nouns (nouns made up of more than one word):

náhm	*water*	
núm kǎirng	*ice*	(water + hard)
núm sôm	*orange juice*	(water + orange)
núm bplah	*fish sauce*	(water + fish)

But when it is the second word in a compound, the vowel is pronounced long:

hôrng náhm	*toilet, bathroom*	(room + water)
mâir náhm	*river*	(mother + water)

6 nǒo

nǒo (*rat*) is widely used as a first-person pronoun (*I*) by young children addressing parents and other adults, and girls and women addressing superiors (such as teachers, bosses or older relatives). It is used as a second-person pronoun (*you*) by parents and adults addressing young children, and people of higher social status addressing servants, cleaners, waitresses and junior colleagues:

nŏo mâi bpai. *I'm not going.* (child speaking)
nŏo kŏr doo nòy dâi mái? *Could I see it?* (child speaking)
nŏo bpai mâi dâi. *You can't go.* (parent to child)

7 dtung

dtung is a shortened form of 'satang'. It has the more general meaning, 'money' in the expressions **gèp dtung** (literally, *collect the money*) and **mâi mee dtung** (*I haven't any money*). The satang is the smallest unit of Thai currency. There are 100 satang in one baht, although today it exists only in the 25-satang and 50-satang coins.

8 'Where?' questions

Where? questions follow the pattern verb + **têe-năi?** (*where?*). Note that **têe-năi?** always occurs at the end of a sentence in Thai:

hôrng náhm yòo têe-năi? *Where is the toilet?*
kOOn tum ngahn têe-năi? *Where do you work?*
káo jòrt rót têe-năi? *Where did he park the car?*
lée-o sái têe-năi? *Where do you turn left?*

Answers to *where?* questions often take the form verb + **têe** (*at*) + location:

yòo têe-nôhn. *It is over there.*
chún tum ngahn têe chee-ung mài. *I work in Chiang Mai.*

If the verb is **bpai** (*to go*) or **mah jàhk** (*to come from*), the word **têe** is normally dropped, both in questions and answers:

kOOn bpai năi? *Where are you going?*
– bpai sa-yăhm sa-kwair. *– I'm going to Siam Square.*

káo mah jàhk năi? *Where does she come from?*
– mah jàhk chee-ung mài. *– She comes from Chiang Mai.*

In informal spoken Thai, **têe** is also commonly dropped when the verb is **yòo** (*to be situated at*):

rót yòo năi? *Where's your car?*
káo yòo chee-ung mài. *He lives in Chiang Mai.*

9 Location words: tahng and kûng

Besides têe, **tahng** (*way*) and **kûng** (*side*) can also be used for describing locations.

tahng is used with **sái** (*left*) and **kwăh** (*right*):

hôrng náhm pôo chai yòo tahng sái.	*The men's toilet is on the left.*
hôrng náhm pôo yĭng yòo tahng kwăh.	*The ladies' toilet is on the right.*

kûng commonly occurs before the following prepositions:

bon	*on; upstairs*
kâhng	*side*
lâhng	*under; downstairs*
lŭng	*behind*
nâh	*in front (of)*
nai	*in*
nôrk	*outside*

If a noun follows the preposition, **kûng** is normally dropped:

yòo lŭng rót.	*It's behind the car.*
yòo nai hôrng.	*It's in the room.*

But if there is no noun after the preposition, **kûng** cannot be dropped:

hôrng náhm yòo kûng bon.	*The toilet is upstairs.*
káo bpai kûng nôrk.	*He has gone outside.*

10 Prefix pôo . . .

pôo occurs as the first syllable of numerous nouns in Thai, including **pôo-chai** (*man/boy*) and **pôo-yĭng têe** (*woman/girl*), where it means *person who . . .* :

pôo-chai	*man/boy* (one who is male)
pôo-yĭng	*woman/girl* (one who is female)
pôo-yài	*adult* (one who is big)
pôo-rái	*criminal* (one who is bad)
pôo-jùt-gahn	*manager* (one who arranges things)
pôo-bor-ri-hăhn	*administrator* (one who administers)

Exercises

1 How would you ask for the following?

(a) the menu
(b) three plates of chicken fried rice
(c) two bottles of Singha beer
(d) a glass of water
(e) the bill

2 How would you ask to do the following?

(a) to see something
(b) to taste something
(c) to park your car over there

3 Match the following orders with the right drinks:

(a) bpép-sêe hâh kòo-ut
(b) bee-a sǐng sǎhm kòo-ut
(c) núm kǎirng bplào sǒrng gâir-o
(d) gah-fair sǒrng tôo-ay

4 How would you ask where the following are?

(a) Siam Square
(b) the Reno Hotel
(c) the toilet
(d) Sukhumwit Road Soi 33
(e) Khun Malee

5 Use the picture to make up sentences describing where members of the family are:

(a) . . . yòo kûng nai
(b) . . . yòo kûng nôrk
(c) . . . yòo kûng bon
(d) . . . yòo kûng lâhng
(e) . . . yòo kûng nâh
(f) . . . yòo kûng lǔng/kûng kâhng

Reading and writing

1 Consonants

The new consonants in this unit are all low-class consonants (like those in unit 1). Be careful not to confuse ค (**k**) with ด (**d**) which you learned in unit 2; ช (**ch**) and ซ (**s**) also look very similar, although the latter has an additional 'notch' on its left 'arm':

k **ch** **s** **t** **p** **f**

2 Vowels

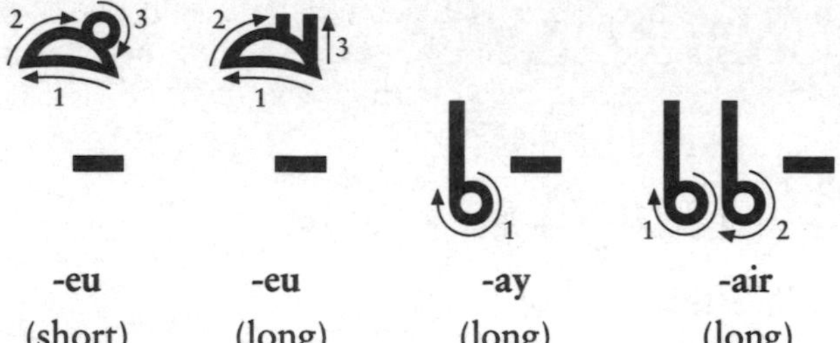

The symbol -ื is unusual in that if there is no final consonant (i.e. the word ends with an '-eu' sound) the zero consonant symbol must be added:

with final consonant		*no final consonant* (add -อ)	
คืน	มืด	คือ	มือ
keun	**mêut**	**keu**	**meu**

The symbol เ- changes from an **-ay** sound to **er-ee** when it occurs with the consonant ย at the end of the word:

เลย	เคย
ler-ee	**ker-ee**

3 Vowel shortener symbol -็

When this symbol, which is identical to the number eight, appears above a consonant and in conjunction with the vowel symbols เ- and แ- the vowels change from long vowels to short vowels; it also occurs above the letter ก with no accompanying written vowel, in which case the syllable is pronounced **gôr**:

เป็น	เล็ก	เก็บ	แช็ก	ก็
bpen	**lék**	**gèp**	**cháirk**	**gôr**

4 Words with no vowel symbol

When a word consists of two consonant symbols with no written vowel symbol, a short **o** vowel must be supplied:

คน	มด	จน	กด
kon	**mót**	**jon**	**gòt**

Remember that the tone rules from unit 3 have to be applied. **kon** and **mót** both begin with a low-class consonant, but **mót** has a high tone because it is a dead syllable and the vowel is short. **gòt** has a mid-class initial consonant and, because it is a dead syllable, it is pronounced with a low tone.

Reading practice

1 Words

This exercise gives you practice in reading words containing some of the new letters you have learned in this unit. Don't forget to distinguish between 'live' and 'dead' syllables'! Look back to your tone rules chart in unit 3. Better still, make a copy of it so that you can keep referring to it when reading Thai words. This will ease some of the burden of memorization and you will find that you gradually absorb the rules through practice.

ชาย ชาม ซอย บาท คำ
ชอบ ทาง พา พัก ทำ
ทุก คืน ดึง ตึก คือ
เคย เลย แพง แดง แปด
เย็น เล็ก เป็น เจ็ด เก็บ
เป็ด ก็ เมนู คน ลง

2 Some short sentences

แปด แปดบาท แปดบาทแพง แปดบาทแพงไป
จีน คนจีน เป็นคนจีน ลุงเป็นคนจีน
ไป มากไป เจ็ดจานมากไป กินเจ็ดจานมากไป

3 Public signs

You may not be able to read very much Thai yet, but already you can make practical use of what you do know. You can, for example:

(i) choose the cheapest bottle of beer:

(a) ๔๙ บาท (b) ๗๓ บาท (c) ๖๕ บาท

(ii) find your way to your friend's house on Soi 19:

(a) ซอย ๑๕ (b) ซอย ๑๗ (c) ซอย ๑๙

(iii) go through the correct door at restaurant toilets:

(a) ชาย (b) หญิง

How are you progressing?

One of the potentially frustrating things about learning to read and write Thai is that you have to absorb so many rules initially before you can read even the simplest dialogue or passage. One good piece of news, however, is that once you have learned these rules, you will find that in Thai there is a much closer match between the spelling of a word and the way it is pronounced than there is in English. Another good piece of news is that you are nearly halfway there. By the end of unit 8 you should be able to read most of the dialogues in the book and by unit 10 you will be attempting special reading passages. So keep working through the script sections, retracing your steps if necessary, reviewing earlier material until it becomes second nature, and 'doodling' until your writing becomes reasonably elegant.

tǎir-o née mee bprai-sa-nee mái?

is there a post office around here?

แถวนี้มีไปรษณีย์ไหม

In this unit you will learn

- **simple post office transactions**
- **more questions about the location of things**
- **noun classifiers**
- **want and want to**
- **consonants: ข ฉ ถ ผ ฝ ศ ส ษ ห**

Dialogues

Sue is trying to find out if there is a post office nearby.

Sue	ขอโทษค่ะ แถวนี้ มีไปรษณีย์ไหม	kŏr-tôht ká tăir-o née mee bprai-sa-nee mái?
Passer-by	ไปรษณีย์หรือ มีค่ะ อยู่ซอย ๑ ใกล้ ๆ ธนาคารกรุงเทพ ฯ	bprai-sa-nee lĕr? mee kâ. yòo soy nèung glâi glâi ta-na-kahn grOOng-tâyp.
Sue	ไกลไหมคะ	glai mái ká?
Passer-by	ไม่ไกลหรอกค่ะ เดินไปทางนี้ สักสองสามนาที เท่านั้น	mâi glai ròrk kâ. dern bpai tahng née sùk sŏrng săhm nah-tee tâo-nún.
Sue	ขอบคุณมากค่ะ	kòrp-kOOn mâhk kâ.
Passer-by	ไม่เป็นไรค่ะ	mâi bpen rai kâ.

tăir-o née	*(in) this vicinity*	แถวนี้
bprai-sa-nee	*post office*	ไปรษณีย์
ta-na-kahn	*bank*	ธนาคาร
grOOng-tâyp	*Bangkok*	กรุงเทพ ฯ
glai	*far*	ไกล
dern	*walk*	เดิน
tahng née	*this way*	ทางนี้
sùk	(see Language notes)	สัก
sŏrng săhm	*two or three; a few*	สองสาม
nah-tee	*minute*	นาที
tâo-nún	*only*	เท่านั้น
mâi bpen rai	*never mind*	ไม่เป็นไร

Sue is at the post office to send some postcards and a package.

Sue	โปสการ์ดส่ง ไปอังกฤษเท่าไรคะ	bpóht-gáht sòng bpai ung-grìt tâo-rài ká?
PO clerk	สิบสองบาทครับ	sìp-sŏrng bàht krúp.
Sue	เอาแสตมป์สิบสองบาท สี่ดวงค่ะ เดี๋ยว . . . ต้องการจดหมายอากาศ แผ่นหนึ่งด้วยค่ะ	ao sa-dtairm sìp-sŏrng bàht sèe doo-ung kâ. dĕe-o . . . dtôrng-gahn jòt-măi ah-gàht pàirn nèung dôo-ay kâ.
PO clerk	หกสิบบาทครับ	hòk-sìp bàht krúp.
Sue	แล้วนี่ส่งไป อเมริกาเท่าไรคะ	láir-o nêe sòng bpai a-may-ri-gah tâo-rài ká?
PO clerk	ส่งไปทางอากาศ หรือทางเรือครับ	sòng bpai tahng ah-gàht réu tahng reu-a krúp?
Sue	ทางอากาศค่ะ อยาก จะลงทะเบียนด้วย	tahng ah-gàht kâ. yàhk ja long ta-bee-un dôo-ay.
PO clerk	ร้อยเจ็ดสิบบาทครับ . . .	róy-jèt-sìp bàht krúp . . .
Sue	ทั้งหมดเท่าไรคะ	túng mòt tâo-rài ká?

bpóht-gáht	*postcard*	โปสการ์ด
sòng	*send*	ส่ง
doo-ung	(classifier for stamps)	ดวง
dĕe-o . . .	*wait a moment*	เดี๋ยว . . .
jòt-măi ah-gàht	*aerogramme*	จดหมายอากาศ
pàirn	(classifier for aerogrammes)	แผ่น
sa-dtairm	*stamp*	แสตมป์
a-may-ri-gah	*America*	อเมริกา
tahng ah-gàht	*by air*	ทางอากาศ
tahng reu-a	*by sea*	ทางเรือ
yàhk (ja)	*to want to*	อยาก(จะ)
long ta-bee-un	*register*	ลงทะเบียน

1 Where is the nearest post office for Sue?
2 What is near the post office?
3 How long will it take Sue to walk there?
4 How many postcards is Sue going to send to England?
5 How many aerogrammes does she buy?
6 Does she plan to send the package to America by air or sea?

i It is unrealistic at this stage to expect to be able to understand complicated directions given in Thai. Asking directions, however, is an excellent way of practising speaking Thai with strangers, even if you don't always catch the answer. You can always start by asking the way to somewhere you know, so that you can say 'thank you' and walk off confidently in the right direction even if you actually understood very little. Repeat the exercise a number of times, however, and you will find your listening skills steadily improve.

Post offices in Thailand are open from 8.30 a.m. to 4.30 p.m. on weekdays but are closed at weekends. In Bangkok, the Central Post Office, located on New Road, is open on both Saturday and Sunday. Post office facilities are available in many of the larger Bangkok hotels and also on university campuses.

Key phrases and expressions

How to:

1 ask if there is . . . in the vicinity

tăir-o née mee . . . mái?	แถวนี้มี . . . ไหม

2 express and acknowledge thanks

kòrp-kOOn (mâhk)	ขอบคุณ (มาก)
mâi bpen rai	ไม่เป็นไร

3 ask how much it costs to send X somewhere

X sòng bpai . . . tâo-rài?	X ส่งไป . . . เท่าไร

4 ask how much it costs to send X by air

X sòng bpai	X ส่งไป
tahng ah-gàht tâo-rài?	ทางอากาศเท่าไร

5 ask to send something by registered mail

yàhk ja long ta-bee-un	อยากจะลงทะเบียน

Language notes

1 Location word: tǎir-o

The question **tǎir-o née mee . . . mái?** is used for asking whether something is located in the vicinity. In statements you will quite often hear the noun **tǎir-o** reduplicated to convey a sense of vagueness about the location of something:

káo jòrt rót tǎir-o tǎir-o soy sǎhm-sìp. *He parked in the Soi 30 area.*
yòo tǎir-o tǎir-o bahng lum-poo. *It is in the Banglampu area.*

2 Bangkok

The Thai word for *Bangkok* is **grOOng-tâyp** which can be translated as 'City of Angels'. This is a hugely abbreviated form of the full name of the city, which is recorded in the *Guinness Book of Records* as the world's longest place name. 'Bangkok' was the name of a small village on the Chao Phya River which became Thailand's capital after 1782.

3 Location words: 'near' and 'far'

To any westerner learning Thai it seems particularly perverse that two words with opposite meanings should sound almost identical. To a Thai, of course, there is a world of difference between **glâi** *near* and **glai** *far*. But if you have difficulty hearing the difference between mid tones and falling tones, don't despair; you will often hear the *near* word in its reduplicated form, **glâi glâi**.

4 Direction verbs

The verbs **pay** (*to go*) and **mah** (*to come*) occur after a number of verbs to show whether the action is directed towards or away from the speaker. They commonly occur with verbs of motion, such as *walk*, *run*, *fly*, *move house* and also *to telephone*. The first two examples, taken from this unit, indicate movement away from the speaker; the second two indicate movement towards the speaker, examples of which you will meet in later units:

dern bpai tahng née. *Walk this way.*
sòng bpai ung-grìt tâo-rài? *How much does it cost to send to England?*

mah-lee toh mah.	*Malee telephoned.*
rao yái mah yòo têe nêe.	*We moved here.*

5 sùk + number + classifier

The word **sùk** occurs in the pattern **sùk** + number + classifier (+ **tâo-nún**) to convey the idea of 'just' or 'as little/few as'. It usually does not need to be translated in English. When **sùk** occurs immediately before the classifier, then the omitted number word is understood to be *one*. **sùk** also occurs with the question word **tâo-rài:**

sùk sŏrng săhm nah-tee tâo-nún	*(just) two or three minutes*
rao gin bia sùk kòo-ut sŏrng kòo-ut.	*We had a bottle of beer or two.*
sùk tâo-rài?	*how much?*

6 mâi bpen rai

mâi pen rai is an idiomatic expression meaning *never mind, don't worry about it, it doesn't matter*. The phrase is often cited by both Thais and foreigners alike as evidence of Thais' 'easy-going' attitude to life; it can also be used as a response to **kòrp-kOOn** (*thank you*), when it means *you're welcome, don't mention it*.

7 Classifiers

One striking difference between Thai and English is the way nouns and numbers are combined. In unit 4 we noted how uncountable nouns could be counted by the container, just as in English (e.g. *three plates of fried rice*) and that the word order in Thai was noun + number + container (i.e. fried rice-three-plate).

When it comes to countable nouns, like *stamps*, *mangoes*, *doctors*, Thai follows this same basic pattern, replacing the container word with a special category of words, called classifiers, in the pattern noun + number + classifier:

sa-dtairm sèe doo-ung	*four stamps* (stamp-four-classifier for stamps)
jòt-măi ah-gàht sŏrng pàirn	*two aerogrammes* (aerogrammes-two-classifier for aerogrammes)
ma-môo-ung hòk bai	*six mangoes*
mŏr jèt kon	*seven doctors*

However **nèung** (*one*), as in the case of container words in unit 4, can occur either before the classifier or after (i.e. noun + classifier + **nèung**) when it occurs after the classifier it can be translated by the indefinite article, *a/an*:

sa-dtairm doo-ung nèung	*a stamp*
kŏr ma-môo-ung bai nèung.	*I'd like a mango, please.*

Some common classifiers and nouns they are used with include:

bai	*individual fruits, eggs, bowls, slips of paper*
doo-ung	*stamps, stars, lights*
dtoo-a	*animals*
hàirng	*places*
hôrng	*rooms*
kon	*people*
kun	*vehicles*
lêm	*books*
lŭng	*houses*
lôok	*fruit*
pàirn	*aerogrammes, flat objects*
un	*small objects*

All container words and measure words such as *kilometre*, *kilogram*, *day* and so on, can also be regarded as classifiers.

8 'Want' and 'want to'

(a) **yàhk (ja)** is an auxiliary verb, meaning *want to*, *would like to*; **ja** is optional. **yàhk (ja)** is followed by another verb:

pŏm yàhk (ja) bpai dôo-ay.	*I want to go, too.*
káo mâi yàhk (ja) mah.	*He doesn't want to come.*

Would you like to . . . ? questions are answered **yàhk** (*yes*) or **mâi yàhk** (*no*):

káo yàhk (ja) bpai dôo-ay mái?	*Does he want to go, too?*
– yàhk/mâi yàhk.	*– Yes/no.*
kOOn yàhk (ja) lorng chim mái?	*Do you want to try tasting it?*
– yàhk/mâi yàhk.	*– Yes/no.*

(b) The verb **ao** also means *want*, but it is followed by a noun:

chún ao bpép-sêe sŏrng kòo-ut.	*I want two bottles of Pepsi.*
káo ao jòt-măi ah-gàht pàirn nèung.	*He wants an aerogramme.*

(c) **dtôrng-gahn** can be either the auxiliary verb *want/need to*, when it is followed by a verb, or it can mean *need/want* and be followed by a noun:

káo dtôrng-gahn long ta-bee-un.	*He wants/needs to register.*
chún dtôrng-gahn sa-dtairm doo-ung nèung.	*I need a stamp.*

9 Verb serialization

One way in which Thai differs markedly from English is the use of noun classifiers; another difference is the way in which several verbs can follow one another in Thai without any intervening words. By using a directional verb (e.g. **bpai** or **mah**) and an auxiliary verb (e.g. **yàhk (ja)** or **dtôrng-gahn**) we can construct simple three-verb sentences:

rao yàhk dern bpai.	*We'd like to walk.* (we-want-walk-go)
chún dtôrng-gahn sòng bpai.	*I need to send it.* (I-need-send-go)

This process of stringing a number of verbs together is called verb serialization. Series of four or five verbs are normal in Thai, but longer combinations are possible.

Exercises

1 How would you ask if there was one of the following in the vicinity:

(a) post office
(b) bank
(c) toilet
(d) telephone (**toh-ra-sùp**)

2 How would you:

(a) ask how much it costs to send a postcard to America?
(b) ask how much it costs to send something by airmail?
(c) ask for five twelve-baht stamps?
(d) ask for one aerogramme?
(e) ask how much it all comes to?

3 Supply the correct classifier in these phrases:

(a) sa-dtairm sìp bàht hâh . . .
(b) jòt-mǎi ah-gàht . . . nèung

(c) ga-fair sǒrng . . .
(d) kâo pùt gài . . . nèung
(e) hôrng náhm sǎhm . . .
(f) núk sèuk-sǎh . . . nèung

4 How would you say:

(a) I would like to park over there.
(b) I would like to go to Siam Square.
(c) I would like an aerogramme.
(d) I would like fried rice.

Reading and writing

1 Consonants

All the new consonants in this unit are high-class consonants. High-class consonants are pronounced with an inherent **rising** tone; so when reading the following letters, we would say **kǒr**, **chǒr**, **tǒr**, **pǒr** etc. You will notice that there are three different high-class 's' symbols. Of these, the most common is the third, with the first two appearing mainly in words of foreign origin.

If you compare the consonants in this unit with the low-class consonants you met in unit 4, you will see that they can be paired up. The basic consonant sound is the same with only the inherent rising tone distinguishing the high-class consonants from the low-class consonants.

low class	ค	ช	ท	พ	ฟ	ซ
	kor	**chor**	**tor**	**por**	**for**	**sor**
high class	ข	ฉ	ถ	ผ	ฝ	ส,ศ,ษ
	kŏr	**chŏr**	**tŏr**	**pŏr**	**fŏr**	**sŏr**

2 High-class consonants at the beginning of live syllables

Live syllables with an initial high-class consonant are pronounced with a *rising* tone:

ขาย ผม สอง

kăi **pŏm** **sŏrng**

A rare exception is the female word for *I*, **di-chún** and **chún** where the tone on **chún** is high.

ดิฉัน ฉัน

di-chún **chún**

3 High-class consonants at the beginning of dead syllables

Dead syllables that begin with a high-class consonant are always pronounced with a *low* tone, regardless of whether the vowel is long or short:

หก สิบ ถูก ขาด

hòk **sìp** **tòok** **kàht**

4 Silent ห at the beginning of a word

There are a number of words in Thai that are spelt with an initial ห which is not pronounced. The function of this 'silent h' is to convert the consonant that follows into a high-class consonant. All such words then follow the tone rules of words with an initial high-class consonant:

ไหน หยุด หลอด

năi **yÒOt** **lòrt**

An important exception to note is the question particle **mái?** which is spelt as if it should have a rising tone, although in normal speech is pronounced with a high tone: ไหม **mái?**

5 Summary of tone rules

The tone rules for syllables and words with initial high-class consonants can be summarized as follows:

Consonant class	Live syllable	Dead syllable Short vowel	Dead syllable Long vowel
High class	**Rising tone**	**Low tone**	**Low tone**

Reading practice

1 Words

Here are some common words that begin with a high-class consonant. The live syllables will have a rising tone and dead syllables a low tone. Read through the exercise several times until you can do it quickly and accurately.

ขาย ขอ ขับ ฉีด ถาม
ถูก ผิด ฝาก สี สุด
สอน สาว สัก สิบ หัก
หา หลัง หวัด หลาย หนู

2 Spot the word

You should now be able to read all these words from the dialogues. Turn back to the beginning of this unit and try to find each one without referring to the romanized section.

ขอโทษ แถว มี ไหม* หรือ
ซอย หรอก ไป ทาง สัก
สอง สาม นาที มาก เป็นไร
สิบสอง บาท ทาง อากาศ จดหมาย
อเมริกา** ลง เจ็ดสิบ หมด

* Remember, this is pronounced with a high tone in normal speech.
** 'zero' consonant at the beginning of this word is pronounced **a.**

3 Match the numbers

(i)	๒	(a)	แปด
(ii)	๓	(b)	หก
(iii)	๖	(c)	สิบ
(iv)	๗	(d)	สาม
(v)	๘	(e)	เจ็ด
(vi)	๑๐	(f)	สอง

4 Sentences

Read across the page, building up to four-word sentences:

ไทย*	คนไทย	เป็นคนไทย	ลุงเป็นคนไทย
ตาก	จังหวัดตาก	จากจังหวัดตาก	มาจากจังหวัดตาก
มาก	หลานมาก	มีหลานมาก	ยายมีหลานมาก
คน	สิบคน	ลูกสิบคน	มีลูกสิบคน
คน	สามคน	สาวสามคน	ลูกสาวสามคน

* Note that the final consonant is redundant in this word.

kǒr pôot gùp . . . nòy, dâi mái?

could I speak to . . ., please?

ขอพูดกับ . . . หน่อย ได้ไหม

In this lesson you will learn

- **the language of telephone transactions**
- **who? questions**
- **when? questions**
- **talking about the future: ja + verb**
- **verbs of thinking and saying with wâh**
- **script review**

Dialogues

Sue is telephoning Malee, but it is the maid at Malee's home who picks up the receiver.

Sue	ฮันโล ขอพูดกับ	hun-loh kŏr pôot gùp
	คุณมาลีหน่อย	kOOn mah-lee nòy
	ได้ไหมคะ	dâi mái ká?
Maid	ใครพูดคะ	krai pôot ká?
Sue	ฉัน Sue พูดค่ะ	chún Sue pôot kâ.
Maid	ใครนะ	krai ná?
	ช่วยพูดดัง ๆ	chôo-ay pôot dung dung
	หน่อยได้ไหม สายไม่ดี	nòy dâi mái? săi mâi dee.
Sue	ค่ะ ฉัน Sue พูดค่ะ	kâ. chún Sue pôot kâ.
	เป็นเพื่อนคุณมาลี	bpen pêu-un kOOn mah-lee.
Maid	รอสักครู่นะคะ . . .	ror sùk krôo ná ká . . .
	คุณมาลีไม่อยู่ค่ะ	kOOn mah-lee mâi yòo kâ.
	ออกไปข้างนอกแล้ว	òrk bpai kûng nôrk láir-o.
Sue	อ้อ หรือคะ	ôr lĕr ká?
	จะกลับมาเมื่อไรคะ	ja glùp mah mêu-rài ká?
Maid	ไม่ทราบค่ะ	mâi sâhp kâ.
	คิดว่าจะกลับมาตอนบ่าย	kít wâh ja glùp mah dtorn bài.
	ตอนบ่ายโทรมาใหม่นะคะ	dtorn bài toh mah mài ná ká.
Sue	ค่ะ ขอบคุณค่ะ	kâ. kòrp-kOOn kâ.
	สวัสดีค่ะ	sa-wùt dee kâ.

hun-loh	*hello* (on telephone)	ฮันโล
pôot	*to speak*	พูด
krai	*who?*	ใคร
dung	*loud*	ดัง
săi	*(telephone) line*	สาย
dee	*good*	ดี
mâi dee	*bad*	ไม่ดี
pêu-un	*friend*	เพื่อน
ror	*to wait*	รอ
krôo	*a moment*	ครู่
òrk	*to go out*	ออก
kûng nôrk	*outside*	ข้างนอก
ja	(future time marker)	จะ
glùp	*to return*	กลับ
mêu-rài?	*when?*	เมื่อไร
sâhp	*to know*	ทราบ
kít	*to think*	คิด
wâh	(see Language notes)	ว่า
dtorn	*period of time*	ตอน
bài	*afternoon*	บ่าย
dtorn bài	*afternoon*	ตอนบ่าย
toh	*to telephone*	โทร
mài	*again; new*	ใหม่

Peter is trying to call Khun Somchai, but Somchai's daughter answers.

Daughter	ฮันโล	hun-loh.
Peter	ฮันโล	hun-loh.
	ที่โน่นบ้านคุณ	têe-nôhn bâhn kOOn
	สมชายใช่ไหมครับ	sŏm-chai châi mái krúp?
Daughter	ใช่ค่ะ	châi kâ.
	แต่คุณพ่อไม่อยู่ค่ะ	dtàir kOOn pôr mâi yòo kâ.
	ไปทำงานแล้ว	bpai tum ngahn láir-o.
Peter	อ้อ หรือครับ	ôr lĕr krúp?
Daughter	คุณต้องการ เบอร์	kOOn dtôrng-gahn ber
	โทรศัพท์มือถือไหม	toh-ra-sùp meu tĕu mái?
Peter	ไม่เป็นไรครับ	mâi bpen rai krúp.
	ตอนเย็นจะโทรมาใหม่	dtorn yen ja toh mah mài.
	ช่วยบอกคุณพ่อว่า	chôo-ay bòrk kOOn pôr wâh
	Peter เพื่อนฝรั่งโทรมา	Peter pêu-un fa-rùng toh mah.
Daughter	ค่ะ	kâ.
Peter	ขอบคุณมากครับ	kòrp-kOOn mâhk krúp.
	สวัสดีครับ	sa-wùt dee krúp.

bâhn	*house, home*	บ้าน
dtàir	*but*	แต่
yòo	*to be in* (e.g. home,work)	อยู่
ber	*number*	เบอร์
toh-ra-sùp	*telephone*	โทรศัพท์
toh-ra-sùp meu tĕu	*mobile phone*	โทรศัพท์มือถือ
dtorn yen	*evening*	ตอนเย็น
bòrk	*to tell*	บอก
pôr	*father*	พ่อ
fa-rùng	*westerner, farang*	ฝรั่ง

1 Why does the maid have a problem understanding Sue?
2 How does Sue describe herself to the maid?
3 Where is Malee?
4 When does the maid think she will be back?
5 What does she advise Sue to do?
6 Where is Somchai?
7 What does Somchai's daughter offer to give Peter?
8 What does Peter decide to do?
9 What message does he leave?

i At this stage any telephone transactions you might need to make in Thai will probably be limited to asking to speak to someone.

The word **toh-ra-sùp** in Thai is both the noun *telephone* and the verb *to telephone*. As a verb it is often shortened to **toh**. You will see this abbreviated form at the end of newspaper advertisements – the equivalent of 'tel.'.

The English word 'hello' is used at the beginning of phone calls and the Thai greeting/farewell **sa-wùt dee** at the end. When giving telephone numbers or extension numbers, Thais usually use the word **toh** for 'two' instead of **sŏrng** as it is felt that **sŏrng** and **săhm** 'three' might easily be confused over the phone. **toh** is Sanskrit* for 'two'. Although it is pronounced the same way as the abbreviated word for *to telephone* it is spelt differently:

โทร.	โท
tel.	*two*

* Sanskrit is the language of classical India from which Thai has borrowed many words in the same way that English has borrowed from Latin.

Key phrases and expressions

1 Could I speak to . . . , please?

kŏr pôot gùp kOOn . . . nòy dâi mái? ขอพูดกับคุณ . . . หน่อยได้ไหม

2 Who's speaking, please?/Is that . . . ?

krai pôot krúp (ká)? ใครพูดครับ (คะ)

têe-nôhn . . . châi mái krúp (ká)? ที่โน่น . . . ใช่ไหมครับ (คะ)

3 This is . . . speaking

pŏm (chún) . . . pôot ผม (ฉัน) . . . พูด

4 Could you speak up a little please?

(chôo-ay) pôot dung dung nòy dâi mái? (ช่วย)พูดดัง ๆ หน่อยได้ไหม

5 The line is bad/isn't free

săi mâi dee สายไม่ดี

săi mâi wâhng สายไม่ว่าง

6 Could you hold on a moment, please?

ror sùk krôo รอสักครู่

7 Could I have extension . . . , please?

kŏr dtòr ber . . . ขอต่อเบอร์ . . .

8 I'll ring back later

dĕe-o ja toh mah mài เดี๋ยวจะโทรมาใหม่

9 Sorry, I've got the wrong number

kŏr-tôht toh pìt ber ขอโทษ โทรผิดเบอร์

Language notes

1 'Who?' questions

The question word **krai** (*who?*) can occur at either the beginning or the end of a sentence, depending on its function. A name alone is often sufficient answer to **krai?** questions, but longer answers follow the same order of words as the question:

krai bòrk káo?	*Who told him?* (who-tell-he)
– sŏm-chai.	*– Somchai.*
– sŏm-chai bòrk.	*– Somchai did.*
– sŏm-chai bòrk káo.	*– Somchai told him.*
káo bòrk krai?	*Who did he tell?* (he-tell-who)
– sŏm-chai.	*– Somchai.*
– bòrk sŏm-chai.	*– (He) told Somchai.*
– káo bòrk sŏm-chai.	*– He told Somchai.*

kOOn bpai gùp krai? *Who are you going with?* (you-go-with-who)

– sŏm-chai. *– Somchai.*
– gùp sŏm-chai. *– With Somchai.*
– bpai gùp sŏm-chai. *– (I'm) going with Somchai.*
– pŏm bpai gùp sŏm-chai. *– I'm going with Somchai.*

2 Polite requests: asking someone to do something

When asking someone to do something, the pattern **chôo-ay** + verb + **nòy** is used. . . . **dâi mái?** can be added at the end of the request for additional politeness:

chôo-ay pôot dung dung nòy dâi mái? *Please speak up.*
chôo-ay bòrk kOOn pôr wâh Peter toh mah. *Please tell your father that Peter rang.*

Be careful to distinguish between **chôo-ay . . .**, used when asking someone else to do something and **kŏr . . .** (unit 4), used when asking to do something oneself:

chôo-ay pôot gùp . . . nòy. *Please speak to . . .*
kŏr pôot gùp . . . nòy? *Can I speak to . . . , please?*

chôo-ay jòrt rót têe-nêe nòy. *Please park here.*
kŏr jòrt rót têe-nêe nòy? *Can I park here, please?*

3 Possession

There are no special words for *his*, *hers*, *my*, *yours* etc. in Thai. Ownership or possession is expressed by the pattern noun + **kŏrng** (*of*) + owner; the word **kŏrng**, however, is frequently omitted:

bâhn (kŏrng) kOOn sŏm-chai *Khun Somchai's home*
bpen pêu-un (kŏrng) kOOn mah-lee. *I'm a friend of Malee.*

The pattern noun + (**kŏrng** +) **krai** (*who?*) means *whose . . . ?*:

rót (kŏrng) krai? *Whose car?*
káo bpen pêu-un (kŏrng) krai? *Whose friend is he/who is he a friend of?*

4 lĕr?

You have already met the question particle **lĕr?** in unit 2; when it occurs on its own, it means 'really?' and can be used both as a genuine expression of surprise and as a bland conversational rejoinder to assure the speaker that you are still listening!

5 Talking about the future: ja + verb

As we have already mentioned, Thai verbs do not change their endings to indicate tense in the same way as verbs in European languages. Often it is only from the context that you can tell whether a Thai is talking about events in the future or the past. When you want to be quite specific about referring to the future, however, add the word **ja** in front of the verb:

káo ja glùp mah dtorn bài.	*She will return in the afternoon.*
dtorn yen ja toh mah mài.	*I'll ring again in the evening.*
pŏm ja jòrt rot têe soy yêe-sìp gâo.	*I'll park the car on Soi 29.*

6 'When?' questions

The question word **mêu-rài?** (*when?*) normally occurs at the end of a sentence; a time expression alone is often sufficient answer, but this may be preceded by a verb:

ja glùp mah mêu-rài?	*When will she be back?*
– (ja glùp mah) dtorn bài.	*– (She'll be back) in the afternoon.*
káo bpai mêu-rài?	*When did he go?*
– (káo bpai) dtorn yen.	*– (He went) in the evening.*
káo toh mah mêu-rài?	*When did he ring?*
– (káo toh mah) dtorn cháo.	*– (He rang) in the morning.*

mêu-rài? may also occur at the beginning of a sentence, often to convey a sense of urgency or irritation:

mêu-rài káo ja glùp mah?	*When **will** she be back?*
mêu-rài káo ja toh mah?	*When **is** he going to ring?*
mêu-rài kOOn ja bòrk káo?	*When **are** you going to tell him?*

7 'Know'

sâhp is a polite, formal word for *to know* which you would use when speaking to strangers or people of obviously higher social status. In less formal situations **róo** is widely used. Be careful to distinguish these from **róo-jùk** (unit 3) which means *to know* in the sense of being acquainted with a person or place.

8 Verbs of thinking/saying + wâh

wâh links verbs of speaking (e.g. **bòrk** *to say)*, mental activity (e.g **kít** *to think*) and perception (e.g. **róo** *to know*), to a following clause, like English 'that' in *you said that . . . , he thinks that . . . , I know that . . .* :

chún kít wâh ja glùp mah dtorn bài.	*I think he'll be back in the afternoon.*
káo bòrk wâh Peter toh mah.	*She said that Peter phoned.*
pŏm róo wâh káo mâi yòo.	*I know he's not in.*

When **wâh** occurs with **bòrk,** it can introduce both indirect and direct speech; in indirect speech it is equivalent to *that* and in direct speech it serves the same function as inverted commas:

káo bòrk wâh (káo) ja mâi bpai.	*He said (that) he would not go.*
káo bòrk wâh (pŏm) ja mâi bpai.	*He said, 'I'm not going.'*

Notice that when the pronouns in the second clause are omitted, indirect and direct speech are identical.

9 Parts of the day

dtorn means *section* or *period of time*. It occurs commonly with the words for *morning*, *afternoon*, *evening* etc. Note that when referring to the time when an action takes place, Thai does not need the word for 'in'.

dtorn cháo	*morning, in the morning*
dtorn bài	*afternoon, in the afternoon*
dtorn yen	*evening, in the evening*
dtorn glahng wun	*daytime, in the daytime*
dtorn glahng keun	*night time, at night*

Time expressions can occur at the beginning or end of a sentence, as in English:

dtorn yen pŏm bpai kûng nôrk.	*In the evening I'm going out.*
pŏm bpai kûng nôrk dtorn yen.	*I'm going out in the evening.*

10 kOOn pôr

Somchai's daughter's use of the title **kOOn** before **pôr** is the deferential way of referring to one's own or another person's father:

kOOn pôr yòo mái krúp? *Is your father at home?*
– kOOn pôr bpai tum ngahn láir-o. *– He's gone to work.*

Exercises

1 How would you:

(a) ask to speak to Malee?
(b) ask someone to speak a little louder?
(c) ask someone to hang on for a moment?
(d) ask who is speaking?
(e) ask when Malee will return?

2 You are thinking of doing a number of things in the near future. Use **pŏm/chún kít wâh ja . . .** to state your plans for:

(a) going out.
(b) going to the post office in the morning.
(c) going to Somchai's house in the afternoon.
(d) returning in the evening.

3 Somchai has told you his plans for the day. Pass on the information to Malee, beginning **kOOn sŏm-chai bòrk wâh . . .**:

(a) I'll go to the bank in the morning.
(b) I'm going to a friend's house in the afternoon.
(c) I'll park my car in Soi 33.
(d) I'll return home in the evening.

4 Ask when Khun Somchai is going to do these things:

(a) return.
(b) be in.
(c) know.
(d) ring (you).
(e) tell (you).
(f) ring and tell (you).

Reading and writing

At this stage it is worth pausing to review the key points that you have learned so far.

1 Consonants

You have learned the following consonants (note that the consonant sound of each letter is given when it occurs both as an initial and as a final consonant):

Low class	น	ม	ง	ร	ล	ย	ว
initial	**n**	**m**	**ng**	**r**	**l**	**y**	**w**
final	**n**	**m**	**ng**	**n**	**n**		
	ค	ช	ซ	ท	พ	ฟ	
initial	**k**	**ch**	**s**	**t**	**p**	**f**	
final	**k**	**t**	**t**	**t**	**p**	**p**	
Mid class	ก	จ	ด	ต	บ	ป	อ
initial	**g**	**j**	**d**	**dt**	**b**	**bp**	zero
final	**k**	**t**	**t**	**t**	**p**	**p**	
High class	ข	ฉ	ถ	ผ	ฝ	ศ,ส,ษ	ห
initial	**k**	**ch**	**t**	**p**	**f**	**s**	**h**
final	**k**	**t**	**t**	**p**	**p**	**t**	

2 Vowels

You have learned the following vowels:

Long vowels	-า	-อ	โ-	-ี	-ู	-ื	เ-	แ-
	-ah	**-or**	**-oh**	**-ee**	**-oo**	**-eu**	**-ay**	**-air**
Short vowels	-ั-	ไ-	ใ-	-ิ	-ุ	-ึ	เ-็	แ-็
	-u	**-ai**	**-ai**	**-i**	**-OO**	**-eu**	**-e**	**-air**

3 Live syllables and dead syllables

You have learned the difference between live syllables and dead syllables:

Live syllables	syllables that end with a *long vowel* or a **m**, **n**, **ng** sound or the short vowels **ai** and **ao**. e.g. มี รอ ดู ปี ดำ จาน ยัง
Dead syllables	syllables that end with a *short vowel* or a **p**, **t**, **k** sound. e.g. ดุ ติ กด ดับ สิบ จาก หมด

4 Summary of tone rules

Consonant class	Live syllable	Dead syllable Short vowel	 Long vowel
Low class	**Mid tone**	**High tone**	**Falling tone**
Mid class	**Mid tone**	**Low tone**	**Low tone**
High class	**Rising tone**	**Low tone**	**Low tone**

5 Reading words

By now, whenever you read a Thai word or syllable, you will have learned to ask yourself three questions: (i) is it a live or dead syllable?, (ii) what class is the initial consonant? and (iii) is the vowel long or short? Once you have answered these questions you should be able to identify the tone of a word correctly.

At this stage, don't worry if you are finding it difficult to memorize the tone rules: simply copy the chart and keep it handy for subsequent lessons (the act of copying itself will help you to memorize it). After a while, you will find you need to refer to it less and less and when you feel ready, you can dispense with it altogether.

Reading practice

ยุพาเป็นคนไทย
มาจากจังหวัดเลย
ดำรงเป็นสามีของยุพา
ดำรงมาจากจังหวัดตาก
ยุพากับดำรงมีลูก ๕ คน
มีลูกชาย ๒ คน มีลูกสาว ๓ คน

สามี	*husband*
จังหวัด	*province*
ตาก	*name of a province in northern Thailand*
เลย	*name of a province in northern Thailand*
กับ	*and, with*
ลูกชาย	*son*
คน	*(classifier for people)*
ลูกสาว	*daughter*

1 Where does Yupa come from?
2 What is her husband's name?
3 What province does he come from?
4 How many sons do they have?
5 How many daughters do they have?

kOOn pôot tai gèng

you speak Thai well

คุณพูดไทยเก่ง

In this lesson you will learn

- **how to talk about your knowledge of Thai**
- **how to talk about actions that happened in the past: ker-ee + verb**
- **how to talk about continuous actions: gum-lung + verb + yòo**
- **how to compare things**
- **tone marks: mái àyk**

Dialogues

A taxi driver strikes up a conversation with Peter.

Taxi	คุณเป็นคนอเมริกัน ใช่ไหมครับ	kOOn bpen kon a-may-ri-gun châi mái krúp?
Peter	ไม่ใช่ครับ เป็นคนอังกฤษ	mâi châi krúp. bpen kon ung-grìt.
Taxi	อ้อ คนอังกฤษหรือ อยู่เมืองไทยนานไหม	ôr kon ung-grìt lěr? yòo meu-ung tai nahn mái?
Peter	ไม่นานครับ	mâi nahn krúp.
Taxi	คุณพูดไทยเก่ง	kOOn pôot tai gèng.
Peter	ไม่เก่งหรอกครับ พูดได้นิดหน่อยเท่านั้น	mâi gèng ròrk krúp. pôot dâi nít-nòy tâo-nún.
Taxi	เก่งซีครับ มีแฟน คนไทยใช่ไหมครับ	gèng see krúp. mee fairn kon tai châi mái krúp?
Peter	ไม่ใช่ครับ เคยเรียนที่อังกฤษ	mâi châi krúp. ker-ee ree-un têe ung-grìt.
Taxi	แล้วคุณอ่านและเขียน ภาษาไทยเป็นไหม	láir-o kOOn àhn láir kěe-un pah-săh tai bpen mái?
Peter	เป็นนิดหน่อยครับ กำลังเรียนอยู่	bpen nít-nòy krúp. gum-lung ree-un yòo.

meu-ung	*country* (informal); *town*	เมือง
meu-ung tai	*Thailand* (informal)	เมืองไทย
nahn	*(for) a long time*	นาน
gèng	*to be good at*	เก่ง
nít-nòy	*a little bit*	นิดหน่อย
tâo-nún	*only*	เท่านั้น
see	*particle*	ซี
fairn	*husband; wife; partner*	แฟน
ker-ee	*used to; to have ever done something*	เคย
ree-un	*to study, learn*	เรียน

sŏrn	*to teach*	สอน
àhn	*to read*	อ่าน
kĕe-un	*to write*	เขียน
pah-săh	*language*	ภาษา
bpen	*can, know how to*	เป็น
gum-lung . . . yòo	*to be in the process of . . .*	กำลัง . . . อยู่

Chanida, meanwhile, is asking Sue how she finds learning Thai.

Chanida	คุณซูพูดไทยเก่งนะ	kOOn Sue pôot tai gèng ná.
	ภาษาไทยยากไหม	pah-săh tai yâhk mái?
Sue	ฉันรู้สึกว่าพูดยาก	chún róo-sèuk wâh pôot yâhk
	เพราะว่ามี	prór wâh mee
	เสียงสูงเสียงต่ำ	sĕe-ung sŏong sĕe-ung dtùm.
	กลัวว่าจะพูดผิดเสมอ	gloo-a wâh ja pôot pìt sa-mĕr.
Chanida	ไม่ต้องกลัวหรอก	mâi dtôrng gloo-a ròrk.
	คุณซูพูดชัดจริง ๆ	kOOn Sue pôot chút jing jing.
	คุณซูเรียนที่ไหน	kOOn Sue ree-un têe-năi?
Sue	เคยเรียนที่ลอนดอน	ker-ee ree-un têe lorn-dorn
	ค่ะ ที่มหาวิทยาลัย	kâ. têe ma-hăh-wít-ta-yah-lai.
Chanida	มีคนไทยสอนไหม	mee kon tai sŏrn mái?
Sue	มีค่ะ	mee kâ.
Chanida	แล้วคุณซู เรียนอ่าน	láir-o kOOn Sue ree-un àhn
	และเขียนด้วยใช่ไหม	láir kĕe-un dôo-ay châi mái?
Sue	ใช่ค่ะ	châi kâ.
	ฝรั่งบางคนคิดว่า	fa-rùng bahng kon kít wâh
	อ่านภาษาไทยยาก	àhn pah-săh tai yâhk.
	ฉันว่าไม่ค่อยยาก	chún wâh mâi kôy yâhk
	เท่าไร ความจริงคิด	tâo-rài. kwahm jing kít
	ว่าอ่านและเขียนง่าย	wâh àhn láir kĕe-un ngâi
	กว่าพูด	gwàh pôot.

yâhk	*difficult*	ยาก
róo-sèuk (wâh)	*to feel (that)*	รู้สึก (ว่า)
prór wâh	*because*	เพราะว่า
sěe-ung	*sound; tone*	เสียง
sŏong	*high*	สูง
dtùm	*low*	ต่ำ
sěe-ung sŏong sěe-ung dtùm	tones	เสียงสูงเสียงต่ำ
gloo-a (wâh)	*to be afraid (that)*	กลัว (ว่า)
pìt	*wrong*	ผิด
sa-měr	*always*	เสมอ
dtôrng	*must*	ต้อง
mâi dtôrng	*there's no need (to)*	ไม่ต้อง
chút	*clear*	ชัด
ma-hăh-wít-ta-yah-lai	*university*	มหาวิทยาลัย
lálr	*and*	และ
bahng	*some*	บาง
wâh	*to think, say*	ว่า
mâi kôy . . . tâo-rài	*not very . . .*	ไม่ค่อย . . . เท่าไร
kwahm jing	*(in) truth; actually*	ความจริง
ngâi	*easy*	ง่าย
ngâi gwàh	*easier*	ง่ายกว่า

1 What wrong assumptions does the taxi driver make about Peter?
2 Where did Peter learn Thai?
3 Who taught him?
4 Can Peter read Thai?
5 Why does Sue find it hard to speak Thai?
6 What is she afraid of?
7 How does Chanida reassure her?
8 How easy does Sue find the Thai script?

One of the most enjoyable aspects of speaking Thai in Thailand is that there always seem to be lots of Thais eager to tell you how well you speak their language. Even the most faltering attempts are likely to prompt a complimentary **pôot tai gèng** (*you speak Thai well*). Such encouragement is a wonderful incentive to practise more. But don't take it too literally. Mutual compliments are an important part of Thai social relations and Thais are simply trying to be friendly and express their appreciation that a foreigner has made an effort to learn something of their language rather than to objectively evaluate his or her linguistic competence. The appropriate response is a suitably modest one of denial such as **mâi gèng ròrk** or **bplào** or **pôot dâi nít-nòy tâo-nún**. Generally speaking, it doesn't hurt to compliment Thais on their command of English; unless, of course, they spent their formative years in an English boarding school or have just returned from the United States with an MBA, in which case you risk sounding a little condescending.

Key phrases and expressions

How to say:

1 I only speak a little (Thai)

pôot (pah-săh tai) dâi nít-nòy tâo-nún พูด(ภาษาไทย)ได้นิดหน่อยเท่านั้น

2 I studied it before

ker-ee ree-un เคยเรียน

3 I am studying it

gum-lung ree-un กำลังเรียน

4 it's difficult to speak because it has tones

pôot yâhk prór wâh mee sĕe-ung sŏong sĕe-ung dtùm พูดยากเพราะว่ามีเสียงสูงเสียงต่ำ

5 I'm always afraid I'll make a mistake

gloo-a wâh ja pôot pìt sa-mĕr กลัวว่าจะพูดผิดเสมอ

Language notes

1 Countries

meu-ung and **bpra-tâyt** both mean *country* and occur before the name of a specific country; **meu-ung** is the informal word, normally used in conversation, while **bpra-tâyt** is normally used when writing or speaking formally:

meu-ung jeen	*China*
bpra-tâyt yêe-bpÒOn	*Japan*

In informal speech, **meu-ung** is often dropped, although it is never dropped before **tai**:

pŏm ker-ee ree-un têe ung-grìt.	*I studied it in England.*
yòo meu-ung tai nahn mái?	*Have you lived in Thailand long?*

2 verb + bpen

In unit 1 you met the pattern **bpen** + noun (e.g. **bpen kon ung-grìt**) where **bpen** meant *is/are*.

When **bpen** occurs in the pattern verb + **bpen**, the meaning of **bpen** is *to know how to do something* or *can*. When it has this meaning it occurs in the same position, after a verb, as **dâi** (*to be able to do something, can*; see unit 2); verb + **bpen mái?** (*can you . . . ?*) questions are answered **bpen** (*yes*) or **mâi bpen** (*no*):

káo pôot pah-săh tai bpen	*He speaks/can speak Thai.*
chún àhn pah-săh tai mâi bpen	*I cannot read Thai.*
kĕe-un pah-săh tai bpen mái?	*Can you read and write Thai?*
– bpen/mâi bpen	*– Yes/no.*

3 verb + bpen/dâi + adverb

Adverbs and adjectives are identical in form in Thai; thus **dee** is both the adjective *good* and the adverb *well*. To describe how competently someone can do something, the pattern verb + **bpen/dâi** + adverb can be used:

pŏm pôot dâi nít-nòy.	*I can speak a little.*
kOOn kĕe-un pah-săh tai dâi dee.	*You can write Thai well.*
káo àhn pah-săh tai bpen nít-nòy.	*She can read Thai a little.*

With the adverbs **gèng** (*expertly*) and **klôrng** (*fluently*) it is normal to drop **bpen/dâi:**

káo pôot tai gèng/klôrng. *He speaks Thai well/fluently.*

4 see

The particle see is used in a number of different ways. One use (illustrated in the dialogue) is at the end of a sentence which contradicts a negative statement:

kOOn pôot tai gèng. *You speak Thai well.*
– mâi gèng ròrk krúp. *– No I don't.*
gèng see krúp. *Yes you do.*

dern bpai mâi glai. *It's not far to walk.*
– glai see. *– Yes it is.*

mâi pairng. *It's not expensive.*
– pairng see. *– Yes it is.*

5 fairn

The word **fairn** derives from the English 'fan' (as in 'supporter', not 'cooling device') and is the normal word for *boyfriend* or *girlfriend*; its meaning is extended to include *husband* and *wife* which can occasionally lead the westerner into unworthy speculation: is that ultra-respectable, middle-aged lady with the nice husband telling you she went to the cinema with him last night . . . or with a secret boyfriend?

6 ker-ee + verb

The pattern **ker-ee** + verb is used to indicate that the action of the verb has (a) occurred at least once in the past or (b) occurred habitually in the past:

káo ker-ee bpai têe-o (*to visit*) **poo-gèt** *He has visited Phuket.*
pǒm ker-ee ree-un pah-săh tai. *I used to study Thai.*

The negative **mâi ker-ee** + verb, means *have never . . .* :

rao mâi ker-ee bpai. *We have never been there.*
chún mâi ker-ee tum. *I have never done it.*

Questions that follow the pattern **ker-ee** + verb + **mái?** (*Have you ever . . . ?*) are answered either **ker-ee** (*yes*) or **mâi ker-ee** (*no*):

ker-ee ree-un mái?	*Have you ever studied it?*
- ker-ee/mâi ker-ee.	*– Yes/no.*
ker-ee gin ah-hăhn tai mái?	*Have you ever eaten Thai food?*
– ker-ee/mâi ker-ee.	*– Yes/no.*

7 gum-lung + verb + yòo

The pattern **gum-lung** + verb + **yòo** is used to indicate continuous actions, either in the present (*I am learning Thai*) or in the past (*I was learning Thai*); either **gum-lung** or **yòo** may be dropped:

káo gum-lung doo tee-wee yòo.	*He is/was watching TV.*
káo gum-lung doo tee-wee.	*He is/was watching TV.*
káo doo tee-wee yòo.	*He is/was watching TV.*
pŏm gum-lung ree-un pah-săh tai yòo.	*I am/was studying Thai.*
chún gum-lung kít yòo.	*I'm thinking.*
rao gum-lung gin kâo yòo.	*We are/were eating.*
kOOn tum a-rai yòo?	*What are you doing?*

8 'Must'

dtôrng (*must*) occurs before another verb:

dtôrng bpai tum ngahn dtorn yen.	*I have to go to work in the evening.*

Questions asking whether someone must do something are answered **dtôrng** (*yes*) or **mâi dtôrng** (*no*):

dtôrng ree-un kěe-un mái?	*Do I have to learn to write?*
– dtôrng/mâi dtôrng.	*– Yes/no.*

dtôrng can be negated in two ways: (a) **mâi dtôrng** + verb means *there is no need to . . .* :

mâi dtôrng gloo-a.	*There's no need to be afraid.*
káo mâi dtôrng bpai.	*There's no need for him to go.*

(b) **dtôrng mâi** + verb means *must not . . .* :

kOOn dtôrng mâi gloo-a.	*You must not be afraid.*
káo dtôrng mâi bpai.	*He must not go.*

9 mâi kôy . . . tâo-rài

mâi kôy . . . tâo-rài (*not very . . .*) is a useful expression for 'softening' negative statements or responses; the word **tâo-rài** is optional and may be omitted:

mâi kôy yâhk (tâo-rài).	*It's not very difficult.*
mâi kôy pairng (tâo-rài).	*It's not very expensive.*
káo pôot tai mâi kôy chút (tâo-rài).	*He doesn't speak Thai very clearly.*
yòo meu-ung tai nahn mái?	*Have you lived in Thailand long?*
– mâi kôy nahn (tâo-rài).	*– Not very long.*

10 kwahm + verb

The pattern **kwahm** + verb is used to form abstract nouns. In the dialogue **kwahm jing** can be translated as *the truth is* or *actually*. Some common examples include:

jing	*to be true*	**kwahm jing**	*truth*
dee	*to be good*	**kwahm dee**	*goodness*
kít	*to think*	**kwahm kít**	*idea*
rúk	*to love*	**kwahm rúk**	*love*
sÒOk	*to be happy*	**kwahm sÒOk**	*happiness*

11 Comparisons

Comparisons are made using the pattern X + adjective + **gwàh** (+ Y):

nêe pairng gwàh.	*This is more expensive.*
pah-săh yêe-bpOOn yâhk gwàh.	*Japanese is more difficult.*
àhn ngâi gwàh pôot.	*Reading is easier than speaking.*
káo pôot gèng gwàh chún.	*She speaks better than me.*

Comparisons can be modified by adding **mâhk** (*a lot*) or **nít-nòy** (*a little bit*) to the end of the sentence:

káo pôot gèng gwàh chún mâhk.	*She speaks much better than me.*
nêe pairng gwàh nít-nòy.	*This is a little bit more expensive.*

Exercises

1 How would you respond to the following questions?

(a) kOOn pôot pah-săh tai bpen mái?
(b) ree-un pah-săh tai nahn mái?
(c) àhn pah-săh tai bpen mái?
(d) kĕe-un pah-săh tai bpen mái?
(e) pah-săh tai yâhk mái?

2 How would you ask someone if they had ever:

(a) been to England?
(b) studied English?
(c) eaten fish and chips?
(d) visited Phuket?
(e) worked in Bangkok?

3 How would you say that something is:

(a) not very expensive?
(b) not very far?
(c) not very tasty?
(d) not very good?
(e) not very clear?
(f) not very difficult?

4 And how would you say that something is:

(a) more expensive?
(b) further?
(c) tastier?
(d) better?
(e) clearer?
(f) more difficult?

5 This is how a number of languages have been ranked in terms of relative difficulty for the English-speaking learner.

	Speaking	Reading
Difficult	Japanese	Chinese
	Chinese	Japanese
	Thai	Thai
Easy	French	French

Complete the following statements using either **yâhk gwàh** or **ngâi gwàh**:

(**a**) pah-săh tai pôot . . . pah-săh fa-rùng-sàyt.
(**b**) pah-săh jeen pôot . . . pah-săh yêe-bpÒOn.
(**c**) pah-săh fa-rùng-sàyt àhn . . . pah-săh jeen.
(**d**) pah-săh yêe-bpÒOn àhn . . . pah-săh tai.

Reading and writing

The chart summarizing tone rules in unit 6 will help you to read any dead syllable, but it covers only those live syllables that are pronounced with a mid or rising tone.

As you will have realized, there are many live syllables that are pronounced with a falling, high or low tone – words such as **mâi, chêu, láir-o, yòo, nòy** and so on.

In words like these, the tone is represented by a tone mark which is written above the initial consonant. If the initial consonant has an ิ or ี vowel above it, then the tone mark is written above the vowel. The two most common tone marks are **mái àyk**, which you are about to meet, and **mái toh** which will be introduced in the next unit.

1 mái àyk (่): tone rules

This tone mark looks like the number 1. It is written above the initial consonant and in line with the right-hand perpendicular stroke. Unfortunately for the learner, due to changes in the language that have occurred over hundreds of years, this one tone mark can represent two different tones! As with dead syllables, the determining factor is the class of the initial consonant. If **mái àyk** occurs on an low-class initial consonant, the tone will be falling:

Low class	ไม่	ที่	ชื่อ
	mâi	**têe**	**chêu**

If the initial consonant is either mid or high class, then the tone is low:

Mid class	ไก่	ต่อ	จ่าย
	gài	**dtòr**	**jài**

High class	สี่	หนึ่ง*	หน่อย*
	sèe	**nèung**	**nòy**

* Remember that silent ห 'converts' the next consonant to high class.

2 Silent อ at the beginning of a word

In unit 5 you met words that began with a silent ห. There are also a very small number of words – only four in fact – that begin with a silent อ. These are all pronounced with a *low tone*. All four word are very common and it is well worth copying them down and memorizing them at this stage. Two of them – **yòo** and **yàhk** – have already occurred in the dialogues:

อยู่	อย่า	อย่าง	อยาก
yòo	**yàh**	**yàhng**	**yàhk**
to be situated at	*don't*	*like, kind*	*to like to*

Reading practice

1 Words

All these words are written with **mái àyk**. This means they will be pronounced with either a falling tone or a low tone:

ไม่	นี่	พ่อ	แม่	หนึ่ง	คู่
อยู่	ไก่	แต่	สั่ง	หน่อย	ต่อ
ชื่อ	ใช่	พี่	ที่	อ่าน	ว่า

2 Phrases

Next, some short phrases using words with **mái àyk**:

ใช่ไหม	ไม่ใช่	นี่เท่าไร	ยี่สิบบาท
แพงไปหน่อย	จอดที่นี่	ไม่แพงหรอก	อยู่ที่โน่น
ไม่เป็นไร	อยู่ที่ไหน	อ่านไม่ยาก	คิดว่าไม่มา

3 Dialogue

And finally, here is Peter negotiating with a tuk-tuk driver:

Peter ไปซอยสามสิบสามเท่าไร

Tuk-tuk ซอยสามสิบสามหรือ คิดแปดสิบบาท

Peter แปดสิบบาทหรือ แพงไปหน่อย

Tuk-tuk ไม่แพงหรอก รถติดมาก

1 Where does Peter want to go?
2 How much does the tuk-tuk driver ask for?
3 What is Peter's reaction?
4 What is the tuk-tuk driver's justification?

mee pêe nórng mái?

do you have any brothers and sisters?

มีพี่น้องไหม

In this unit you will learn

- how to greet people
- kin terms: brothers and sisters, sons and daughters
- why? questions
- how many? questions
- . . . yet? questions
- tone marks: **mái toh**, **mái dtree** and **mái jùt-dta-wah**

Dialogues

Sue and her husband Peter are visiting Sue's friend Chanida at her home.

Chanida	สวัสดีค่ะ คุณซู	sa-wùt dee kâ kOOn Sue.
	เชิญข้างในซิคะ	chern kûng nai sí ká.
Sue	ขอบคุณค่ะ นี่ปีเตอร์	kòrp-kOOn kâ. nêe Peter
	แฟนฉันกับลูก	fairn chún gùp lôok.
Chanida	สวัสดีค่ะ คุณ Peter	sa-wùt dee kâ. kOOn Peter
	สบายดีหรือคะ	sa-bai dee lĕr ká?
Peter	สบายดีครับ	sa-bai dee krúp.
	แล้วคุณชนิดาล่ะครับ	láir-o kOOn cha-ní-dah lâ krúp?
Chanida	สบายดีเหมือนกันค่ะ	sa-bai dee mĕu-un gun kâ.
	ทำไมคุณ Peter	tum-mai kOOn Peter
	พูดไทยเก่ง	pôot tai gèng?
	อยู่เมืองไทยนานไหม	yòo meu-ung tai nahn mái?
Peter	ไม่ค่อยนานเท่าไรครับ	mâi kôy nahn tâo-rài krúp.
Chanida	เก่งนะ พูดไทยชัด	gèng ná. pôot tai chút.
	แล้วลูกล่ะ	láir-o lôok lâ.
	พูดภาษาไทยเป็นไหม	pôot pah-săh tai bpen mái?
Sue	เป็นนิดหน่อยค่ะ	bpen nít-nòy kâ.

chern . . . sí	*please . . .*	เชิญ . . . ซิ
kûng nai	*inside*	ข้างใน
fairn	*boy/girlfriend; spouse*	แฟน
lôok	*child* (one's own)	ลูก
sa-bai	*to be well, comfortable*	สบาย
sa-bai dee lĕr?	*How are you?*	สบายดีหรือ
láir-o . . . lâ?	*And how about . . . ?*	แล้ว . . . ล่ะ
mĕu-un gun	*likewise*	เหมือนกัน

Chanida and Sue are looking through some old family snapshots of Sue's.

Chanida	คุณซูมีพี่น้อง	kOOn Sue mee pêe-nórng
	ไหมคะ	mái ká?
Sue	มีค่ะ มีสี่คน	mee kâ. mee sèe kon.
	มีพี่ชายคนหนึ่ง	mee pêe-chai kon nèung,
	พี่สาวคนหนึ่ง	pêe-săo kon nèung,
	น้องชายคนหนึ่ง	nórng-chai kon nèung
	แล้วก็น้องสาว	láir-o gôr nórng-săo
	คนหนึ่ง	kon nèung.
Chanida	นี่พี่ชายใช่ไหมคะ	nêe pêe-chai, châi mái ká?
Sue	ใช่ค่ะ	châi kâ.
Chanida	รูปหล่อนะ	rôop lòr ná
	อายุเท่าไรคะ	ah-yÓO tâo-rài ká?
Sue	อายุสามสิบสองค่ะ	ah-yÓO săhm-sìp-sŏrng kâ.
Chanida	แต่งงานแล้วหรือยัง	dtàirng ngahn láir-o réu yung?
Sue	แต่งงานแล้ว	dtàirng ngahn láir-o.
Chanida	มีลูกแล้วหรือยังคะ	mee lôok láir-o réu yung ká?
Sue	มีแล้ว	mee láir-o.
Chanida	มีลูกกี่คน	mee lôok gèe kon?
Sue	สองคนค่ะ	sŏrng kon kâ.
	ลูกชายอายุสามขวบ	lôok chai ah-yÓO săhm kòo-up
	ลูกสาวอายุสองขวบ	lôok săo ah-yÓO sŏrng kòo-up
	แล้วคุณชนิดาล่ะ	láir-o kOOn cha-ní-dah lâ.
	มีพี่น้องไหม	mee pêe-nórng mái?

pêe-nórng	*brothers and sisters*	พี่น้อง
pêe-chai	*older brother*	พี่ชาย
pêe-săo	*older sister*	พี่สาว
nórng-chai	*younger brother*	น้องชาย
nórng-săo	*younger sister*	น้องสาว
rôop	*shape, appearance*	รูป
lòr	*handsome*	หล่อ
ah-yÓO	*age*	อายุ
dtàirng ngahn	*to be married*	แต่งงาน
. . . láir-o réu yung?	*. . . yet (or not)?*	แล้วหรือยัง
gèe	*how many?*	กี่
lôok chai	*son*	ลูกชาย
kòo-up	*year(s old)*	ขวบ
lôok săo	*daughter*	ลูกสาว

1 Has Peter been in Thailand long?
2 What compliments does Chanida pay Peter?
3 Do Peter and Sue's children speak Thai?
4 How many brothers and sisters does Sue have?
5 How old is her older brother?
6 How old are his children?

i If you are invited to a Thai home, you should normally remove your shoes before entering the house. The traditional Thai greeting is the **wâi**, in which the head is bowed slightly and the hands held in prayer-like position in front of the face at approximately chin height. How low the head is bowed and the height at which the hands are held reflect the degree of respect conveyed by the person *wai*-ing. A child *wai*-ing an adult, for example, may hold their hands so that the tips of the fingers are close to the forehead, while an adult responding may keep their own fingertips well below their chin.

Thais also show respect for older people by trying to keep their head at a lower level when passing or talking to them. For very tall people this can be tricky, if not impossible, and this requirement should not be taken too literally; an obvious attempt to bend forward a little is quite sufficient. It should be mentioned that for Thais, the head is a taboo area: never attempt to ruffle a Thai's hair in jest or offer a friendly pat on the head.

If it is second nature for you to sit with one or both legs stretched out in front of you, you risk unwittingly causing offence, for to point your feet directly towards someone is considered extremely impolite. Practise keeping your feet firmly on the ground or demurely tucked to one side but as inconspicuous as possible!

Key phrases and expressions

How to:

1 ask how someone is

(formal) **sa-bai dee lěr krúp** (**ká**)? สบายดีหรือครับ (คะ)

(informal) **bpen yung-ngai bâhng?** เป็นอย่างไรบ้าง

2 ask how many brothers and sisters a person has

mee pêe-nórng gèe kon? มีพี่น้องกี่คน

3 ask about a person's age

ah-yÓO tâo-rài? อายุเท่าไร

4 ask whether a person is married or not

dtàirng ngahn láir-o réu yung? แต่งงานแล้วหรือยัง

5 ask whether a person has any children or not

mee lôok láir-o réu yung? มีลูกแล้วหรือยัง

Language notes

1 Polite invitations

The pattern **chern** (*to invite*) + verb + **sí** is used when inviting someone to do something such as come in, sit down, go first, start eating and so on.

The mood particle **sí** following a verb, often conveys the sense of a mild command:

chern kûng nai sí krúp/ká.	*Please come in.*
chern nûng sí krúp/ká.	*Please sit down.*
chern sí krúp/ká.	*Please go ahead.*

Note the female polite particle in **chern . . .** invitations is **ká**, not **kâ**.

2 'How are you?'

The question **sa-bai dee lěr?** (*are you well?*) is normally answered **sa-bai dee.** The same answer is appropriate for the more informal enquiry **bpen yung-ngai bâhng?** (*how are things?*)

3 láir-o . . . lâ? questions

The expression **láir-o . . . lâ?** means '(And) how/what about . . . ?'; the speaker assumes that the listener understands the context of the question, which remains unspecified:

láir-o kOOn lâ?	*And how about you?*
láir-o lôok lâ?	*And how about the children?*
láir-o dtorn yen lâ?	*And what about the evening?*

4 'Why?' questions

The question word **tum-mai?** (*why?*) can occur either at the beginning or the end of the question:

tum-mai kOOn pôot tai gèng?	*Why do you speak Thai so well?*
bpai tum-mai?	*Why are you going?*

You can answer 'why?' questions using **prór wâh** (*because*):

prór wâh mâir bpen kon tai.	*Because my mother is Thai.*
prór wâh yàhk bpai.	*Because I'd like to go.*

5 'Brothers and sisters'

pêe-nórng (*brothers and sisters*) literally means *older siblings–younger siblings* and makes no reference to gender at all. You may hear someone referring to a member of their family as **pêe** and you will not know whether it is an older brother or older sister. When it is necessary to be specific, the word **chai** (male) or **săo** (female) is added after **pêe** or **nórng.** These same gender words are also used with **lôok** (*child*) to distinguish between sons and daughters:

pêe-chai	*older brother*
pêe-săo	*older sister*
nórng-chai	*younger brother*
nórng-săo	*younger sister*

Both **pêe** and **nórng** are also used as *I* and *you* pronouns to create a sense of both hierarchy and intimacy. **pêe** has an especially wide range of usage, which includes younger work colleagues addressing older colleagues, shop assistants addressing older customers, wives addressing husbands and complete strangers striking up a conversation with someone older. **nórng** is often used in restaurants, as an alternative to **nǒo** (unit 3) to summon a waiter or waitress; but it can also convey closeness or intimacy between the two speakers.

6 Age

Age is stated using the verb **ah-yÓO** (*age*) + number + **kòo-up/ (bpee)** (*years*). **kòo-up** is used when talking about children up to the age of 13 or 14; for people older than that, **bpee** may be used, although it is often omitted. **láir-o** (*already*) may also occur at the end of the expression. The question word **tâo-rài?** (*how much?*) is used when asking someone's age:

ah-yÓO tâo-rài?	*How old is he?*
ah-yÓO hòk kòo-up (láir-o)	*six years old*
ah-yÓO yêe-sìp hâh bpee (láir-o)	*25 years old*

7 . . . láir-o réu yung? questions

Questions that end in **. . . láir-o réu yung?** ask whether something has happened yet; the word **láir-o** is often omitted and the question abbreviated to **. . . réu yung?**:

dtàirng ngahn (láir-o) réu yung?	*Is he married (yet)?*
mee lôok (láir-o) réu yung?	*Do they have any children (yet)?*
gin kâo (láir-o) réu yung?	*Have you eaten yet?*

A *yes* answer to a **. . . láir-o réu yung?** question is formed by verb + **láir-o**; a *no* answer is **yung krúp/kâ**:

dtàirng ngahn (láir-o) réu yung? **– dtàirng ngahn láir-o /yung krúp/kâ.**	*Is he married?* *Yes/no.*
mee lôok (láir-o) réu yung? **– mee láir-o/yung krúp/kâ.**	*Do they have any children?* *Yes/no.*
gin kâo (láir-o) réu yung? **– gin láir-o/yung krúp/kâ.**	*Have you eaten yet?* *Yes/no.*

8 'How many?' questions

How many? questions are formed by the pattern verb + (noun) + gèe (*how many?*) + classifier; the answer will normally take the form (noun) + number + classifier:

mee lôok gèe kon?	*How many children do you have?*
– mee (lôok) sŏrng kon.	*– Two.*
ao bpép-sêe gèe kòo-ut?	*How many bottles of Pepsi do you want?*
– hâh kòo-ut.	*– Five.*
séu (*buy*) **sa-dtairm gèe doo-ung?**	*How many stamps did you buy?*
– sìp doo-ung.	*– Ten.*
bpai gèe wun?	*How many days are you going for?*
– săhm wun.	*– Three.*

9 Children

The word **lôok** (*child, children*) refers only to children in the sense of offspring. Thais would use **lôok** in sentences like *How many children do you have?*, *Her children are lovely!*, *Whose child is that?* and so on. When talking about children as an age category in statements such as *Thai children are very polite*, *Children under 12 not admitted* and so on, the word **dèk** is used.

The gender of one's children are specified in the same way as brothers and sisters, namely **chai** for males and **săo** for females:

lûuk chai	*son*
lûuk săo	*daughter*

Exercises

1 How would you ask someone if they have:

(a) parked the car yet?
(b) eaten yet?
(c) spoken to Khun Somchai yet?
(d) told Khun Malee yet?
(e) been out yet?

2 How would you ask someone:

(a) how many brothers and sisters they have?
(b) how many older sisters they have?
(c) how many younger brothers they have?
(d) how many children they have?
(e) how many sons they have?
(f) how many daughters they have?

3 How would you respond if a Thai said to you:

(a) sa-bai dee lěr krúp?
(b) kOOn pôot pah-sǎh tai bpen mái?
(c) yòo meu-ung tai nahn mái?
(d) kOOn pôot tai gèng.
(e) chern kûng nai sí krúp.
(f) mee pêe-nórng mái?
(g) kǒr-tôht, kOOn dtàirng ngahn láir-o réu yung?

4 How would you ask someone:

(a) how many cups of coffee they drank?
(b) how many plates of shrimp fried rice they ate?
(c) how many bottles of beer they drank?
(d) how many stamps they want?
(e) how many mangoes they ate?

5 Sue has gone to register at a local clinic. A receptionist is taking down details from the answers Sue gives. What questions did the secretary ask?

Receptionist	________ .
Sue	chêu Susan Ford kâ.
Receptionist	________ .
Sue	ah-yÓO sǎhm-sìp-hâh bpee láir-o.
Receptionist	yòo ________ .
Sue	mâi nahn kâ. sǒrng sǎhm deu-un tâo-nún.
Receptionist	kǒr-tôht ________ .
Sue	kâ, dtàirng ngahn láir-o.
Receptionist	________________________ .
Sue	mee láir-o. mee lôok chai sǒrng kon láir-o gôr lôok sǎo kon nèung.
Receptionist	________________________ .
Sue	ah-yÓO sìp kòo-up, bpàirt kòo-up láir-o gôr hâh kòo-up.

Reading and writing

In the last unit you met the tone mark **mái àyk**. The other main tone mark is **mái toh** which is introduced in this unit together with the much less common **mái dtree** and **mái jùt-dta-wah**. Scan through some of the earlier dialogues to see how frequently **mái àyk** and **mái toh** tone marks occur. Once you have mastered these, you are well on the way to being able to read the dialogues in Thai script.

1 mái toh (-้): tone rules

This tone mark looks like the number 2 with an elongated tail and is written above the initial consonant. Like **mái àyk**, this single tone mark also represents two different tones.

When **mái toh** occurs on a low class initial consonant, the tone is high:

Low class	รู้	แล้ว	น้อง
	róo	**láir-o**	**nórng**

If the initial consonant is either mid or high class, then the tone is falling:

Mid class	ได้	แก้ว	ต้อง
	dâi	**gâir-o**	**dtôrng**
High class	ข้าง	ให้	ถ้า
	kâhng	**hâi**	**tâh**

2 mái dtree (-๊) and mái jùt-dta-wah (-๋): tone rules

In addition to **mái àyk** and **mái toh** there are two other tone marks to learn. But these are much less frequently encountered than the tone marks you have already learned. **mái dtree** looks like the number 7: it always produces a *high* tone. The symbol for **mái jùt-dta-wah** is a cross; words with this mark are always pronounced with a rising tone:

เป๊ปซี่	ต๋อย
bpép-sêe	**dtŏy**

3 Summary of tone mark rules

Tone marks are used, where necessary, to indicate tones in live syllables. (There are only a few exceptions where a tone mark is used in a dead syllable.)

The following chart summarizes these rules:

Initial consonant class	**mái àyk** (-่)	**mái toh** (-้)	**mái dtree** (-๊)	**mái jùt-dta-wah** (-๋)
Low class	**Falling**	**High**	**High**	**Rising**
Mid class	**Low**	**Falling**	**High**	**Rising**
High class	**Low**	**Falling**	**High**	**Rising**

Again, as a learning aid, you might find it helpful to make your own copy of this chart and keep it handy for reference rather than trying to memorize everything immediately.

Reading practice

1 Words

All these words are written with **mái toh** and are therefore pronounced with either a falling tone or a high tone:

ต้อง ทิ้ง บ้าน ให้ รู้

ส้ม นี้ ถ้า เก้า น้ำ

แล้ว กุ้ง ร้อน ห้อง ซื้อ

ข้าว โน้น แก้ว หน้า ได้

2 Phrases

And now some phrases from this and earlier units, using words with **mái toh**:

ได้ไหม ไม่ได้ สามสิบห้า

รู้จักไหม ก็แล้วกัน ข้าวผัดกุ้ง

แก้วหนึ่ง แถวนี้ สองร้อยบาท

3 Dialogue

And finally, here is Somchai ordering lunch in a noodle shop for himself and a couple of friends:

Somchai ขอข้าวผัดกุ้งสองจาน
แล้วก็ข้าวหน้าเป็ดจานหนึ่ง

Waiter ข้าวหน้าเป็ดไม่มี
มีข้าวหน้าไก่แล้วก็ข้าวหมูแดง

Somchai ขอข้าวหมูแดงก็แล้วกัน
แล้วก็น้ำส้มสามแก้ว

Waiter น้ำส้มไม่มี
มีเป๊ปซี่เท่านั้น

ข้าวหน้าเป็ด	*duck rice*
ข้าวหน้าไก่	*chicken rice*
ข้าวหมูแดง	*red pork rice*
น้ำส้ม	*orange juice*
เท่านั้น	*only*

1 What did Somchai order?
2 Which food dish did the restaurant not have?
3 What did Somchai choose instead?
4 What is the only drink that the restaurant has?
5 What drinks did Somchai originally order?

tahn ah-hăhn pèt bpen mái?

can you eat hot food?

ทานอาหารเผ็ดเป็นไหม

In this lesson you will learn

- **more about food and restaurant transactions**
- **anything, anywhere, anyone**
- **the verb hâi**
- **if clauses**
- **consonants: ฆ ธ ภ ญ ณ**
- **vowels: เ-า เ-ีย เ-ือ -ัว เ-ิ -ะ**

Dialogues

Waiter	สั่งหรือยังครับ	sùng réu yung krúp?
Chanida	ยังค่ะ	yung kâ.
	ขอดูเมนูหน่อย	kŏr doo may-noo nòy.
	คุณปีเตอร์ชอบทาน	kOOn Peter chôrp tahn
	อะไร	a-rai?
Peter	อะไรก็ได้ครับ	a-rai gôr dâi krúp.
	ให้คุณชนิดา	hâi kOOn cha-ní-dah
	สั่งดีกว่า	sùng dee gwàh.
Chanida	คุณ Sue	kOOn Sue
	ทานเผ็ดเป็นไหม	tahn pèt bpen mái?
Sue	เป็นค่ะ	bpen kâ,
	ถ้าไม่เผ็ดเกินไป	tâh mâi pèt gern bpai.
Chanida	แกงไก่เผ็ดมากไหมคะ	gairng gài pèt mâhk mái ká?
Waiter	ไม่ค่อยเผ็ดเท่าไรครับ	mâi kôy pèt tâo-rài krúp.
Chanida	ถ้าอย่างนั้น	tâh yàhng nún
	ก็ขอแกงไก่	gôr kŏr gairng gài
	เนื้อผัดน้ำมันหอย	néu-a pùt núm mun hŏy
	แล้วก็ต้มยำกุ้ง	láir-o gôr dtôm yum gÔOng.
	ต้มยำไม่เอาเผ็ด	dtôm yum mâi ao pèt
	มากนะ เอาข้าวด้วยนะ	mâhk ná. ao kâo dôo-ay ná.
Waiter	ครับ	krúp.
	แล้วรับน้ำอะไรครับ	láir-o rúp náhm a-rai krúp?
Chanida	ขอน้ำส้มคั้น	kŏr núm sôm kún
	สองแก้วค่ะ	sŏrng gâir-o kâ.
	แล้วคุณ Peter	láir-o kOOn Peter
	รับเบียร์ ใช่ไหม	rúp bee-a châi mái?

sùng	*to order*	สั่ง
tahn	*to eat*	ทาน
a-rai gôr dâi	*anything*	อะไรก็ได้
hâi	*to get someone to do something*	ให้
pèt	*spicy*	เผ็ด
tâh	*if*	ถ้า
. . . gern bpai	*too . . .*	. . . เกินไป
gairng	*curry*	แกง
gairng gài	*chicken curry*	แกงไก่
tâh yàhng nún	*in that case*	ถ้าอย่างนั้น
néu-a	*beef*	เนื้อ
pùt	*to stir fry*	ผัด
núm mun hŏy	*oyster sauce*	น้ำมันหอย
néu-a pùt núm mun hŏy	*beef fried in oyster sauce*	เนื้อผัดน้ำมันหอย
dtôm yum gÔOng	*shrimp 'tom yam'*	ต้มยำกุ้ง
rúp	*to receive, take*	รับ
núm sôm	*orange juice*	น้ำส้ม
núm sôm kún	*fresh orange juice*	น้ำส้มคั้น

After the main course the waiter returns.

Waiter	รับของหวานไหมครับ	rúp kŏrng wăhn mái krúp?
Chanida	มีอะไรบ้างคะ	mee a-rai bâhng ká?
Waiter	มีผลไม้ ขนม แล้วก็ไอศครีม	mee pŏn-la-mái ka-nŏm láir-o gôr ai dtim.
Chanida	ขนมที่นี่อร่อยนะ คุณ Sue ทานขนมไหม	ka-nŏm têe-nêe a-ròy ná. kOOn Sue tahn ka-nŏm mái?
Sue	ไม่ค่ะ อิ่มแล้ว	mâi kâ. ìm láir-o.

Chanida	แล้วคุณ Peter ล่ะ	láir-o kOOn Peter lâ?
Peter	ทานขนม	tahn ka-nŏm
	ไทยไม่เป็นครับ	tai mâi bpen krúp.
	คิดว่าไม่อร่อย	kít wâh mâi a-ròy.
	หวานเกินไป	wăhn gern bpai.

kŏrng wăhn	*sweet, dessert*	ของหวาน
. . . bâhng	(see Language notes)	. . . บ้าง
pŏn-la-mái	*fruit*	ผลไม้
ka-nŏm	*cake, dessert*	ขนม
ai dtim	*ice cream*	ไอศครีม
ìm	*to be full*	อิ่ม

At the end of the meal, Khun Somchai offers Peter a cigarette.

Somchai	สูบบุหรี่ไหมครับ	sòop bOO-rèe mái krúp?
Peter	ไม่สูบครับ เลิกแล้ว	mâi sòop krúp. lêrk láir-o.
Somchai	เก่งนะ	gèng ná.
	ไม่สูบผมก็เครียด	mâi sòop pŏm gôr krêe-ut.
	เลิกไม่ได้ น้อง ๆ	lêrk mâi dâi. nórng, nórng!
	ขอที่เขี่ยบุหรี่หน่อย	kŏr têe-kèe-a bOO-rèe nòy.
	เช็คบิลด้วย	chék bin dôo-ay.
Waiter	ครับผม	krúp pŏm.

bOO-rèe	*cigarette*	บุหรี่
sòop bOO-rèe	*to smoke*	สูบบุหรี่
lêrk	*to cease, give up*	เลิก
krêe-ut	*to be stressed, tense*	เครียด
nórng, nórng	*waiter!*	น้อง ๆ
têe-kèe-a bOO-rèe	*ashtray*	ที่เขี่ยบุหรี่
chék bin	*can I have the bill?*	เช็คบิล
krúp pŏm	(male polite particle)	ครับผม

1 Can Sue eat hot food?
2 What dishes does Khun Chanida order?
3 What do they have to drink with their meal?
4 Why doesn't Sue want any dessert?
5 Why doesn't Peter like Thai desserts?
6 What does Somchai ask the waiter for?

i If you are eating alone in a restaurant, you are most likely to order a rice or noodle dish (see unit 4) which are served quickly. But if you go out for an evening meal with a number of friends, you are more likely to order rice and a variety of side dishes. These may be brought to the table once they are cooked and the meal can begin before all the dishes have arrived. If you are invited to select one of the dishes, you should be aware that it is not for your exclusive consumption but is supposed to blend in with all the other dishes. If you are not very confident about what to choose, you can always relinquish the responsibility by saying, **hâi kOOn X sùng dee gwàh** (*it's better to let Khun X order*). But even if you opt out, watch what Thais order, so that on future occasions you will be able to make appropriate combinations. Thais use a spoon and fork (although chopsticks are used in noodle shops) to eat. After rice has been served onto the plate, a spoonful or two is normally taken from one of the side dishes and mixed with the rice before eating. A meal is thus a constant 'dipping-in' process. In some restaurants a serving spoon will be provided with each side dish, but in others, you simply use the spoon and fork that you eat with. Expect to be asked questions about whether you can eat Thai food (**tahn ah-hăhn tai bpen mái?**), whether you can eat spicy food (**tahn ah-hăhn pèt bpen mái?**, often abbreviated to **tahn pèt bpen mái?**), whether Thai food is tasty (**ah-hăhn tai a-ròy mái?**), whether Thai food is spicy (**ah-hăhn tai pèt mái?**) and so on. At the end of a meal, the host, or senior person present will normally pick up the bill.

Although Thai cigarette packets carry health warnings, many Thais, especially men, smoke. Smoking is still seen as manly in men and sophisticated in *some* women. When offering a cigarette, a Thai may ask **sòop bOO-rèe mái?** or, more surprisingly to the English speaker, **sòop bOO-rèe *bpen* mái?** (literally,'***Can*** you smoke?'). The latter question does not require a pedantic explanation along the lines of 'Yes-I-*can*-but-actually-I-don't-anymore-because-it's-bad-for-the-health'; a simple **mâi sòop krúp (kâ)** or, if accepting, **kòrp-kOOn krúp (kâ)** is quite sufficient. If you are a smoker, turn to page 168 and learn to recognise the Thai words for 'No smoking' in exercise 3(c).

Key phrases and expressions

How to:

1 ask your friend to order for you

hâi kOOn X sùng dee gwàh ให้คุณ X สั่งดีกว่า

2 ask if a dish is very spicy

. . . pèt mâhk mái? . . . เผ็ดมากไหม

3 tell the waiter you don't want it too hot

mâi ao pèt mâhk ná ไม่เอาเผ็ดมากนะ

4 say you are full

ìm láir-o อิ่มแล้ว

5 say you can't eat something

tahn (gin) . . . mâi bpen ทาน (กิน) . . . ไม่เป็น

6 say something is too sweet/spicy

wăhn/pèt gern bpai หวาน/เผ็ดเกินไป

7 say you don't smoke

mâi sòop krúp (kâ) ไม่สูบครับ(ค่ะ)

Language notes

1 'Like'

It is important not to confuse **chôrp** (*to like*) with **yàhk (ja)** (*to want to, would like to*) which you met in unit 5. **chôrp** can be followed by either a verb or a noun, but **yàhk ja** is always followed by a verb:

chôrp yòo têe-nêe. *I like living here.*
yàhk ja yòo têe-nêe. *I would like to live here.*

chôrp (gin) ah-hăhn tai. *I like (eating) Thai food.*
yàhk ja gin ah-hăhn tai. *I would like to eat Thai food.*

2 . . . gôr dâi

The question words **arai?** (*what?*), **tâo-rài?** (*how much?*), **têe-năi?** (*where?*), **krai?** (*who?*) and **mêu-rài?** (*when?*) also act as indefinite pronouns, *anything*, *however much*, *anywhere*, *anyone* and *whenever*, respectively; they are followed by **. . . gôr dâi** to show amenability or indifference, similar to English *anything/anyone/whenever you like*:

pŏm tahn a-rai gôr dâi.	*I can eat anything you like.*
kOOn bòrk krai gôr dâi.	*You can tell anyone you like.*
jòrt têe-năi gôr dâi.	*Park anywhere you like.*
rao bpai mêu-rài gôr dâi.	*We can go any time you like.*

3 hâi

hâi is an important verb in Thai with a number of distinct usages. One use is as a causative verb, which ranges in meaning from the mildly coercive *to get someone to do something*, to the more benevolent *to let someone do something*; the listener has to judge from the context which sense is implied:

(pŏm) hâi kOOn cha-ní-dah sùng.	*I'll let Khun Chanida order.*
chún hâi káo toh mah mài.	*I got him to ring back.*
káo hâi pŏm jòrt rót dtrong née.	*He let me park right here.*
kOOn ja hâi káo tum arai?.	*What will you get him to do?*

4 Polite vocabulary

One way of indicating politeness in Thai is to use polite particles, such as **krúp** and **kâ/ká** (unit 1). Another way is to select the more formal of two words with the same meaning, such as **sâhp** instead of **róo**. This unit introduces two more 'formal' words, **tahn** (*to eat*) and **rúp** (*to receive, want*) used by restaurant staff when taking orders:

	Formal	*Informal*
to know	**sâhp**	**róo**
to eat	**tahn**	**gin**
to want	**rúp**	**ao**

You may also meet **tahn** in the polite greeting **tahn kâo (láir-o) réu yung?** (*Have you eaten yet?*).

5 'If'

Sentences including an 'if' clause, typically follow the pattern **tâh** (*if*) . . . **gôr** (*then*) + verb:

tâh yàhng nún gôr kŏr gairng gài.	*If that's the case, I'd like chicken curry.*
tâh mâi pèt chún gôr gin dâi.	*If it's not hot, I can eat it.*
tâh mâi mah gôr mâi bpen rai.	*If you don't come, it doesn't matter.*
tâh rót dtìt rao gôr mâi bpai.	*If the traffic is bad, we're not going.*

Confusingly, for the learner, the word **tâh** is commonly omitted:

(tâh) mâi sòop pŏm gôr krêe-ut.	*If I don't smoke, I get stressed.*
(tâh) mâi mah gôr mâi bpen rai.	*If you don't come, it doesn't matter.*

gôr may also be omitted:

tâh mâi pèt (gôr) gin dâi.	*If it's not hot, I can eat it.*

And in abrupt speech both **tâh** and **gôr** can disappear:

mâi pèt gin dâi.	*If it's not hot, I can eat it.*
rót dtìt mâi bpai.	*If the traffic is bad, we're not going.*

6 Wh- question + bâhng

The wh- question words (i.e. *what?*, *who?*, *where?* etc.) occur with **bâhng** (*some, somewhat*) in the pattern verb + wh-question + **bâhng** to indicate that a list of things is anticipated in the answer:

mee kŏrng wăhn a-rai bâhng?	*What desserts do you have?*
káo róo-jùk krai bâhng?	*Who does he know?*
bpai têe-o (*visit*) **têe-năi bâhng?**	*Where did you visit?*

Answers to such questions usually take the form X + Y + **láir-o gôr** (*and*) + Z:

mee pŏn-la-mái ka-nŏm láir-o gôr ai dtim.	*There's fruit, cake and ice cream.*

7 Too . . .

Too . . . is expressed by the pattern adjective + **(gern) bpai**; the word **gern** is optional and frequently omitted in spoken Thai:

wăhn (gern) bpai	*too sweet*
pèt (gern) bpai	*too hot, spicy*
nahn (gern) bpai	*too long (in time)*

The words **mâhk** (*much*), **nòy** (*a little*) or **nít nòy** (*a little bit*) can be added to convey the idea of *much too . . . , a little too . . .* and so on, in which case **gern** is normally omitted. Note that **mâhk** normally occurs before **bpai**, while **nòy** and **nít nòy** occur after:

glai mâhk bpai	*much too far*
pèt bpai nít-nòy	*a little bit too spicy*
pairng bpai nòy	*a little too expensive* (see unit 2)

8 krúp pŏm

krúp pŏm is an alternative to **krúp** as a polite *yes* response for male speakers; it has only become popular in the last decade or so.

Exercises

1 How would you answer if a Thai asked you:

(a) tahn ah-hăhn tai bpen mái?
(b) ah-hăhn tai pèt mái?
(c) tahn pèt bpen mái?
(d) ah-hăhn tai a-ròy mái?
(e) sòop bOO-rèe mái?

2 Answer the following questions using . . . **gôr dâi** to show that you have no special preference:

(a) kOOn yàhk ja bpai mêu-rài?
(b) kOOn yàhk ja gin náhm a-rai?
(c) kOOn yàhk ja pôot gùp krai bâhng?
(d) kOOn yàhk ja bpai têe-o têe-năi bâhng?

3 Translate the following sentences, using the pattern adjective + **(gern) bpai** to justify the initial negative comment:

(a) We can't walk. It's too far.
(b) Thai desserts aren't tasty. They are too sweet.
(c) I don't want it. It's too expensive.
(d) He doesn't like Thai food. It's too spicy.
(e) I can't speak Thai. It's too difficult.

4 Use the pattern (**tâh**) . . . **gôr** . . . to join the two sentences:

(a) glai bpai — mâi dtôrng dern
(b) mâi a-ròy — mâi dtôrng gin
(c) mâi yàhk bpai — mâi dtôrng
(d) mâi pèt mâhk — kít wâh gin dâi

5 Use the pattern **hâi kOOn sŏm-chai** + verb + **dee gwàh** to suggest that it would be better if Somchai did the following:

(a) parked the car.
(b) ordered the food.
(c) spoke to Malee.
(d) made the telephone call.

Reading and writing

1 Consonants

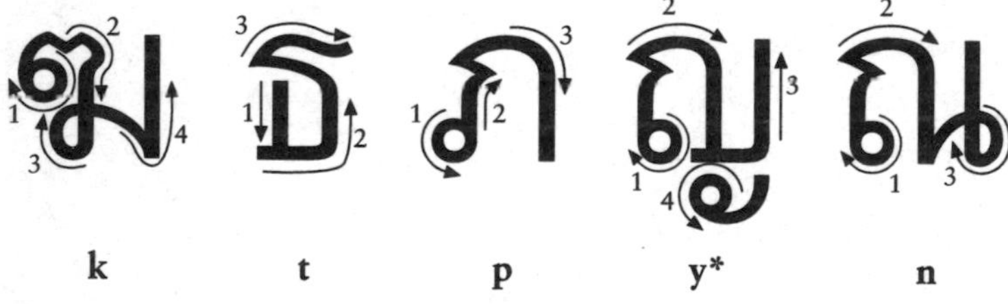

k **t** **p** **y*** **n**

* pronounced 'n' at the end of a word.

This third group of low-class consonants have the same sounds as other low-class consonants that you have already learned in units 1 and 4. The new consonants do not occur as frequently as those you met earlier, but they cannot be ignored as they are appear in a number of common words. These include:

ฆ่า	ภาษา	หญิง	ใหญ่	ญี่ปุ่น	คุณ
kâh	**pah-săh**	**yĭng**	**yài**	**yêe-bpÒOn**	**kOOn**
to kill	*language*	*lady*	*big*	*Japan*	*you, Khun*

2 Vowels

เ-า	เ-ีย	เ-ือ	-ัว*	เ-ิ**	-ะ
-ao	-ee-a	-eu-a	-oo-a	-er	-a
(short)	(long)	(long)	(long)	(long)	(short)

Several new vowels are now being added, most of which are made up of combinations of symbols you have already met. Many learners worry that when reading words where a vowel surrounds a consonant, such as เ-า, they will try to read it as two separate vowels (เ- and -า) instead of recognizing it as a single vowel. In fact, most find the problem evaporates as soon as they start to practise reading. Even so, it is worth remembering that whenever you encounter the symbol เ- you need to scan the next couple of letters briefly to see whether it is a vowel in its own right or just a part of a 'wrap-around' vowel.

* When -ัว is followed by another consonant symbol it omits the top part (-ั) of the vowel symbol.

หัว	ตัว	วัว
hŏo-a	**dtoo-a**	**woo-a**

but

ด้วย	สวน	ขวด
dôo-ay	**sŏo-un**	**kòo-ut**

** When เ-ิ is *not* followed by a consonant it drops the top part of the vowel symbol (-ิ) *but adds* the zero consonant symbol (อ) at the end of the word:

เดิน	เปิด	เกิด
dern	**bpèrt**	**gèrt**

but

เธอ	เจอ
ter	**jer**

Reading practice

1 Words

ภาค ภาษา ใหญ่ หญิง คุณ ฆ่า
เรา เขา เอา เข้า เท่าไร เท่านั้น
เรียน เขียน เลี้ยว เมื่อ เหมือน เพื่อน
ตัว หัว วัว สวย ช่วย ด้วย
เกิน เกิด เชิญ เดิน เจอ เธอ
จะ คะ ค่ะ นะ อะไร บะหมี่

2 Phrases

These phrases from earlier units include some of the new letters from this unit.

คุณชื่ออะไรคะ
โลละเท่าไร
แล้วเลี้ยวซ้าย
เอาบะหมี่น้ำชามหนึ่ง
เดินไปสองนาทีเท่านั้น
เป็นเพื่อนคุณมาลี
เรียกว่าน้อยหน่า
แล้วคุณชนิดาล่ะครับ
ลูกชายอายุสามขวบ

สีแดงสวยมากนะคะ
เก้าสิบเอ็ดบาทค่ะ
เอาน้ำอะไรคะ
เอาเป๊ปซี่ขวดใหญ่
อยากจะลงทะเบียนด้วย
จะไปเมื่อไรคะ
อยู่เมืองไทยนานไหม
พูดภาษาไทยเป็นไหม

3 Menus

Thai food has become extremely popular in the West following the tourist boom of the 1980s. Menus in Thai restaurants often list dishes both in Thai script and romanized Thai, although systems of romanizing Thai words will vary considerably from one restaurant to another. Cover up the romanized Thai and see how well you can read basic menu items.

Curries and soups

แกง	**gairng**	*'wet' curry* (i.e. with a lot of liquid)
แพนง	**pa-nairng**	*'dry' curry*
แกงไก่	**gairng gài**	*chicken curry*
แกงเนื้อ	**gairng néu-a**	*beef curry*
แกงจืด	**gairng jèut**	*bland, clear soup*
ต้มยำ	**dtôm yum**	*'tom yam' – a spicy soup made with lemon grass*
ต้มยำกุ้ง	**dtôm yum gÔOng**	*shrimp 'tom yam'*
ต้มยำปลา	**dtôm yum bplah**	*fish 'tom yam'*

Meat, fish and egg

ไก่	**gài**	*chicken*
เนื้อ	**néu-a**	*beef*
หมู	**mŏo**	*pork*
เป็ด	**bpèt**	*duck*
ปู	**bpoo**	*crab*
ปลา	**bplah**	*fish*
กุ้ง	**gÔOng**	*shrimp*
ไข่	**kài**	*egg*

ไก่/หมู/เนื้อ/กุ้งผัดพริก	**gài/mŏo/néu-a/gÔOng pùt prík** *chicken/pork/beef/shrimp fried with chillies*
ไก่/หมู/เนื้อ/ผัดขิง	**gài/mŏo/néu-a pùt kĭng** *chicken/pork/beef fried with ginger*
ไก่/หมูผัดหน่อไม้	**gài/mŏo pùt nòr-mái** *chicken/pork fried with bamboo shoots*
ไก่/หมู/กุ้งผัดใบกระเพรา	**gài/mŏo/gÔOng pùt bai gra-prao** *chicken/pork/shrimp fried with basil leaves*

ไก่/หมู/ปลาผัดเปรี้ยวหวาน	**gài/mǒo/bplah pùt bprêe-o wăhn** *sweet and sour chicken/pork/fish*
เนื้อผัดน้ำมันหอย	**néu-a pùt núm mun hǒy** *beef fried in oyster sauce*
ไก่ทอดกระเทียมพริกไทย	**gài tôrt gra-tee-um prík tai** *chicken fried with garlic and pepper*
ไก่/เป็ดย่าง	**gài/bpèt yâhng** *barbecued chicken/duck*
ไข่ดาว	**kài dao** *fried egg*
ไข่เจียว	**kài jee-o** *omelette*
ไข่ยัดไส้	**kài yút sâi** *stuffed omelette*

mâi kâo jai

I don't understand

ไม่เข้าใจ

In this unit you will learn

- **coping strategies when you don't understand**
- **how? questions**
- **don't . . .**
- **initial consonant clusters**
- **words with no written vowel symbol**

Dialogues

Sue has accompanied some Thai friends to a restaurant.

Chanida	ปลาเค็มมากไหมคะ คุณซู	bplah kem mâhk mái ká kOOn Sue?
Sue	อะไรนะคะ	a-rai ná ká?
	พูดอีกทีได้ไหม	pôot èek tee dâi mái?
Chanida	ปลาเค็มมากไหม	bplah kem mâhk mái?
Sue	ไม่เข้าใจ พูดช้า ๆ หน่อยได้ไหม	mâi kâo jai. pôot cháh cháh nòy dâi mái?
Chanida	ปลา – เค็ม – ไหม	bplah – kem – mái?
Sue	ไม่รู้จักคำว่า 'เค็ม' ภาษาอังกฤษ แปลว่าอะไร	mâi róo-jùk kum wâh 'kem'. pah-săh ung-grìt bplair wâh a-rai?
Chanida	แปลว่า salty	bplair wâh 'salty'.
Sue	อ้อ เข้าใจแล้ว เค็มค่ะ	ôr kâo jai láir-o. kem kâ.
	'เค็ม' สะกดอย่างไร	'kem' sa-gòt yung-ngai?

bplah	*fish*	ปลา
kem	*salty*	เค็ม
tee	*time*	ที
èek tee	*again*	อีกที
kâo jai	*to understand*	เข้าใจ
cháh	*slow*	ช้า
kum	*word*	คำ
bplair	*to translate*	แปล
. . . bplair wâh a-rai?	*what does . . . mean?*	แปลว่าอะไร
sa-gòt	*to spell*	สะกด
yung-ngai?	*how?*	อย่างไร

Peter is also in a restaurant. His Thai companions are busy chattering away in Thai until Somchai suddenly turns to him.

Somchai	คุณ Peter	kOOn Peter
	ฟังรู้เรื่องไหม	fung róo rêu-ung mái?
Peter	อะไรนะครับ	a-rai ná krúp?
Malee	ฝรั่งงง	fa-rùng ngong.
Somchai	ฟังรู้เรื่องไหม	fung róo rêu-ung mái?
Peter	ไม่รู้เรื่อง	mâi róo rêu-ung.
	ถ้าพูดเร็วมาก	tâh pôot ray-o mâhk
	ผมก็ไม่รู้เรื่องเลย	pŏm gôr mâi róo rêu-ung ler-ee.
Malee	ไม่เป็นไรหรอก	mâi bpen rai ròrk.
	เรานินทาคุณเท่านั้น	rao nin-tah kOOn tâo-nún.
Peter	'นินทา'	'nin-tah'
	หมายความว่าอะไร	măi-kwahm wâh a-rai?
Somchai	แปลว่า gossip	bplair wâh 'gossip'.
	แต่อย่าไปเชื่อ	dtàir yàh bpai chêu-a
	มาลีนะ คุณมาลี	Malee ná. kOOn Malee
	ชอบพูดเล่นเสมอ	chôrp pôot lên sa-mĕr.

fung	*to listen*	ฟัง
rôo rêu-ung	*to understand*	รู้เรื่อง
ngong	*to be dazed, confused*	งง
ray-o	*quick*	เร็ว
mâi . . . ler-ee	*not . . . at all*	ไม่ . . . เลย
nin-tah	*to gossip*	นินทา
. . . măi-kwahm wâh a-rai?	*what does . . . mean?*	. . . หมายความว่าอะไร
yàh	*don't*	อย่า
chêu-a	*to believe*	เชื่อ
pôot lên	*to joke*	พูดเล่น

1 What was the Thai word that Sue did not know?
2 How did she try to ensure that she would remember it?
3 How did she answer Chanida's original question?
4 Why couldn't Peter understand what his companions were saying?
5 What joke did Malee make?
6 Why didn't Peter get the joke?

i Although you will find Thais extremely complimentary about your attempts to learn Thai, you will almost certainly feel that your linguistic inadequacies are exposed with alarming frequency in the initial stages. One obvious problem is vocabulary. Thai words sound quite unlike any European language and so there is little scope for latching onto a familiar word and then guessing what people are talking about. Even when you stay within your linguistic limitations, you may find a Thai looking absolutely bewildered by your best attempts, only to repeat, with a sudden expression of enlightenment, *exactly* what you just said. Well, *almost* exactly. Maybe you got a tone wrong, a vowel not quite right, or maybe your Thai friend was simply more accustomed to foreigners speaking Thai with a German accent. The important thing is not to get discouraged by these little setbacks. Relax. Recognize that on some days you are on better form than on others. Don't worry if everything is going over your head. Be prepared to laugh at yourself. But, most important of all, have some positive strategy for dealing with communication breakdowns and try to analyse where your individual weaknesses lie. Learn different ways of asking someone to repeat something – for even the most patient of Thais may tire of the farang whose every other utterance is **a-rai ná?** A knowledge of Thai script is invaluable here, because you can always ask how something is written in Thai (**pah-săh tai kĕe-un yung-ngai?**); and if you weren't sure what tone the word was when you heard it, you can check from the spelling.

Key phrases and expressions

How to say:

1 Pardon?

a-rai ná? อะไรนะ

2 Could you say that again?

pôot èek tee dâi mái? พูดอีกทีได้ไหม

3 I don't understand

mâi kâo jai ไม่เข้าใจ

mâi róo rêu-ung ไม่รู้เรื่อง

4 Could you speak slowly please?

pôot cháh cháh nòy dâi mái? พูดช้า ๆ หน่อยได้ไหม

5 I don't know the word

mâi róo-jùk kum wâh . . . ไม่รู้จักคำว่า . . .

6 What's that in English?

pah-săh ung-grìt bplair wâh a-rai? ภาษาอังกฤษแปลว่าอะไร

7 How do you spell/write it?

sa-gòt yung-ngai? สะกดอย่างไร

kĕe-un yung-ngai? เขียนอย่างไร

8 What does . . . mean?

. . . măi kwahm wâh a-rai? . . . หมายความว่าอะไร

. . . bplair wâh a-rai? . . . แปลว่าอะไร

Language notes

1 'What does that mean?'

There are two ways of asking what something means: **bplair wâh a-rai?** is, literally, a request for a translation, while **măi kwahm wâh a-rai?** is asking for clarification or an explanation:

pah-săh ung-grìt bplair wâh a-rai? *What's that in English?*
kOOn măi kwahm wâh a-rai? *What do you mean?*

2 How? questions

How? questions which ask about the manner in which something is done follow the pattern verb + **yung-ngai?** (*how?*):

sa-gòt yung-ngai? *How do you spell it?*
bpen yung-ngai (bâhng)? *How are things?*
bpai yung-ngai? *How are we going?*

If the sentence includes a grammatical object, this commonly occurs before the verb:

kem **sa-gòt yung-ngai?**	*How do you spell 'salt'?*
ma-môo-ung gin yung-ngai?	*How do you eat mangoes?*

The Thai spelling of *how?* suggests that the correct pronunciation is **yàhng-rai** rather than **yung-ngai**. In normal speech, however, the first vowel is shortened, the low tone changes to a neutral mid tone and the final **ng** in the first syllable and initial **r** in the second syllable are assimilated into a **ng** sound. In fact, when greeting each other informally, Thais will often go a step further and say, simply, **bpen ngai?**

How? questions which ask how tall/heavy/long (in linear measurement or time) something is use **tâo-rài?** (*how much?*):

sŏong (*high/tall*) **tâo-rài?**	*How high/tall is it?*
kOOn nùk (*heavy*) **tâo-rài?**	*How heavy are you/What do you weigh?*
ree-un pah-săh tai nahn tâo-rài?	*How long have you studied Thai?*

3 róo rêu-ung

róo rêu-ung like **kâo jai** means *to understand*. It often occurs after the verbs **fung** (*to listen*) and **àhn** (*to read*) as a 'resultative verb', where it indicates the 'result' (i.e. understanding) that follows the action of the first verb (i.e. listening, reading):

róo rêu-ung mái?	*Do you understand?*
fung róo rêu-ung mái?	*Do you understand?* (by listening)
àhn róo rêu-ung mái?	*Do you understand?* (by reading)

It is the resultative verb that is used for 'yes' answers and which is negated for 'no' answers:

fung róo rêu-ung mái?	*Do you understand?* (by listening)
– róo rêu-ung/mâi róo rêu-ung.	– *Yes/no.*

Similarly, in negative statements, it is the resultative verb that is negated:

mâi róo rêu-ung.	*I don't understand.*
fung mâi róo rêu-ung.	*I don't understand.* (what I hear)
àhn mâi róo rêu-ung.	*I don't understand.* (what I read)

4 'Not . . . at all'

The pattern **mâi** + verb + **ler-ee** (*not . . . at all*) is used to intensify negative statements:

pŏm mâi róo rêu-ung ler-ee.	*I don't understand at all.*
mâi nâh yòo ler-ee.	*It's not very nice to live in at all.*
mâi mee ler-ee.	*There aren't any at all.*
mâi pairng ler-ee.	*It's not at all expensive.*

It is important to distinguish between **mâi . . . ler-ee** and **mâi . . . rork** (see unit 3), for both can be translated as *not . . . at all*. **mâi . . . ler-ee** is a statement of fact or opinion, whereas **mâi . . . ròrk** is a statement of contradiction:

pairng jung ler-ee.	*It's ever so expensive.*
– mâi pairng ròrk.	*– No it isn't. / Not at all.*

5 yàh

Negative commands follow the pattern **yàh** (*don't*) + verb; they can be made milder by the addition of the mood particle **ná** (*right?*, *OK?*):

yàh leum ná?	*Don't forget, OK?*
yàh tum pèt mâhk ná?	*Don't make it very spicy, OK?*
yàh kùp ray-o ná?	*Don't drive fast, OK?*

In the second dialogue, Somchai says **yàh** ***bpai*** **chêu-a kOOn Malee ná**. This usage of **bpai** has an exact equivalent in English: *Don't go believing Khun Malee.*

6 pôot lên

When the word **lên** (*to play*) follows another verb, it indicates that the action of the first verb is being carried out for fun:

pôot	*to speak*	**pôot lên**	*to joke*
dern	*to walk*	**dern lên**	*to go for a walk*
àhn	*to read*	**àhn lên**	*to read for pleasure*
gin	*to eat*	**gin lên**	*to eat 'for fun'* (e.g. mid-meal snacks)

Exercises

1 How would you:

(a) tell somone you did not understand?
(b) ask someone to repeat something?
(c) ask someone what something means?
(d) ask someone to speak slowly?
(e) ask someone how to write something?

2 A Korean businessman who speaks no English and less Thai than Peter is having difficulty following a conversation among his Thai hosts. He keeps asking Peter what various words mean. What alternative Thai words can Peter suggest?

(a) *bpra-tâyt* bplair wâh a-rai?
(a) *tahn* bplair wâh a-rai?
(b) *sâhp* bplair wâh a-rai?
(d) *mâi róo rêu-ung* bplair wâh a-rai?

3 Use **. . . yung-ngai?** to seek advice on how to do the following, making the italicized word the first word in your question:

(a) go to *Chiangmai*.
(b) to eat *mangoes*.
(c) use (**chái**) the *telephone*.
(d) to write *sa-bai*

4 Answer these questions with an emphatic *no*, using the pattern **mâi . . . ler-ee**:

(a) chôrp mái?
(b) dee mái?
(c) ao mái?
(d) kâo jai mái?
(e) fung róo rêu-ung mái?

5 Here's Peter, locked in conversation with Malee and stubbornly refusing to be defeated by his limited vocabulary. What do you think he said?

Malee ker-ee bpai doo nǔng tai mái?
Peter ________ .
Malee ker-ee bpai doo nǔng tai mái?
Peter ________ .
Malee ker-ee – bpai – doo – nǔng – tai – mái?
Peter ________ .
Malee nǔng bplair wâh 'movie'.
kâo jai mái?

Peter	_______ .
Malee	ker-ee bpai doo mái?
Peter	mâi ker-ee.

Reading and writing

1 Words beginning with consonant clusters

All the words that you have read up to now have begun with either a single consonant or a vowel sound. In this unit we are going to learn how to read words that begin with a consonant cluster (two consonant sounds) – words like **krúp, glùp, gwàh** and so on. The following consonant clusters exist in Thai; knowing which consonant clusters can exist at the beginning of a word will help you to avoid misreading certain two-syllable words:

กร-	คร-	ขร-	ตร-	ปร-	พร-
gr-	**kr-**	**kr-**	**dtr-**	**bpr-**	**pr-**
กล-	คล-	ขล-		ปล-	พล-
gl-	**kl-**	**kl-**		**bpl-**	**pl-**
กว-	คว-	ขว-			
gw-	**kw-**	**kw-**			

When it comes to reading a word like ครับ, the tone should clearly be high, since (i) it is a dead syllable, (ii) both consonants in the cluster are low class and (iii) the vowel is short.

But in many words the two consonants at the beginning of a word belong to different classes. In such cases, it is the class of the *first* consonant that determines the tone:

ขวา	ใกล้	ปลูก
kwăh	**glâi**	**bplòok**

2 Words with no vowel symbols

In unit 4 you met words like **kon** and **gòt** which consisted of two consonants but no written vowel symbol. Two-syllable words, consisting of three consonant symbols and no vowel symbols are much less common. In such cases, the first vowel is **-a** and the second **-o**:

ถนน สงบ ขนม

ta-nǒn sa-ngòp ka-nǒm

More common are words in which there is a vowel symbol in the second syllable, but where a short **-a** vowel has to be supplied in the first:

ตลาด สนาม สบาย ชนิดา

dta-làht sa-năhm sa-bai cha-ní-dah

Since these words begin with two consonants, they look very similar to those that begin with a consonant cluster. But if you check the consonant cluster chart, you will see that the *sounds* **dtl-, sn-** and **sb-** do not exist at the beginning of Thai words. So the short **-a** vowel has to be added after the initial consonant. The first syllable in words like this is pronounced with a mid tone.

The tone of the second syllable is determined by the *second* consonant in the cluster unless it is one of those consonants you learned in unit 1 (i.e. ง น ม ร ย ล ว); if the second consonant is a unit 1 consonant then the class of the *first* consonant determines the tone:

ขบวน สภาพ สนาม สง่า

ka-boo-un sa-pâhp sa-năhm sa-ngàh

Note: Words beginning บร- are pronounced with an **-or** vowel between the first and second consonants, not an **-a** vowel:

บริการ บริเวณ บริษัท

bor-ri-gahn bor-ri-wayn bor-ri-sùt

Reading practice

1 Words

The first two letters in these words form a consonant cluster:

กว่า ขวา กรุง ประตู ปลา
เปล่า ตรง ไกล ใกล้ กลับ
ใคร คล้าย ครับ ความ ประเทศ

The first two letters in the following words do not form a consonant cluster and therefore require a vowel to be supplied:

ถนน ตลก ขยัน สยาม สภาพ
ขนาด สนุก สถาน สบาย บริษัท
ฉลอง ฉลาด ฝรั่ง ขยะ บริการ

2 Conversation

Interviewer คุณอยู่เมืองไทยนานไหมครับ
Businessman ไม่นานครับ
ประมาณ ๖ เดือนเท่านั้น
Interviewer คุณพูดไทยเก่งมากครับ
เหมือนเป็นเจ้าของภาษา
Businessman ไม่หรอกครับ
เวลาคนไทยพูด
บางครั้งผมก็ฟังไม่รู้เรื่องเลย
แล้วถ้าผมพูดภาษาไทย
คนไทยก็ฟังไม่รู้เรื่องเหมือนกัน
Interviewer คุณเรียนภาษาไทยที่ไหน
Businessman เรียนที่โรงเรียนสอนภาษาอยู่แถว
ถนนสุขุมวิทแล้วใช้ตำรากับเทปที่บ้าน
Interviewer ภาษาไทยยากไหมครับ
Businessman ยากครับ
แต่ถ้าไม่มีเทปฟัง ก็คงยากกว่า
Interviewer แล้วคุณอ่านและเขียนภาษาไทยเป็นไหม
Businessman อ่านเป็นนิดหน่อยครับ ถ้าเป็นคำง่าย ๆ
แต่เขียนไม่ค่อยได้

เหมือน	*like, similar*
เจ้าของภาษา	*native speaker* (literally, owner of the language)
เวลา	*time*
บางครั้ง	*sometimes*
เหมือนกัน	*likewise*
โรงเรียน	*school*
ใช้	*to use*
ตำรา	*textbook*
กับ	*with, and*
เทป	*tape*
ที่บ้าน	*at home*
คง	*sure to, bound to*
คำ	*word*

1 How long has the businessman been in Thailand?
2 What communication problems does he sometimes encounter?
3 How did he learn Thai?
4 Can he read and write Thai?

chôrp yòo grOOng-tâyp mái?

do you like living in Bangkok?

ชอบอยู่กรุงเทพฯไหม

In this unit you will learn

- **how to talk about living and working in Bangkok**
- **how to talk about things that happened in the past**
- **some ways of intensifying adjectives and adverbs**
- **some more uses of gôr**
- **consonants: ฌ ฎ ฏ ฐ ฑ ฒ ฬ ฮ**
- **vowels: เ-ะ แ-ะ โ-ะ เ-อะ เ-าะ**

Dialogues

Chanida is asking Sue how she likes living in Bangkok.

Chanida	คุณซูชอบอยู่	kOOn Sue chôrp yòo
	กรุงเทพฯไหม	grOOng-tâyp mái?
Sue	ชอบค่ะ	chôrp kâ.
	คิดว่าน่าสนใจมาก	kít wâh nâh sǒn jai mâhk.
Chanida	จริงหรือคะ	jing lěr ká?
	ฉันว่ากรุงเทพฯ	chún wâh grOOng-tâyp
	ตอนนี้ไม่น่าอยู่เลย	dtorn née mâi nâh yòo ler-ee.
	พ่อแม่บอกว่า	pôr mâir bòrk wâh
	เมื่อก่อนรถไม่ค่อยมี	mêu-a gòrn rót mâi kôy mee,
	ตึกสูง ๆ	dtèuk sǒong sǒong
	ก็ไม่ค่อยมี	gôr mâi kôy mee.
	ตอนนั้นมีคลอง	dtorn nún mee klorng
	มีต้นไม้สวย ๆ	mee dtôn-mái sǒo-ay sǒo-ay
	แล้วอากาศสะอาด	láir-o ah-gàht sa-àht.
Sue	คุณชนิดาเป็นคน	kOOn cha-ní-dah bpen kon
	กรุงเทพฯใช่ไหมคะ	grOOng-tâyp châi mái ká?
Chanida	ไม่ใช่ค่ะ	mâi châi kâ.
	พ่อแม่ย้ายมาอยู่ที่นี่	pôr mâir yái mah yòo têe-nêe
	เมื่อฉันยังเด็ก	mêu-a chún yung dèk.
	เมื่อก่อนฉันอยู่	mêu-a gòrn chún yòo
	ภาคใต้ เกิดที่จังหวัด	pâhk dtâi. gèrt têe jung-wùt
	ภูเก็ต	poo-gèt.

chôrp	*to like*	ชอบ
dtorn née	*now*	ตอนนี้
nâh yòo	*habitable*	น่าอยู่
mâir	*mother*	แม่
gòrn	*before*	ก่อน
mêu-a gòrn	*formerly, before*	เมื่อก่อน
dtèuk	*building*	ตึก
klorng	*canal*	คลอง
dtôn-mái	*tree*	ต้นไม้
mêu-a	*when*	เมื่อ
yung	*still*	ยัง
dèk	*child*	เด็ก
pâhk dtâi	*the South*	ภาคใต้
gèrt	*to be born*	เกิด
poo-gèt	*Phuket*	ภูเก็ต

Peter is asking Khun Somchai about his job.

Peter	งานตอนนี้	ngahn dtorn née
	เป็นอย่างไร	bpen yung-ngai?
Somchai	ก็ . . . ดีเหมือนกัน	gôr . . . dee měu-un gun.
	เงินเดือนก็ใช้ได้	ngern deu-un gôr chái dâi.
	แต่บางครั้งคิด	dtàir bahng krúng kít
	ว่าน่าเบื่อ	wâh nâh bèu-a.
	ต้องตื่นแต่เช้า	dtôrng dtèun dtàir cháo
	แล้วกลับบ้านดึก	láir-o glùp bâhn dèuk.
	รถมันติดจังเลย	rót mun dtìt jung ler-ee.
	ทุกวันกลับบ้าน	tÓOk wun glùp bâhn
	เสียเวลา	sěe-a way-lah
	สองชั่วโมงกว่า	sǒrng chôo-a-mohng gwàh.
	รู้สึกว่าแย่นะ	róo-sèuk wâh yâir ná.

Peter	ใช่ แย่จริง ๆ	châi. yâir jing jing.
Somchai	แล้วอากาศมันไม่ดี	láir-o ah-gàht mun mâi dee.
	บางครั้งคิดว่า	bahng krúng kít wâh
	อยากจะย้ายไปอยู่	yàhk ja yái bpai yòo
	ต่างจังหวัด	dtàhng jung-wùt.
	อากาศมันดีกว่า	ah-gàht mun dee gwàh,
	สะอาดกว่า . . . แล้ว	sa-àht gwàh . . . láir-o
	รถไม่ติด คนไม่แน่น	rót mâi dtìt, kon mâi nâirn
	เหมือนที่กรุงเทพ ฯ	měu-un têe grOOng-tâyp.

ngahn	*work*	งาน
bpen yung-ngai?	*how is it?*	เป็นอย่างไร
gôr . . .	*well . . .*	ก็ . . .
. . . měu-un gun	*fairly . . .*	เหมือนกัน
ngern deu-un	*salary*	เงินเดือน
chái dâi	*reasonable, acceptable*	ใช้ได้
dtàir	*but*	แต่
krúng	*time(s)*	ครั้ง
nâh bèu-a	*boring*	น่าเบื่อ
dtèun	*to wake up*	ตื่น
(dtàir) cháo	*(from) early morning*	(แต่)เช้า
bâhn	*house, home*	บ้าน
dèuk	*late at night*	ดึก
mun	*it*	มัน
jung ler-ee	*really, very*	จังเลย
tÓOk	*every*	ทุก
wun	*day*	วัน

sěe-a	*to spend, waste*	เสีย
way-lah	*time*	เวลา
chôo-a-mohng	*hour*	ชั่วโมง
. . . gwàh	*more than . . .*	กว่า
yâir	*to be a nuisance, a hassle*	แย่
ah-gàht	*air, weather, climate*	อากาศ
yái	*to move*	ย้าย
dtàhng jung-wùt	*up country, outside Bangkok*	ต่างจังหวัด
sa-àht	*clean*	สะอาด
nâirn	*to be crowded*	แน่น
měu-un	*like, similar, as*	เหมือน

1 Does Chanida like Bangkok?
2 Where does she come from?
3 When did she move to Bangkok?
4 How does she describe what Bangkok was like in the past?
5 What does Somchai feel about his salary?
7 How long does it take Somchai to get home from work?
8 What advantages does Somchai believe that working upcountry has over Bangkok?

i Bangkok has the reputation of being one of the world's most congested cities; while special bus lanes, elaborate one-way detours and the wide-scale construction of flyovers and elevated bypasses has improved things considerably over the last decade, the traffic situation continues to seriously affect the quality of life of everyone in the city.

Bangkok residents appear resigned to this and few would consider forgoing the economic opportunies afforded by the capital in favour of a better living environment upcountry. The massive building boom of the late 1980s and early 1990s, during which multistorey office blocks, shopping centres and condominiums seemed to spring up, chaotically, almost overnight, further added to the environmental nightmare. Desplte this, many people, both Thai and foreigner, find Bangkok has a richness and vitality that are quite unique.

Key phrases and expressions

How to:

1 ask someone's opinion of something and state one's own opinion

. . . bpen yung-ngai?	. . . เป็นอย่างไร
pŏm/chún wâh . . .	ผม/ฉันว่า . . .
kít wâh . . .	คิดว่า . . .
róo-sèuk wâh . . .	รู้สึกว่า . . .

2 talk about things that happened in the past

mêu-a gòrn . . .	เมื่อก่อน . . .
mêu-a chún yung dèk . . .	เมื่อฉันยังเด็ก . . .
mêu-a chún ah-yÓO hâh kòo-up . . .	เมื่อฉันอายุห้าขวบ . . .
mêu-a săhm bpee gòrn . . .	เมื่อสามปีก่อน . . .

3 express approval in different ways

dee (mâhk) jing jing	ดี (มาก) จริงๆ
dee (mâhk) jung ler-ee	ดี (มาก) จังเลย
dee mâhk ler-ee	ดีมากเลย
dee mâhk	ดีมาก

Language notes

1 nâh + verb

nâh occurs before a verb to form an adjective that carries the sense *worthy of . . .* :

bèu-a	*to be bored*	**nâh bèu-a**	*boring*
sŏn jai	*to be interested in*	**nâh sŏn jai**	*interesting*
yòo	*to live*	**nâh yòo**	*habitable, nice to live in*
rúk	*to love*	**nâh rúk**	*lovable, sweet, cute*
gin	*to eat*	**nâh gin**	*tasty*

chún kít wâh nâh sŏn jai mâhk.	*I think it is very interesting.*
grOOng-tâyp mâi nâh yòo ler-ee.	*Bangkok is not a habitable place at all.*
ngahn dtorn née nâh bèu-a.	*Work at the moment is boring.*

2 mêu-a

mêu-a (*when*) is used when talking about things that happened in the past; *previously/before* can be expresed by **mêu-a gòrn,** while **mêu-a** + time expression + **gòrn** is one of several ways of expressing . . . *ago*:

mêu-a gòrn rót mâi kôy mee.	*Before, there were hardly any cars.*
mêu-a gòrn chún yòo pâhk tâi.	*Before, I lived in the South.*
mêu-a chún yung dèk.	*when I was still a child*
mêu-a chún ah-yÓO hâh kòo-up.	*when I was five years old*
mêu-a săhm bpee gòrn.	*three years ago*

3 gôr

gôr has occurred several times, in idiomatic expressions such as **. . . gôr láir-o gun** (unit 2) and **. . . gôr dâi** (unit 9) and in conditional sentences (**tâh . . . gôr . . .**, unit 9). Three further uses are illustrated in this unit. First, **gôr** can mean *too, also*:

rót mâi mee, dtèuk sŏong gôr mâi mee.	*There were no cars and no tall buildings either/too.*
kon tai yér, fa-rùng gôr yér	*lots of Thais and lots of farangs, too*

Second, it occurs at the beginning of a sentence as a hesitation device, rather like English *well/er . . .* :

ngahn dtorn née bpen yung-ngai?	*How's work these days?*
– gôr . . . dee mĕu-un gun.	*– Well, . . . it's OK.*

Third, when the topic of the sentence occurs at the beginning of the sentence, **gôr** often occurs in the pattern **sòo-un** (*as for*) + topic + **gôr** + verb:

sòo-un ah-hăhn tai pŏm gôr chôrp.	*As for Thai food, I like it.*
sòo-un pah-săh jeen gôr yâhk bpai.	*As for Chinese, it's too difficult.*

In spoken Thai, **sòo-un** is often dropped:

ngern deu-un gôr chái dâi.	*As for the salary, it's alright.*
ah-hăhn tai gôr a-ròy.	*As for Thai food, it's tasty.*

4 . . . mĕu-un gun

mĕu-un gun literally means *likewise, similarly* and is often used in this way:

mĕu-un gun mâhk.	*They are very similar.*
mâi mĕu-un gun.	*They are not the same.*

The phrase also has an idiomatic usage, illustrated in the dialogue, indicating a qualified or lukewarm 'yes' response:

dee mái? *Is it good?*
– gôr dee mĕu-un gun. *– Well, it's quite good.*

chôrp mái? *Do you like it?*
– gôr chôrp mĕu-un gun. *– Well, yes, I quite like it.*

5 Noun + pronoun + verb

The pattern noun + pronoun + verb, where the pronoun refers to the noun, occurs commonly in spoken Thai. You may hear some Thais carry the construction across to English, with statements like *My teacher he is not nice*:

rót mun dtìt. *The traffic is jammed.* (traffic-it-stuck)
ah-gàht mun dee gwàh. *The air is better.* (air-it-better)
sŏm-chai káo mâi mah. *Somchai is not coming.* (Somchai-he-not-come)

6 Intensification

The easiest way to intensify an adjective or adverb is to add **mâhk** (*very, much*) after it. In this unit two additional ways of intensification are introduced, adding **jing jing** or **jung ler-ee** after the adjective, both of which can be translated as *really* . . . or *ever so*. . . . You can also use **mâhk** in front of **jing jing** and **jung ler-ee**; in the latter case it is very often abbreviated in speech to **. . . mâhk ler-ee.** You now have quite a selection of ways for intensifying adjectives, in both positive and negative ways:

dee (mâhk) jing jing. *It's really (very) good.*
dee (mâhk) jung ler-ee. *It's really (very) good.*
dee mâhk ler-ee. *It's really very good.*
dee mâhk. *It's very good.*
dee. *It's good.*
gôr . . . dee mĕe-un gun. *Well . . . it's good.* (some reservations)

mâi kôy dee (tâo-rài). *It's not very good.*
mâi dee. *It's not good/it's bad.*
mâi dee ler-ee. *It's not good at all/it's very bad.*

7 'More than . . .'

The basic pattern expressing the idea of *more than . . .* is (noun +) **mâhk gwàh** + number + classifier:

mee fa-rùng mâhk gwàh sìp kon.	*There were more than ten farangs.*
chún gin gah-fair mâhk gwàh sèe tôo-ay.	*I drank more than four cups of coffee.*

Note that the pattern (noun +) number + classifier + **gwàh** conveys the idea of a fraction – but not a whole unit more:

sŏrng chôo-a-mohng gwàh	*more than two hours* (but not three)

8 Regions

Thailand is divided into four regions (**pâhk**), each of which has its own distinct dialect and traditional customs:

pâhk nĕu-a	*the North*	ภาคเหนือ
pâhk dtâi	*the South*	ภาคใต้
pâhk glahng	*the Central Region*	ภาคกลาง
pâhk ee-săhn	*the Northeast*	ภาคอีสาน

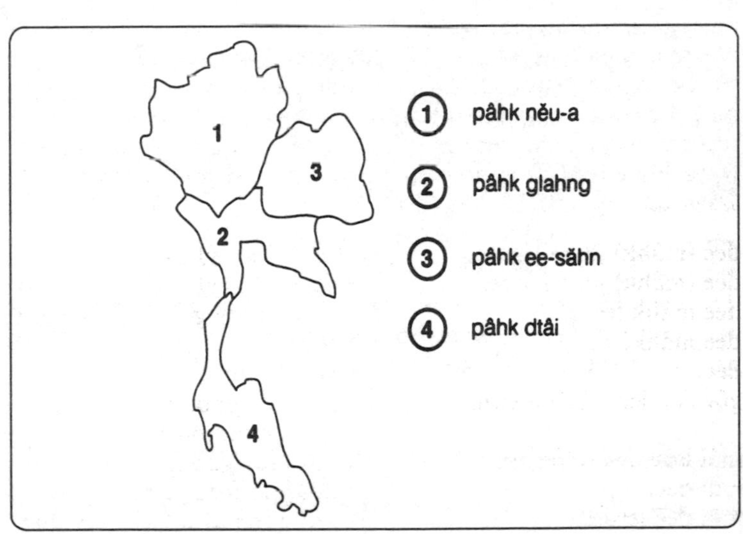

Exercises

1 Answer these questions with an emphatic *yes*, using the pattern . . . **mâhk jing jing** or . . . **mâhk jung ler-ee:**

(a) chôrp mái?
(b) dee mái?
(c) nâh bèu-a mái?
(d) gairng gài pèt mái?
(e) ree-un têe a-may-ri-gah pairng mái?

2 You are weighing up the advantages and disadvantages of living in Bangkok with living outside the capital. Which statements would you list under each heading?

(a) yòo grOOng-tâyp. . . . **(b) yòo dtàhng jung-wùt. . . .**

(i) ah-gàht sa-àht gwàh.
(ii) ngern deu-un gôr chái dâi.
(iii) kon nâirn.
(iv) dtôrng dtèun dtàir cháo láir-o glùp bâhn dèuk.
(v) rót mâi dtìt.
(vi) ah-gàht mâi dee.
(vii) kon mâi kôy nâirn.
(viii) rót dtìt jung ler-ee.
(ix) dtèuk sŏong sŏong mâi kôy mee.
(x) ngern deu-un mâi kôy dee.

3 Complete the following sentences:

(a) pŏm/chún gèrt têe . . .
(b) mêu-a pŏm/chún yung dèk bâhn pôr mâir yòo têe . . .
(c) mêu-a pŏm/chún ah-yÓO hâh kòo-up bpai ree-un têe . . .
(d) mêu-a pŏm/chún ah-yÓO . . . bpee yái bpai yòo . . .

Reading and writing

1 Consonants

The consonants in this unit are not very common and at this stage you need not worry about memorizing them. The class of each consonant is indicated beneath the symbol:

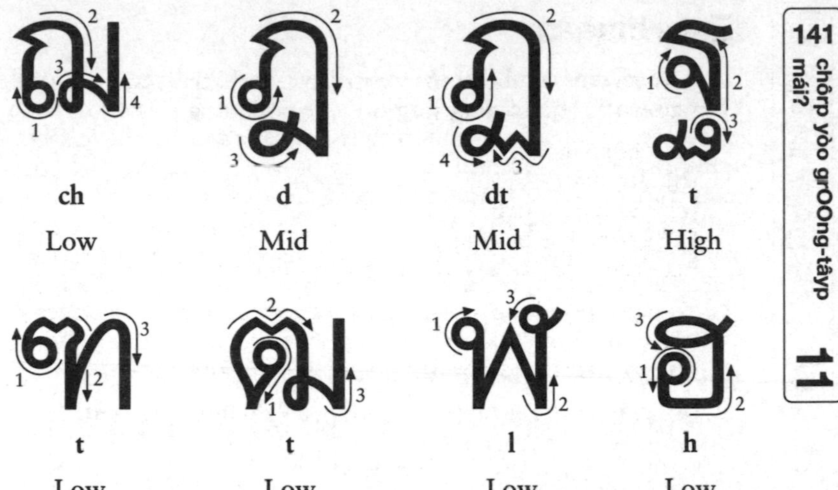

2 Vowel shortener: -ะ

You have already met the vowel symbol -ะ as a short **a** vowel (unit 9).

The same symbol also has a completely different function, in shortening the following long vowels: เ-, แ-, โ-, เ-อ, and in changing the pronunciation of เ-า:

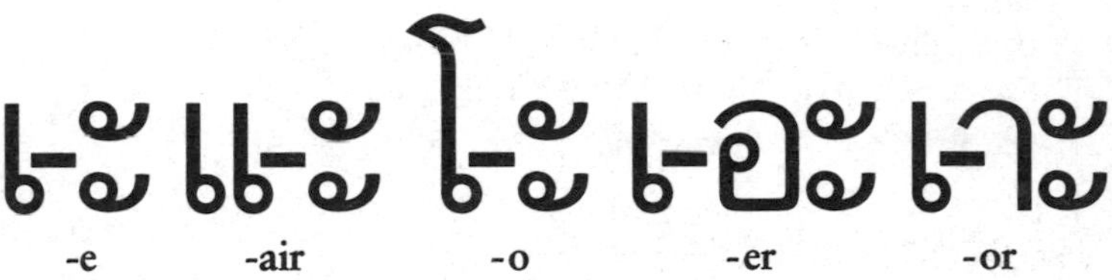

Reading practice

1 Words

เยะ	เละเทะ	เตะ	เกะกะ
และ	แกะ	แพะ	แตะ
โต๊ะ	เลอะเทอะ	เยอะ	เยอะแยะ
เพราะ	เกาะ	เหมาะ	หัวเราะ

2 Passage

Each year thousands of people leave their villages in rural Thailand and flock to Bangkok in search of work. While some are seasonal migrants, others, through either poverty or ambition, will never return. In this passage, a young girl, Tui, talks about leaving home and going to work in a noodle shop in Bangkok. Notice that she refers to herself as *Tui* rather than using **chún**. Using one's name or nickname instead of *I* is very common in girls' speech; a lot of foreign men pick up the habit and sound rather strange to Thais.

ตุ๋ยเป็นคนอีสานค่ะ อยู่หมู่บ้านเล็กๆ ที่จังหวัดหนองคาย เมื่อก่อนตุ๋ยทำนา แต่ไม่ชอบ เพราะว่าเป็นงานหนักมาก ตุ๋ยก็คิดว่าย้ายมาทำงานที่นี่ดีกว่า ตอนนี้ทำงานอยู่ที่ร้านก๋วยเตี๋ยวอยู่แถวสุขุมวิท ล้างชามล้างจานทั้งวัน บางวันคิดว่าน่าเบื่อ แต่ไม่อยากกลับบ้านเพราะว่า ไม่อยากทำนาและเงินเดือนที่นี่ก็ใช้ได้ ดีกว่าต่างจังหวัด

คนอีสาน	*a Northeasterner*
หมู่บ้าน	*village*
เล็ก ๆ (lék lék)	(the symbol ๆ means 'repeat' the previous word)
หนองคาย	*Nongkhai*
ทำนา	*rice farming*
หนัก	*heavy; hard* (work)
ร้านก๋วยเตี๋ยว	*noodle shop*
ล้าง	*to wash*
ทั้งวัน	*all day*

(a) What work did Tui do in her village?
(b) Why didn't she like it?
(c) What does she do all day long in the noodle shop?
(d) Is she happy in her work?
(e) Why doesn't she want to go home?

3 Passage

Here is a little more information about Chanida's family:

คุณชนิดาเป็นคนภาคใต้ เกิดที่จังหวัดภูเก็ต พ่อเป็นตำรวจ แม่เป็นแม่บ้าน มีลูกสามคน พ่อแม่คุณชนิดากับพี่น้องย้ายมาอยู่ที่นี่เมื่อคุณชนิดาอายุห้าขวบ ตอนนี้น้องชายคุณชนิดาเรียนอยู่ที่มหาวิทยาลัยมหิดล เขาอยากจะเป็นหมอ คุณพ่อชนิดาอยากจะให้น้องชายไปเรียนต่อที่ประเทศอเมริกา

ตำรวจ	*policeman* **(dtum-ròo-ut*)**
แม่บ้าน	*housewife*
มหาวิทยาลัยมหิดล	*Mahidol University*
ต่อ	*to continue*
เรียนต่อ	*to continue one's studies*

* The second syllable is pronounced with a low tone, not a falling tone, as might be expected from the rules you have learned.

(a) How many brothers and sisters does Chanida have?
(b) How old was Chanida when the family moved to Bangkok?
(c) What is Chanida's younger brother doing at the moment?
(d) What plans does Chanida's father have for his son's future?

4 Dialogue

And here's Peter asking Somchai about his origins.

Peter คุณสมชายเป็นคนภาคเหนือใช่ไหม

Somchai ใช่ ผมเกิดที่เชียงใหม่ พ่อแม่ย้ายมาอยู่ที่นี่เมื่อสามสิบปีก่อนเมื่อผมยังเด็ก พ่ออยากให้ผมเรียนที่นี่ เพราะว่าพ่อคิดว่าโรงเรียนที่นี่ดีกว่า

Peter ชอบอยู่ที่นี่ไหม

Somchai ไม่ค่อยชอบเท่าไร ที่นี่รถติดจังเลย อยู่เชียงใหม่อากาศสะอาดกว่าและรถไม่ติดเหมือนที่นี่

(a) What province was Somchai born in?
(b) How long ago did his parents move to Bangkok?
(c) Why did the family move to Bangkok?
(d) In what ways does Somchai feel that his place of birth is better than Bangkok?

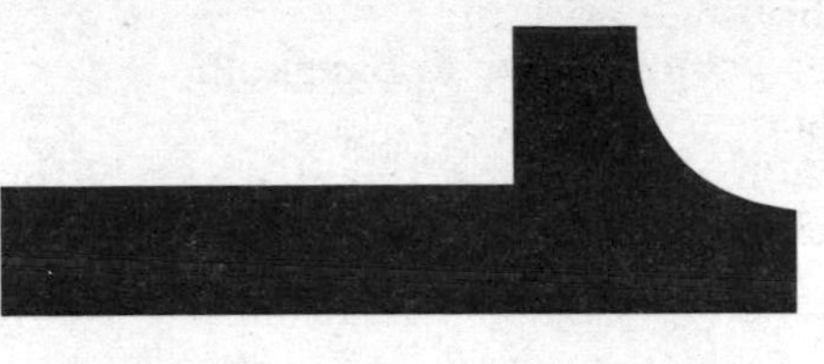

rót òrk gèe mohng?

what time does the coach leave?

รถออกกี่โมง

In this unit you will learn

- **how to make enquiries about travel arrangements**
- **how to tell the time**
- **miscellaneous spelling rules**

Dialogues

Sue	เราคิดจะไปเที่ยว	rao kít ja bpai têe-o
	นครพนมอาทิตย์หน้า	na-korn pa-nom ah-tít nâh.
	ไปรถไฟดีไหม	bpai rót fai dee mái?
Chanida	นั่งรถไฟไป	nûng rót fai bpai
	นครพนมไม่ได้	na-korn pa-nom mâi dâi.
	ถ้าอยากไปรถไฟ	tâh yàhk bpai rót fai
	ก็ต้องต่อรถทัวร์ที่	gôr dtôrng dtòr rót too-a têe
	ขอนแก่น	kŏrn-gàirn.
Sue	อ้อ หรือคะ	ôr lĕr ká?
	ขอนแก่นอยู่ห่างจาก	kŏrn-gàirn yòo hàhng jàhk
	นครพนมกี่กิโลคะ	na-korn pa-nom gèe gi-loh ká?
Chanida	คิดว่าต้องนั่งรถทัวร์	kít wâh dtôrng nûng rót too-a
	ประมาณ ๖ ชั่วโมง	bpra-mahn hòk chôo-a-mohng.
Sue	โอ้โฮ นานจริง ๆ	ôh hoh nahn jing jing.
Chanida	ค่ะ ฉันว่านั่งรถทัวร์	kâ. chún wâh nûng rót too-a
	จากกรุงเทพฯ ดีกว่า	jàhk grOOng-tâyp dee gwàh
	แต่ควรจะจองตั๋ว	dtàir koo-un ja jorng dtŏo-a
	ล่วงหน้า	lôo-ung nâh.

têe-o	*to visit, go out*	เที่ยว
na-korn pa-nom	*Nakhorn Phanom*	นครพนม
ah-tít	*week*	อาทิตย์
nâh	*next*	หน้า
rót fai	*train*	รถไฟ
nûng	*to sit; travel by*	นั่ง
dtòr	*to continue*	ต่อ
rót too-a	*tour bus*	รถทัวร์
kŏrn-gàirn	*Khonkaen*	ขอนแก่น
hàhng jàhk	*to be far from*	ห่างจาก

gi-loh	*kilometre*	กิโล
koo-un (ja)	*should*	ควร(จะ)
jorng	*to book*	จอง
dtŏo-a	*ticket*	ตั๋ว
lôo-ung nâh	*in advance*	ล่วงหน้า

Peter is at the Northern Bus Terminal in Bangkok, trying to book tickets for a trip to the Northeast.

Peter	ขอโทษครับ	kŏr-tôht krúp.
	ไปนครพนมจองตั๋ว	bpai na-korn pa-nom jorng dtŏo-a
	ที่ไหน	têe-năi?
Clerk	ที่นี่ค่ะ	têe-nêe kâ.
	จะไปเมื่อไร	ja bpai mêu-rài?
Peter	คิดจะไปพรุ่งนี้	kít ja bpai prÔOng née.
Clerk	พรุ่งนี้เช้าเต็มแล้ว	prÔOng née cháo dtem láir-o.
	คืนพรุ่งนี้ได้ไหมคะ	keun prÔOng née dâi mái ká?
Peter	ได้ครับ	dâi krúp.
	รถออกกี่โมง	rót òrk gèe mohng?
Clerk	ออกสี่ทุ่มครึ่งค่ะ	òrk sèe tÔOm krêung kâ.
Peter	ใช้เวลาเดินทาง	chái way-lah dern tahng
	กี่ชั่วโมงครับ	gèe chôo-a-mohng krúp?
Clerk	ประมาณแปด	bpra-mahn bpàirt
	ชั่วโมงค่ะ	chôo-a-mohng kâ.
	ถึงนครพนม	tĕung na-korn pa-nom
	ประมาณตีห้า	bpra-mahn dtee hâh.
Peter	ตั๋วใบละเท่าไรครับ	dtŏo-a bai la tâo-rài krúp?
Clerk	ใบละสองร้อยห้า	bai la sŏrng róy hâh
	สิบบาทค่ะ	sìp bàht kâ.
Peter	ดีครับ เอาสองใบ	dee krúp. ao sŏrng bai.
	แล้วขึ้นรถที่ไหน	láir-o kêun rót têe-năi?

prÔOng née	*tomorrow*	พรุ่งนี้
cháo	*morning*	เช้า
dtem (láir-o)	*full*	เต็ม(แล้ว)
keun	*night*	คืน
rót may	*bus*	รถเมล์
gèe mohng?	*what time?*	กี่โมง
sèe tÔOm	*10.00 p.m.*	สี่ทุ่ม
krêung	*half*	ครึ่ง
sèe tÔOm krêung	*10.30 p.m.*	สี่ทุ่มครึ่ง
chái	*to use*	ใช้
chái way-lah	*to take time*	ใช้เวลา
dern tahng	*to travel*	เดินทาง
dtee hâh	*5.00 a.m.*	ตีห้า
bai	(classifier for ticket)	ใบ
kêun	*to get on*	ขึ้น

1 When does Peter want to go to Nakhorn Phanom?
2 What time does his bus leave?
3 How long is the journey?
4 How much does his ticket cost?

i Travel outside Bangkok is cheap and convenient. Perhaps the best way to travel up country is by air-conditioned tour bus; if you can arrange for a daytime rather than overnight departure, this will give you a good opportunity to get some impression of the rural landscape in relative comfort. Tour buses are operated both by the state-owned Mass Transport Organization (MTO) and private companies. They operate a frequent and efficient service to every province in the country. Refreshments are served en route and, on longer journeys, a simple meal is provided at a highway cafe on showing your ticket. When travelling up country it is normally necessary to book in advance. MTO buses, or **rót bor kŏr sŏr** as they are known by the Thai acronymn, can be booked at the Northern, Eastern or Southern Bus Terminals.

Key phrases and expressions

How to:

1 ask where to book tickets

jorng dtŏo-a têe-năi? จองตั๋วที่ไหน

2 ask what time the bus leaves/arrives

rót may òrk gèe mohng? รถเมล์ออกกี่โมง

rót may tĕung gèe mohng? รถเมล์ถึงกี่โมง

3 ask how long the journey takes

chái way-lah dern tahng gèe chôo-a mohng? ใช้เวลาเดินทางกี่ชั่วโมง

4 ask where to get on (off) the bus

kêun (long) rót may têe-năi? ขึ้น(ลง)รถเมล์ที่ไหน

Language notes

1 têe-o

têe-o occurs most commonly as a verb meaning *to visit (places)*. **bpai têe-o** (*I'm going out*) is a deliberately vague response to the informal greeting **bpai năi?** (*Where are you going?*) while **têe-o pôo-yĭng** is a common euphemism for *'visiting' prostitutes*. Note that a different verb, **yêe-um**, is used for visiting people:

rao kít ja bpai têe-o na-korn pa-nom.	*We're thinking of visiting Nakhorn Phanom.*
bpai năi?	*Where are you going?*
– bpai têe-o.	*– Out.*
káo chôrp têe-o pôo-yĭng.	*He likes 'visiting' prostitutes.*
wun la sŏrng têe-o	*two trips a day*
chún ja bpai yêe-um pêu-un.	*I'm going to visit a friend.*

2 'By train'

No preposition is needed in Thai to translate *by* in expressions like *by bus*, *by train*, *by car* and so on. It is sufficient to use the pattern **bpai** + vehicle:

rao ja bpai rót may.	*We are going by bus.*

Alternatively, the pattern **nûng** (*to sit*)/**kùp** (*to drive*) + vehicle + **bpai/mah** can be used to specify whether someone is a passenger or driver and whether they are coming or going:

nûng rót fai bpai na-korn pa-nom mâi dâi.	*You can't go to Nakhorn Phanom by train.*
dtôrng nûng rót too-a hòk chôo-a-mohng.	*You have to travel by tour bus for six hours.*
pŏm kùp rót mah.	*I drove here (by car).*

3 Distances

The distance in kilometres between two places is expressed by the pattern place A + **yòo** + **hàhng jàhk** + place B + number + **gi-loh**:

nŏrng-kai yòo hàhng jàhk grOOng-tâyp 614 gi-loh.	*Nongkhai is 614 kilometres from Bangkok.*
rohng ree-un yòo hàhng jàhk bâhn sìp nah-tee.	*The school is ten minutes from home.*

4 'Tomorrow morning/evening'

Notice that **prÔOng née** (*tomorrow*) occurs before **cháo** (*morning*) but after **keun** (*night*):

prÔOng née cháo	*tomorrow morning*
prÔOng née bài	*tomorrow afternoon*
prÔOng née yen	*tomorrow (early) evening*
but	
keun prÔOng née	*tomorrow night*

5 Asking the time

To ask what time something happens, the pattern verb + **gèe mohng?** is used; *what time is it?* is **gèe mohng láir-o?**:

rót òrk gèe mohng?	*What time does the bus leave?*
gèe mohng láir-o?	*What time is it?*

When asking how many hours something takes, the word **chôo-a mohng** (*hour*) is used:

gèe chôo-a mohng?	*how many hours?*
chái way-lah gèe chôo-a mohng?	*How many hours does it take?*

6 Telling the time

Hours

In the traditional Thai system of telling the time, the day is divided into four sections of six hours, whereby 7 a.m. and 7 p.m. both become *one o'clock*, 8 a.m. and 8 p.m. *two o'clock* and so on. In telling the time, a specific word is used to distinguish each of these four periods of the day:

dtee	*1 a.m.–6 a.m.*	**bài**	*1 p.m.–approx 4 p.m.*
		yen	*4 p.m.–6 p.m.*
cháo	*7 a.m.–midday*	**tÔOm**	*7 p.m.–midnight*

However, the hours between 6 a.m. and 11 a.m. can be expressed in two ways:

midnight	**têe-ung keun**	*midday*	**têe-ung (wun)**
1 a.m.	**dtee nèung**	*1 p.m.*	**bài mohng**
2 a.m.	**dtee sŏrng**	*2 p.m.*	**bài sŏrng mohng**
3 a.m.	**dtee săhm**	*3 p.m.*	**bài săhm mohng**
4 a.m.	**dtee sèe**	*4 p.m.*	**bài sèe mohng**
5 a.m.	**dtee hâh**	*5 p.m.*	**hâh mohng yen**
6 a.m.	**dtee hòk**	*6 p.m.*	**hòk mohng yen**
7 a.m.	**mohng cháo**	*7 p.m.*	**tÔOm nèung**
8 a.m.	**sŏrng mohng cháo**	*8 p.m.*	**sŏrng tÔOm**
or	**bpàirt mohng cháo**		
9 a.m.	**săhm mohng cháo**	*9 p.m.*	**săhm tÔOm**
or	**gâo mohng cháo**		
10 a.m.	**sèe mohng cháo**	*10 p.m.*	**sèe tÔOm**
or	**sìp mohng cháo**		
11 a.m.	**hâh mohng cháo**	*11 p.m.*	**hâh tÔOm**
or	**sìp-èt mohng cháo**		

Note that **dtee** and **bài** appear before the number; **dtee** and **tÔOm** do not occur with **mohng**.

Half hours

Half past the hour is expressed by adding the word **krêung** (*half*) to the hour time. For the hours from 7 a.m. to 11 a.m., however, the word **cháo** is usually omitted:

2.30 a.m.	**dtee sŏrng krêung**
8.30 a.m.	**sŏrng mohng krêung**
10.30 a.m.	**sìp mohng krêung**
3.30 p.m.	**bài săhm mohng krêung**
5.30 p.m.	**hâh mohng yen krêung**
11.30 p.m.	**hâh tÔOm krêung**

Minutes past, minutes to the hour

There is no special word for *quarter past* or *quarter to* the hour. Minutes past the hour are expressed as hour time + number + **nah-tee** (*minute*):

11.15 a.m.	**hâh mohng sìp-hâh nah-tee**
3.10 p.m.	**bài săhm mohng sìp nah-tee**
8.15 p.m.	**sŏrng tÔOm sìp hâh nah-tee**

Minutes to the hour are expressed as **èek** (*further, more*) + number + **nah-tee** + hour time:

9.45 a.m.	**èek sìp-hâh nah-tee sèe mohng cháo**
4.40 p.m.	**èek yêe-sìp nah-tee hâh mohng yen**
11.50 p.m.	**èek sìp nah-tee têe-ung keun**

24-hour clock

In the 24-hour clock system the word **nah-li-gah** is used for *hours* and half hours are expressed as *30 minutes past*:

20.00	**yêe-sìp nah-li-gah**
22.30	**yêe-sìp-sŏrng nah-li-gah săhm-sìp nah-tee**

Exercises

1 Match up the following times:

(a) èek sìp hâh nah-tee têe-ung wun	(i) 05.30
(b) hâh tÔOm yêe-sìp hâh nah-tee	(ii) 16.10
(c) bài sèe mohng sìp nah-tee	(iii) 11.45
(d) dtee hâh krêung	(iv) 23.25

2 What time is it?

(a) 09.30
(b) 14.20
(c) 17.00
(d) 21.45

3 How would you ask:

(a) where to book a ticket for Chiangmai?
(b) what time the Chiangmai bus leaves?
(c) how many kilometres Chiangmai is from Bangkok?
(d) how long the journey takes?
(e) where to get on the bus?

Reading and writing

You have now covered the principal features of the Thai writing system. This unit gives examples of the most common spelling irregularities and lists miscellaneous diacritics which you are likely to encounter in reading an ordinary passage of Thai.

1 The letter ร

The letter ร is normally pronounced as **n** at the end of a word:

อาหาร	ควร	ผู้จัดการ
ah-hăhn	**koo-un**	**pôo jùt gahn**
food	*should*	*manager*

In a number of words, however, it is pronounced **orn**:

นคร	ละคร	พร
na-korn	**la-korn**	**porn**
Nakhorn (in place names)	*theatre*	*gift, blessing*

In certain words it is not pronounced at all:

จริง	สระ
jing	**sà**
true	*swimming pool*

When ทร occurs at the beginning of a word, the cluster is pronounced **s**:

ทราบ	ทรง	ทราย
sâhp	**song**	**sai**
to know	*breast*	*sand*

When -รร occurs at the end of a word or syllable it is pronounced **-un** and **-u** if it is followed by a consonant:

รถบรรทุก	พรรค	กรรม
rót bun-tÓOk	**púk**	**gum**
lorry	*(political) party*	*fate, karma*

2 'r' in ung-grìt

The Thai spelling of **ung-grìt** (*English*) uses the rare symbol ฤ to represent the **ri** sound.

อังกฤษ

ung-grìt

English

3 Letters that are not pronounced at the end of a word

When the symbol ์ occurs above a consonant, that consonant is not pronounced. It occurs in words of foreign origin, where the foreign spelling has been retained:

เบอร์	จอห์น	เสาร์	อาทิตย์
ber	**jorn**	**săo**	**ah-tít**
number	*John*	*Saturday*	*Sunday, week*

Sometimes it is not only the consonant below the symbol which is not pronounced but also the one immediately preceding it:

จันทร์	ศาสตร์
jun	**sàht**
Monday, moon	*science*

In some cases, even though there is no 'consonant killer' (์), the final consonant is still not pronounced:

บัตร	สมัคร
bùt	**sa-mùk**
card	*to join*

And in other cases, a final short vowel is not pronounced:

ชาติ	เหตุ
châht	**hàyt**
nation	*reason*

4 Linker syllables

There are a number of words which appear to have two syllables but which are pronounced as three syllables, with a short a vowel in the middle. In such words the final consonant of the first syllable also functions as the initial consonant in the second syllable:

ชนบท	ผลไม้
chon-na-bòt	**pŏn-la-mái**
countryside	*fruit*

5 Mismatch between pronunciation and spelling

There are a few common words that in normal conversation are pronounced with a high tone when the written form suggests the tone should be rising:

ไหม	ฉัน	เขา
mái	**chún**	**káo**
(question particle)	*I*	*he, she, they*

6 Symbols ฯ and ๆ

The symbol ฯ you will probably first meet in the word **grOOng-tâyp** – the Thai name for *Bangkok*. It really means 'etc.' and is used to abbreviate the extremely long full name of the capital. The second symbol indicates that the preceding word should be repeated:

กรุงเทพ ฯ	ช้า ๆ
grOOng-tâyp	**cháh cháh**
Bangkok	*slow*

How are you progressing?

You have now covered the major features of the Thai writing system and you should find that if you cover up the romanized part of the dialogues and study the Thai script sections you can read every word. At this point, it is worth going back over the earlier units and working through the Thai script dialogues. It will almost certainly be slow work at first; but if you keep re-reading the same dialogues, you will find that your reading speed steadily improves and that your eye begins to skim quickly over letters without having to pause to think carefully about each one. The reading speed you develop on familiar passages will gradually transfer itself to new, unseen materials.

Reading practice

1 Here are some words from earlier lessons with the 'killer' symbol over one of the letters. Some of these words are recognizably borrowed from English, while others come from Sanskrit, the classical language of India.

โปสการ์ด	แสตมป์	เบียร์สิงห์
ปีเตอร์	เก็บสตางค์	ไปรษณีย์
เบอร์โทรศัพท์	ซอยเกษมสันต์	

2 A number of provinces include the word **na-korn** in their name. **na-korn** comes from Sanskrit and means *city*. Match the Thai script spelling with the normal romanization of these place names:

(i) นครปฐม	(a) Nakhorn Ratchasima
(ii) นครนายก	(b) Nakhorn Phanom
(iii) นครสวรรค์	(c) Sakol Nakhorn
(iv) นครราชสีมา	(d) Nakhorn Srithammarat
(v) นครพนม	(e) Nakhorn Sawan
(vi) สกลนคร	(f) Nakhorn Nayok
(vii) นครศรีธรรมราช	(g) Nakhorn Pathom

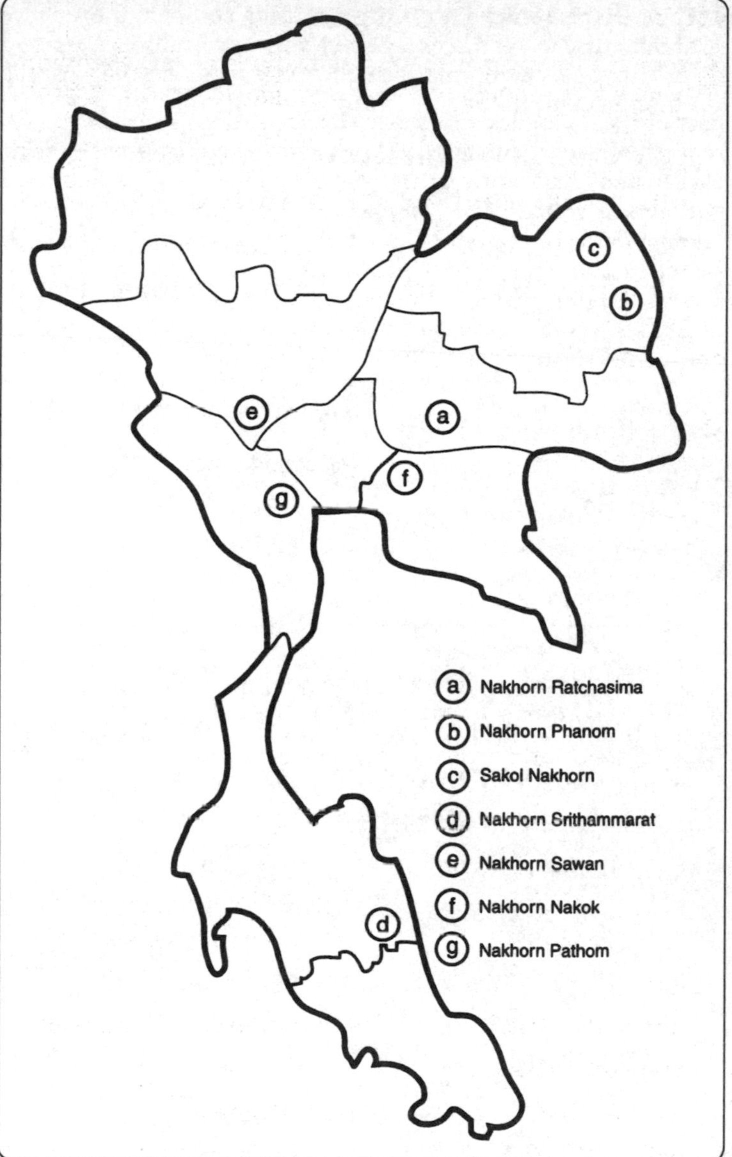
c
b
a
e
f
g
d
a Nakhorn Ratchasima
b Nakhorn Phanom
c Sakol Nakhorn
d Nakhorn Srithammarat
e Nakhorn Sawan
f Nakhorn Nakok
g Nakhorn Pathom

3 Here is some information from a tour company's brochure about trips to Nongkhai. When you have fully understood the passage, write full sentence answers in Thai to the questions that follow.

หนองคายอยู่ห่างจากกรุงเทพ ฯ ๖๑๔ กิโลเมตร บริษัท วี ไอ พี จำกัด มีรถปรับอากาศชั้นหนึ่ง ออกจากกรุงเทพฯ วันละ ๒ เที่ยว เวลา ๐๘.๐๐ และ ๒๑.๓๐ นาฬิกา ใช้เวลาเดินทางประมาณ ๑๐ ชั่วโมง ค่าโดยสารคนละ ๓๘๐ บาท

จำกัด	*Ltd*
ปรับอากาศ	*air conditioned*
ชั้นหนึ่ง	*first class*
เที่ยว	*trip*
ค่าโดยสาร	*fare*

๑ หนองคายอยู่ห่างจากกรุงเทพ ฯ กี่กิโลเมตร
๒ บริษัท วี ไอ พี จำกัด มีรถไปหนองคายวันละกี่เที่ยว
๓ รถไปหนองคายออกกี่โมง
๔ ใช้เวลาเดินทางกี่ชั่วโมง
๕ ค่าโดยสารเท่าไร

13 mee hôrng wâhng mái?

do you have any free rooms?

มีห้องว่างไหม

In this unit you will learn

- **how to book a hotel room**
- **. . . réu bplào? questions**
- **days of the week**
- **another use of hâi**
- **verb + wái**

Dialogues

Peter and Sue have arrived at a small hotel in the provincial capital of Nakhorn Phanom.

Peter	มีห้องว่างไหมครับ	mee hôrng wâhng mái krúp?
Clerk	มีครับ	mee krúp.
	จะพักอยู่กี่วัน	ja púk yòo gèe wun?
Peter	ยังไม่แน่ครับ	yung mâi nâir krúp.
	อาจจะอยู่จนถึง	àht ja yòo jon tĕung
	วันเสาร์ หรือวันอาทิตย์	wun săo réu wun ah-tít.
	ห้องติดแอร์หรือเปล่า	hôrng dtìt air réu bplào?
Clerk	ติดครับ	dtìt krúp.
Peter	ค่าห้องวันละเท่าไรครับ	kâh hôrng wun la tâo-rài krúp?
Clerk	วันละห้าร้อยบาทครับ	wun la hâh róy bàht krúp.
	ถ้าอยู่อาทิตย์หนึ่ง	tâh yòo ah-tít nèung
	ก็จะลดให้สิบเปอร์เซ็นต์	gôr ja lót hâi sìp bper sen.
Peter	ขอดูห้องก่อนได้ไหม	kŏr doo hôrng gòrn dâi mái?
Clerk	ได้ครับ เชิญทางนี้ครับ	dâi krúp. chern tahng née krúp.
Peter	มุ้งลวดมันเสียครับ	mÓOng lôo-ut mun sĕe-a krúp.
	ช่วยแก้ให้หน่อยได้ไหม	chôo-ay gâir hâi nòy dâi mái?
Clerk	ได้ครับ เดี๋ยวจะซ่อมให้	dâi krúp. dĕe-o ja sôrm hâi.
Peter	ช่วยฉีดยากันยุง	chôo-ay chèet yah gun yOOng
	ให้ด้วยได้ไหม	hâi dôo-ay dâi mái?

púk	*to stay*	พัก
nâir	*to be certain*	แน่
àht (ja)	*may*	อาจ(จะ)
jon tĕung	*until*	จนถึง
wun săo	*Saturday*	วันเสาร์
wun ah-tít	*Sunday*	วันอาทิตย์

. . . réu bplào?	*. . . or not?*	. . . หรือเปล่า
dtìt air	*to be air conditioned*	ติดแอร์
(wun) la	*per* (day)	(วัน)ละ
ah-tít	*week*	อาทิตย์
hâi	*for*	ให้
bper sen	*per cent*	เปอร์เซ็นต์
mÓOng lôo-ut	*mosquito screen*	มุ้งลวด
sěe-a	*to be broken*	เสีย
gâir	*to fix, repair, mend*	แก้
sôrm	*to repair, mend*	ซ่อม
chèet	*to spray*	ฉีด
yah gun yOOng	*mosquito repellent*	ยากันยุง

Peter and Sue have agreed to take the room and are now going out for a meal.

Clerk	ไปไหนครับ	bpai năi krúp?
Peter	ไปทานข้าว	bpai tahn kâo.
	ขอโทษครับ	kŏr-tŏht krúp,
	ขอฝากของไว้	kŏr fàhk kŏrng wái
	ที่นี่ได้ไหม	têe-nêe dâi mái?
Clerk	ของอะไรครับ	kŏrng a-rai krúp?
Peter	กล้องถ่ายรูปและ	glôrng tài rôop láir
	กล้องถ่ายวีดีโอ	glôrng tài wee-dee-oh.
Clerk	ได้ครับ ฝากไว้	dâi krúp. fàhk wái
	ที่นี่ปลอดภัย ผมจะ	têe-nêe bplòrt-pai. pŏm ja
	เก็บไว้ให้ในตู้เซฟ	gèp wái hâi nai dtôo sáyf.
Peter	ขอบคุณมากครับ	kòrp-kOOn mâhk krúp.
	ขอฝากกุญแจห้องด้วย	kŏr fàhk gOOn-jair hôrng dôo-ay.

fàhk	*to deposit*	ฝาก
kŏrng	*things*	ของ
glôrng tài rôop	*camera*	กล้องถ่ายรูป
glôrng tài wee-dee-oh	*video camera*	กล้องถ่ายวีดีโอ
bplòrt-pai	*safe* (adj)	ปลอดภัย
gèp wái	*to keep*	เก็บไว้
dtôo sáyf	*safe* (n)	ตู้เซฟ
gOOn-jair	*key*	กุญแจ

1 How long are Peter and Sue thinking of staying at the hotel?
2 Do they want an air-conditioned room or a room with a fan?
3 How much is the room per night?
4 What inducement does the clerk offer the couple to stay longer?
5 What valuables do they want to leave in the hotel safe?

i If you are staying in a large hotel in Bangkok you will find that most of the staff speak English. Since their English will be considerably better than your Thai at this stage, it is more appropriate for you to stick to English when speaking to them. However, in cheaper hotels and guest houses, especially in provincial areas, you may find it necessary to use Thai to book your room.

Hotel rooms will either be air conditioned or have a ceiling fan (**pút lom**). A room with a double bed is confusingly described as a 'single room' (**hôrng dèe-o**) while a 'double room' (**hôrng kôo**) has two single beds. Rooms in modern hotels will include a western-style toilet, shower and wash basin, although in provincial areas you may find a Thai-style toilet and a large earthenware water jar, with a small bowl for scooping up the water and pouring over yourself. If your room has a water jar, you will probably find mosquitoes congregating there and it is well worth being equipped with your own insecticide (**yah gun yOOng**). And while on the subject of mosquitoes (**yOOng**), check that the mosquito screens (**mÓOng lôo-ut**) on the windows are in good condition and, if not, insist on changing the room.

The Thai word for hotel (**rohng rairm**), is also a euphemism for brothel and many of the cheaper hotels that are not brothels are used primarily for illicit liaisons. If you find you get odd looks when you arrive alone and try to book in for a week, you may be at the wrong kind of establishment.

Key phrases and expressions

How to:

1 ask if there are any free rooms
mee hôrng wâhng mái? มีห้องว่างไหม

2 say you will stay until Saturday
ja yòo jon tĕung wun săo จะอยู่จนถึงวันเสาร์

3 ask whether the room is air conditioned
hôrng dtìt air réu bplào? ห้องติดแอร์หรือเปล่า

4 ask what the daily rate is
kâh hôrng wun la tâo-rài? ค่าห้องวันละเท่าไร

5 ask to see the room
kŏr doo hôrng gòrn dâi mái? ขอดูห้องก่อนได้ไหม

6 say X is broken and ask for it to be fixed
X sĕe-a X เสีย
chôo-ay gâir hâi nòy dâi mái? ช่วยแก้ให้หน่อยได้ไหม

7 ask to leave something
kŏr fàhk kŏrng wái têe-nêe dâi mái? ขอฝากของไว้ที่นี่ได้ไหม

Language notes

1 Days of the week

wun jun	*Monday*	วันจันทร์
wun ung-kahn	*Tuesday*	วันอังคาร
wun pÓOt	*Wednesday*	วันพุธ
wun pa-réu-hùt	*Thursday*	วันพฤหัส
wun sÒOk	*Friday*	วันศุกร์
wun săo	*Saturday*	วันเสาร์
wun ah-tít	*Sunday*	วันอาทิตย์

The word **wun** (*day*) usually prefaces the name of the day. When talking about the day on which something happens, Thai does not use a preposition corresponding to English *on*:

wun jun pŏm bpai tum ngahn. — *On Monday I'm going to work.*
káo ja glùp mah wun săo. — *He's coming back on Saturday.*

2 'Air conditioned'

The English word **air** is frequently used to mean *air conditioned*, in expressions like **dtìt air** (*air conditioned*), **hôrng air** (*air-conditioned room*), **rót air** (*air-conditioned bus*). The more formal Thai word for *air conditioned* is **bprùp ah-gàht** (literally, *adjust air*), while an air conditioner is **krêu-ung** (*machine*) **bprùp ah-gàht.**

3 . . . réu bplào? questions

. . . réu bplào? literally means . . . *or not?* although the English translation makes this question form sound rather more abrupt than it is in Thai. There is nothing brusque about **. . . réu bplào?** questions; they simply require a clear *yes* or *no* answer:

bpai réu bplào? — *Are you going (or not)?*
hôrng dtìt air réu bplào? — *Does the room have air conditioning (or not)?*

Yes/no answers are formed as follows:

(a) if the question refers to the present or future:

Yes: verb
No: **(bplào)** + **mâi** + verb

bpai réu bplào? — *Is he going (or not)?*
– bpai/(bplào) mâi bpai. — *– Yes/no.*

a-ròy réu bplào? — *Is it tasty (or not)?*
– a-ròy/(bplào) mâi a-ròy. — *– Yes/no.*

(b) if the question refers to the past, action verbs such as *to go*, *to eat*, *to study* etc. behave differently to stative verbs such as *to be expensive*, *to be bored*, *to be tasty* and so on:

Yes: Action verb + **láir-o**
Stative verb (+ **krúp/kâ**)
No: **(bplào)** + **mâi dâi** + action verb
(bplào) + **mâi** + stative verb

káo toh mah réu bplào?	*Did he phone (or not)?*
– toh mah láir-o/(bplào) mâi dâi toh mah.	*– Yes/no.*
pairng réu bplào?	*Was it expensive (or not)?*
– pairng/(bplào) mâi pairng.	*– Yes/no.*

4 hâi

You met the word **hâi** in unit 9 as a causative verb meaning *to get someone to do something*:

hâi kOOn cha-ní-dah sùng dee gwàh.	*It's better if I let Khun Chanida order.*
chún hâi káo toh mah mài.	*I got him to ring back.*

Another important use of **hâi** is to indicate the beneficiary of an action, when it can be translated as *for*; this usage often confuses the learner, because in spoken Thai the beneficiary is normally understood from the context and therefore omitted. In this unit you will find several examples of **hâi** meaning *for*. Notice that the pronoun, given in brackets in the example, is commonly omitted in speech:

ja lót hâi (kOOn) sìp bper sen.	*I'll reduce by 10% for you.*
chôo-ay gâir hâi (pŏm) nòy dâi mái?	*Please repair it for me.*
dĕe-o ja sôrm hâi (kOOn).	*In a moment I'll repair it for you.*
chôo-ay chèet yah gun yOOng hâi (pŏm) dôo-ay dâi mái?	*Please spray mosquito repellant for me.*
pŏm ja gèp wái hâi (kOOn) nai dtôo sáyf.	*I'll keep it in the safe for you.*

5 Polite requests: asking someone to do something (2)

In unit 6 you met the pattern **chôo-ay** + verb + **nòy** (+ **dâi mái?**) used when asking sombody to do something for you:

chôo-ay pôot dung dung nòy dâi mái? *Please speak up.*

chôo-ay also occurs commonly with the particle **dôo-ay** in polite requests, in the basic pattern **chôo-ay** + verb + **dôo-ay**; this can optionally be expanded by the addition of **nòy** and/or **dâi mái?**:

chôo-ay bòrk káo dôo-ay.	*Please tell him.*
chôo-ay bòrk káo nòy dôo-ay.	*Could you tell him, please?*
chôo-ay bòrk káo nòy dôo-ay dâi mái?	*Could you tell him, please?*

6 Verb + wái

The word **wái** occurs after verbs of action to indicate that the action is being done for future use or reference; it occurs commonly with the verbs **gèp** (*to keep*) and **fàhk** (*to deposit*):

kŏr fàhk kŏrng wái têe-nêe dâi mái?	*Can I leave my things here?*
pŏm ja gèp wái hâi nai dtôo sáyf.	*I'll keep it in the safe for you.*
káo jorng dtŏo-a wái láir-o.	*He has already booked his ticket.*

7 tum-mai lâ?

When Thais ask *why?* in response to a statement, they frequently add the particle **lâ** after **tum-mai**, as a way of pressing for an explanation; in spoken Thai **lâ** is often reduced to **â**:

prÔOng née chún mâi bpai.	*I'm not going tomorrow.*
– tum-mai lâ?	*Why?*

Exercises

1 Use the pattern **chôo-ay** + verb + **hâi** + **nòy** + **dâi mái?** to ask Khun Somchai to do you the following favours:

(a) park the car for you.
(b) buy some cigarettes for you.
(c) order a plate of chicken fried rice for you.
(d) book the train ticket for you.

2 In the last exercise there was no need to use the pronoun **pŏm/chún** after **hâi** because it was clear that you were asking Khun Somchai to do something for you. Now ask Khun Somchai to do the same favours for Khun Malee.

Example:
(a) park the car for Khun Malee.
chôo-ay jòrt rót hâi kOOn mah-lee nòy dâi mái?
(b) buy some cigarettes for Khun Malee.
(c) order a plate of chicken fried rice for Khun Malee.
(d) book the train ticket for Khun Malee.

3 Use the pattern **bplào, mâi dâi** + verb, to signal a firm *no* to the following questions asking whether you did something:

(a) bpai bâhn kOOn sŏm-chai réu bplào?
(b) sùng kâo pùt réu bplào?
(c) séu bee-a réu bplào?
(d) bòrk kOOn mah-lee réu bplào?

4 Use the pattern **bplào krúp (kâ), mâi** + verb, to signal a firm *no* to the following questions:

(a) pairng réu bplào?
(b) bèu-a réu bplào?
(c) pèt réu bplào?
(d) glai réu bplào?

5 How would you ask to leave the following articles in the hotel safe?

(a) keys
(b) camera
(c) mobile phone
(d) aeroplane (**krêu-ung bin**) ticket

Reading practice

1 The clerk at the hotel where Peter and Sue are staying asks whether they have visited the famous temple of Wat That Phanom.

Clerk ไปเที่ยววัดธาตุพนมหรือยังครับ
Sue ที่ไหนนะคะ
Clerk วัดธาตุพนมครับ
Sue ยังค่ะ เราอยากจะไปพรุ่งนี้ แต่ไม่ทราบว่าจะไปอย่างไร
Clerk ไปกับทัวร์ได้ครับ มีรถแอร์ไปทุกเช้ากลับเย็น
Sue หรือคะ ค่าทัวร์เท่าไรคะ
Clerk คนละสี่ร้อยเจ็ดสิบบาทครับ
Sue รถออกกี่โมงคะ
Clerk แปดโมงเช้า ออกจากหน้าโรงแรมนี่เอง แล้วกลับห้าโมงเย็น
Sue แล้วจองตั๋วที่ไหน
Clerk ผมจองให้ก็ได้ ไปหรือเปล่าครับ
Sue เดี๋ยว คิดดูก่อนค่ะ

wút tâht pa-nom	*Wat That Phanom*	วัดธาตุพนม
rót air	*air-conditioned bus*	รถแอร์
. . . nêe eng	*this very . . .*	นี่เอง
kít doo	*to think about, consider*	คิดดู

(a) How does the clerk suggest they get to Wat That Phanom?
(b) How much will it cost?
(c) What time will they leave and return?
(d) What does the clerk offer to do for them?
(e) What decision does Sue make?

2 Once at Wat That Phanom Sue asks a Thai about taking photographs. What message does the official ask the Thai to convey to Sue?

Sue ขอโทษค่ะ ที่นี่ห้ามถ่ายรูปหรือเปล่าคะ

Thai คิดว่าไม่ห้ามครับ แต่จะไปถามเจ้าหน้าที่ให้เดี๋ยว.... ขอโทษครับ ที่นี่ถ่ายรูปได้ใช่ไหม

Official ที่นี่ได้ครับ แต่ข้างในห้ามถ่าย ช่วยบอกฝรั่งว่าต้องถอดรองเท้าก่อนเข้าข้างในด้วย

hâhm	*to forbid*	ห้าม
tài rôop	*to take a photograph*	ถ่ายรูป
tăhm	*to ask*	ถาม
jâo nâh-têe	*official*	เจ้าหน้าที่
tòrt	*to take off*	ถอด
rorng táo	*shoes*	รองเท้า

3 Match the prohibition notices with the correct translation.

(a) ห้ามถ่ายรูป (i) No parking
(b) ห้ามจอดรถ (ii) Sale prohibited
(c) ห้ามสูบบุหรี่ (iii) No entry
(d) ห้ามเข้า (iv) No smoking
(e) ห้ามขาย (v) Photography forbidden

4 On the journey to Nakhorn Phanom the overnight coach stopped at a restaurant/coach park. This is the announcement the courier made:

ท่านผู้โดยสารคะ
เรามาถึงนครราชสีมาเรียบร้อยแล้วค่ะ
แล้วเราจะหยุดพักกินข้าวต้ม สักครึ่งชั่วโมง
เวลานี้ เที่ยงคืนครึ่งนะคะ
รถจะออกใหม่เวลาตีหนึ่งตรงนะคะ
ท่านผู้โดยสารช่วยกลับมาที่รถก่อนเวลานั้นนะคะ
เวลาลงรถแล้วช่วยเอาตั๋วรถไปด้วย
อย่าลืมนะคะเพราะว่าต้องเอาไปแสดงในร้านอาหาร
ไม่มีตั๋วติดตัว ก็ต้องเสียค่าอาหารเองนะคะ

tûn	*you* (polite)	ท่าน
pôo-doy-ee săhn	*passenger*	ผู้โดยสาร
tûn pôo-doy-ee săhn	*'ladies and gentlemen'*	ท่านผู้โดยสาร
mah tĕung	*to reach*	มาถึง
na-korn râht-cha-sĕe-mah	*Nakhorn Ratchasima*	นครราชสีมา
rêe-up róy	*safely*	เรียบร้อย
yÒOt	*to stop*	หยุด
kâo dtôm	*rice porridge*	ข้าวต้ม
krêung chôo-a mohng	*half an hour*	ครึ่งชั่วโมง
dtrong	*straight, exact*	ตรง
long	*to get off* (a bus)	ลง
ao + (noun +) **bpai**	*to take*	เอา . . . ไป
leum	*to forget*	ลืม
sa-dairng	*to show*	แสดง

ráhn ah-hăhn	*restaurant*	ร้านอาหาร
dtoo-a	*body*	ตัว
dtìt dtoo-a	*on you, with you*	ติดตัว
kâh	*cost*	ค่า
eng	*self*	เอง

(a) What time did the bus reach Nakhorn Ratchasima?
(b) What was the purpose of the stop?
(c) What time was the bus going to depart?
(d) What did the courier remind the passengers to take with them?
(e) What would happen if they forgot?

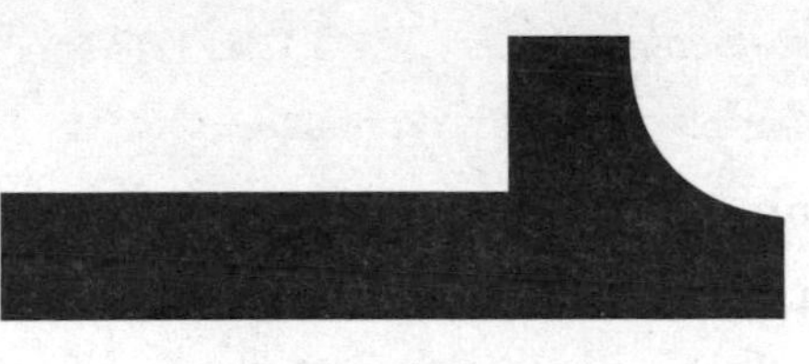

yàhk ja yòo bâhn têe mee sŏo-un

I want to live in a house where there is a garden

อยากจะอยู่บ้านที่มีสวน

In this unit you will learn

- **how to talk about things you are about to do**
- **relative clauses**
- **dates, months and seasons**
- **the verb to give**
- **negative questions**

Dialogues

Sue is telling Malee about her plans for moving house.

Sue	เรากำลังจะย้ายบ้านค่ะ	rao gum-lung ja yái bâhn kâ.
Malee	หรือ อพาร์ทเม้นท์ ที่อยู่ตอนนี้ไม่ดีหรือ	lĕr? a-páht-mén têe yòo dtorn née mâi dee lĕr?
Sue	ก็ . . . ดีซี แต่ว่าเราอยากจะอยู่บ้านที่มีสวน	gôr . . . dee see. dtàir wâh rao yàhk ja yòo bâhn têe mee sŏo-un.
Malee	แล้วไม่กลัวขโมยหรือ	láir-o mâi gloo-a ka-moy lĕr?
Sue	ก็ . . . กลัวเหมือนกัน	gôr . . . gloo-a mĕu-un gun.
Malee	จะย้ายเมื่อไรคะ	ja yái mêu-rài ká?
Sue	วันที่ ๑๕ เดือนหน้า	wun têe sìp hâh deu-un nâh.
Malee	บ้านเป็นอย่างไร	bâhn bpen yung-ngai?
Sue	สวยมากค่ะ เป็นบ้านไม้แบบไทย มีสองชั้นแล้วมีบริเวณบ้านกว้างใหญ่ ข้างบนมีห้องนอน ๓ ห้อง แล้วห้องน้ำห้องส้วม ข้างล่างมีห้องครัวห้องรับแขก แล้วก็ห้องน้ำ	sŏo-ay mâhk kâ. bpen bâhn mái bàirp tai mee sŏrng chún láir-o mee bor-ri-wayn bâhn gwâhng yài. kûng bon mee hôrng norn săhm hôrng láir-o hôrng náhm hôrng sôo-um. kûng lâhng mee hôrng kroo-a hôrng rúp kàirk láir-o gôr hôrng náhm.

gum-lung ja	*to be about to . . .*	กำลังจะ . . .
a-páht-mén	*apartment*	อพาร์ทเม้นท์
têe	*which, where, who*	ที่
see	(mood particle)	ซี
dtàir wâh	*but*	แต่ว่า
sŏo-un	*garden*	สวน
ka-moy	*burglar*	ขโมย

wun têe sìp hâh	*the 15th*	วันที่ ๑๕
deu-un	*month*	เดือน
nâh	*next*	หน้า
mái	*wood*	ไม้
bàirp	*style*	แบบ
bàirp tai	*Thai style*	แบบไทย
chún	*storey, floor*	ชั้น
bor-ri-wayn bâhn	*house compound*	บริเวณบ้าน
gwâhng	*wide*	กว้าง
hôrng norn	*bedroom*	ห้องนอน
hôrng sôo-um	*toilet*	ห้องส้วม
hôrng kroo-a	*kitchen*	ห้องครัว
hôrng rúp kàirk	*living room*	ห้องรับแขก

Malee quizzes Sue a little more about the new house.

Malee	ค่าเช่าแพงไหม	kâh châo pairng mái?
Sue	เดือนละสองหมื่น	de-un la sŏrng mèun
	แต่ต้องให้ค่ามัดจำ	dtàir dtôrng hâi kâh mút-jum
	เขาหกหมื่นด้วย	káo hòk mèun dôo-ay.
Malee	หน้าฝนน้ำท่วมไหม	nâh fŏn náhm tôo-um mái?
Sue	อุ๊ย . . . ลืมถาม	óo-ee . . . leum tăhm.

kâh châo	*rent*	ค่าเช่า
mèun	*10,000*	หมื่น
hâi	*to give*	ให้
kâh mút-jum	*deposit*	ค่ามัดจำ
nâh fŏn	*rainy season*	หน้าฝน
náhm tôo-um	*to flood*	น้ำท่วม
óo-ee . . .	(exclamation of surprise)	อุ๊ย

1 What is wrong with the apartment where Sue lives?
2 When does she plan to move?
3 What is the new house like?
4 How many bedrooms does it have?
5 What rooms does it have downstairs?
6 What is the monthly rent?
7 How much deposit did she have to pay?
8 Does the area flood during the rainy season?

Language notes

1 gum-lung ja + verb

The pattern **gum-lung ja** + verb is used to describe actions that are, or were, about to happen:

rao gum-lung ja yái bâhn.	*We are/were about to move home.*
chún gum-lung ja gin kâo.	*I am/was about to eat.*
káo gum-lung ja séu.	*He is/was about to buy it.*

Be careful not to confuse this pattern with **gum-lung** + verb + **yòo** (unit 7) used to describe continuous actions.

2 Negative questions

Negative questions (*it's not . . ., then?*) can be formed by the pattern **mâi** + verb + **lĕr?**:

a-páht-mén mâi dee lĕr?	*The apartment isn't any good, then?*
káo mâi mah lĕr?	*He's not coming, then?*
kOOn mâi chôrp lĕr?	*You don't like it, then?*

Yes/no answers to negative questions are confusing to English speakers, in that Thais use **krúp/kâ** (*yes*) where English speakers say *no*:

káo mâi mah lĕr?	*He's not coming, then?*
– krúp/kâ (káo mâi mah).	*– No (he's not).*
kOOn mâi chôrp lĕr?	*You don't like it then?*
– krúp/kâ (mâi chôrp).	*– No (I don't).*

A *yes* answer often involves the verb followed by the particle **see** (unit 7) which indicates a contradiction of the negative question:

a-páht-mén mâi dee lĕr?	*The apartment isn't any good, then?*
– gôr . . . dee see.	*Well, yes, it is.*
kOOn mâi chôrp lĕr?	*You don't like it then?*
– chôrp see.	*– Yes (I do).*

3 Relative pronouns

A single relative pronoun **têe** can mean *where, which, who, when*:

a-páht-mén têe yòo dtorn née . . .	*The apartment where you live now . . .*
rao yàhk yòo bâhn têe mee sŏo-un.	*We want to live in a house where there is a garden.*
rót têe káo séu pairng mâhk.	*The car which he bought was very expensive.*
hôrng têe mâi mee air yung wâhng.	*The room which is not air conditioned is still free.*
pêu-un têe chêu jáirk bpen kon tai.	*My friend who is called Jack is Thai.*
kon têe bòrk mah-lee mâi châi pŏm.	*The person who told Malee wasn't me.*
wun têe chún bpai rórn mâhk.	*The day when I went was very hot.*
deu-un têe rao yòo náhm tôo-um.	*The month when we were there, there were floods.*

4 Months

mók-ga-rah-kom	*January*	มกราคม
gOOm-pah-pun	*February*	กุมภาพันธ์
mee-nah-kom	*March*	มีนาคม
may-săh-yon	*April*	เมษายน
préut-sa-pah-kom	*May*	พฤษภาคม
mí-tOO-nah-yon	*June*	มิถุนายน
ga-rúk-ga-dah-kom	*July*	กรกฎาคม
sĭng-hăh-kom	*August*	สิงหาคม
gun-yah-yon	*September*	กันยายน
dtOO-lah-kom	*October*	ตุลาคม
préut-sa-jìk-gah-yon	*November*	พฤศจิกายน
tun-wah-kom	*December*	ธันวาคม

The final syllable is **-kom** for months with 31 days, **-yon** for 30 days and **-pun** for the shortest month, February. In normal speech, the word **deu-un** (*month*) often prefaces the name of the month while the final syllable is omitted. Note that Thai does not use a preposition corresponding to English *in*:

bpai deu-un sĭng-hăh.	*I'm going in August.*
glùp deu-un tun-wah.	*He's coming back in December.*

5 Dates and ordinal numbers and years

Ordinal numbers in Thai are formed by adding **têe** in front of the number:

têe nèung	*first*
têe sŏrng	*second*
têe săhm	*third*

Dates are expressed using the pattern **wun** + ordinal number + month:

wun têe sìp tun-wah-kom	*10th December*
wun têe yêe-sìp may-săh-yon	*20th April*

The year (**bpee**) is normally counted according to the Buddhist era (BE) (**pÓOt-ta-sùk-ka-râht** or **por sŏr** (พศ) for short) which began with the birth of the Buddha, 543 years before the birth of Christ. To convert Thai years to AD (**kor sŏr** (คศ) for short), you simply subract 543 years. Thus, 2500 BE is 1957 AD, while 2000 AD is 2543 BE.

6 'To give'

You have already met the word **hâi** in unit 9, where it had the meaning of *causing someone to do something* and in unit 13 where it meant *for*; a third meaning of **hâi** is *to give*. Unlike English, the order of objects with **hâi** is subject + **hâi** + direct object + indirect object:

chún hâi kâh mút-jum káo hòk mèun.	*I gave them a deposit of 60,000.* (I-give-deposit-they-60,000)
fairn hâi ngern pŏm.	*My wife gave me the money.* (wife-give-money-I)
rao hâi rót káo.	*We gave him a car.* (we-give-car-he)

7 Seasons

There are three seasons in Thailand, the cool season (November to February), the hot season (March to June) and the rainy season (July to October). The formal Thai word for *season* is **reu-doo**, but **nâh** is more commonly used in speech:

nâh năo	*cool season*
nâh rórn	*hot season*
nâh fŏn	*rainy season*

Exercises

1 How would you say you are about to do the following:

(a) order food
(b) go home
(c) go out
(d) buy a new car
(e) book a train ticket to Chiangmai

2 How would you say the following dates:

(a) 9th January
(b) 19th June
(c) 31st August
(d) 5th November
(e) 3rd April

3 Translate the following sentences into English, using the relative pronoun **têe**:

(a) The house where I am staying is not very big.
(b) The food which we eat is not very spicy.
(c) The Thais I know speak English very well.
(d) The school where I study is far away.
(e) The teacher who teaches Thai comes from Chiangmai.
(f) The blouse which I like is too expensive.
(g) Where is the book which I gave you?
(h) The year (when) I studied Thai there were not many pupils.
(i) The day (when) we went to Nakhorn Phanom was not very hot.

Reading practice

1 Noi, a Thai hotel worker, is talking about her work.

น้อยทำงานอยู่ที่นี่เกือบ ๒๐ ปีแล้วค่ะ ทำงานอยู่ที่นี่สบาย ทำความสะอาดห้อง และซักรีดเสื้อผ้า มาทำงานเวลา ๒ โมงเช้าแล้วกลับบ้านบ่าย ๔ โมง แขกที่นี่ส่วนมากเป็นชาวต่างประเทศ ฝรั่งก็มี จีนก็มี ญี่ปุ่นก็มี บางคนก็ใจดีมาก ให้ทิปเป็นร้อยกว่าบาท แต่ตอนนี้เป็นหน้าฝน แขกไม่ค่อยมี งานก็ไม่ค่อยมาก น้อยก็นั่งคุยกับเพื่อนทั้งวัน

เกือบ	*almost*
สบาย	*to be happy, well, comfortable*
ความสะอาด	*cleaning*
ซัก	*to wash*
รีด	*to iron*
เสื้อผ้า	*clothes*
แขก	*guest*
ส่วนมาก	*mostly, for the most part*
ชาวต่างประเทศ	*foreigners*
ใจดี	*to be kind*
ทิป	*tip*
คุย	*to chat*
ทั้งวัน	*all day*

2 Malee and Sue are discussing a visit Sue had made to the seaside.

Malee คุณซู เคยไปเที่ยวชายทะเลที่เมืองไทยหรือยัง

Sue เคยค่ะ เคยไปพัทยาครั้งหนึ่ง
เมื่อสองสามเดือนก่อน

Malee สนุกไหม

Sue ก็ . . . ไม่ค่อยสนุกเท่าไร มีคนเยอะแยะ
ไม่ชอบ ชอบเงียบ ๆ มากกว่า

Malee ถ้าไปชายทะเล ฉันว่าไปหัวหินดีกว่า
เงียบกว่าพัทยาเยอะ นักท่องเที่ยวก็น้อยกว่า
ไม่อย่างนั้น ก็ไปเที่ยวเกาะเสม็ดซิ
เช่าบังกาโลก็สนุกดี

Sue บังกาโลเป็นอย่างไรคะ

Malee ส่วนมากมีแต่ห้องนอนกับห้องน้ำเท่านั้น
แอร์ไม่มี ห้องครัวก็ไม่มี
แต่อยู่ได้สบาย เพราะแถวนั้นมี
ร้านอาหารทะเลเยอะ

chai ta-lay	*seaside*	ชายทะเล
pút-ta-yah	*Pattaya*	พัทยา
yér-yáir	*lots*	เยอะแยะ
ta-lay	*sea*	ทะเล
hŏo-a hĭn	*Hua Hin*	หัวหิน
ngêe-up	*quiet, calm*	เงียบ
gòr sa-mèt	*Koh (island) Samet*	เกาะเสม็ด
bung-ga-loh	*bungalow*	บังกาโล

3 John is having a few problems with his hotel room.

John ขอเปลี่ยนห้องได้ไหมครับ

Clerk ทำไมล่ะครับ

John เครื่องปรับอากาศมันเสีย

Clerk เดี๋ยวจะขึ้นไปดู

John ไม่ต้องครับ
ห้องน้ำใช้ไม่ได้ด้วย ไม่มีน้ำ
อยากเปลี่ยนห้องดีกว่า

Clerk เปลี่ยนไม่ได้ครับ

John ทำไมล่ะครับ

Clerk ห้องอื่นไม่มีครับ

bplèe-un	*to change*	เปลี่ยน
krêu-ung bprùp ah-gàht	*air conditioner*	เครื่องปรับอากาศ
kêun	*to go up*	ขึ้น
èun	*other*	อื่น

4 Lek, a Thai woman, talks about her language problems when she first came to live in England.

เล็กแต่งงานที่กรุงเทพฯ สามีเป็นคนอังกฤษ
ทำงานอยู่ที่บริษัทใหญ่แห่งหนึ่งแถวถนนสุขุมวิท
เรากลับมาอยู่ที่อังกฤษเมื่อสามปีก่อน
ความจริงเล็กไม่อยากมาอยู่อังกฤษเลย
เพราะว่าพูดภาษาอังกฤษไม่ค่อยเป็น

เคยเรียนที่โรงเรียน แต่เรียนไม่เก่ง
คนอังกฤษพูด เล็กฟังไม่รู้เรื่องเลย
สามีก็ให้เล็กไปเรียนภาษาที่โรงเรียนแถว ๆ บ้าน
ที่โรงเรียนมีนักเรียนทุกชาติ ญี่ปุ่นก็มี จีนก็มี
เยอรมันก็มี อาฟริกาก็มี แล้วก็มีอาหรับด้วย
ฉันต้องไปเรียนอาทิตย์ละ ๔ วัน คือวันจันทร์
วันอังคาร วันพุธแล้วก็วันศุกร์ เรียนวันละ ๒-๓
ชั่วโมงตั้งแต่สามโมงเช้าจนถึงเที่ยง เรียนประมาณ ๖
เดือนแล้ว เล็กก็รู้สึกว่า ภาษาอังกฤษดีขึ้นมากเลย

สามี	*husband*
แห่ง	(classifier for companies)
นักเรียน	*pupil*
เยอรมัน	*German*
อาฟริกา	*Africa(n)*
อาหรับ	*Arab*
ดีขึ้น	*to improve*

key to the exercises

Unit 1

Exercise 1

(a) pŏm (di-chún) chêu . . .
(b) nahm sa-gOOn . . .
(c) bpen kon . . .
(d) bpen . . . / tum ngahn gùp . . .

Exercise 2

(a) châi krúp (kâ)
(b) nahm sa-gOOn Green krúp (kâ)
(c) mâi châi krúp (kâ)
(d) bpen kon ung-grìt krúp (kâ)
(e) châi krúp (kâ)
(f) bpen núk tÓO-rá-gìt krúp (kâ)

Exercise 3

(a)–(ii) (b)–(iv) (c)–(i) (d)–(iii)

Exercise 4

2 káo chêu John. nahm sa-gOOn Stevens. bpen kon a-may-ri-gun. mah jàhk new yórk. bpen núk sèuk-săh
3 káo chêu Makoto. nahm sa-gOOn Iwasaki. bpen kon yêe-bpÒOn. mah jàhk dtoh-gee-o. bpen núk tÓO-rá-gìt
4 káo chêu Paula. nahm sa-gOOn Besson. bpen kon fa-rùng-sàyt. mah jàhk bpah-rít. bpen ah-jahn

Exercise 5

(a) bpen – mâi châi
(b) mâi châi – bpen
(c) mâi châi – bpen
(d) bpen – mâi châi

Exercise 6

(a) kŏr-tôht krúp (kâ) kOOn chêu a-rai?
(b) káo chêu sŏm-chai châi mái?
(c) káo nahm sa-gOOn a-rai?
(d) káo bpen kon châht a-rai?
(e) káo bpen kon tai châi mái?
(f) káo bpen ah-jahn châi mái?
(g) káo mâi châi kon tai; bpen kon yêe-bpÒOn
(h) káo mâi châi kon ung-grìt; bpen kon fa-rùng-sàyt

Reading practice

2 Words

mah	nah	nahm	nahn	nahng	ngahn
num	rum	lum	wun	yung	mun
lung	rung	ror	rorng	morng	norn
rai	nai	yai	lao	yao	rao

3 Sentences

yahm	yahm lao	yahm lao mah
nai	nai ror	nai ror nahn
nahng	nahng lah	nahng lah ngahn
yai	yai rum	yai rum nahn

4 Numbers

1 236-4890 2 580-7359 3 225-7381
4 693-2145 5 371-9548

Unit 2

Exercise 1

(b) pairng bpai nòy krúp (kâ) hâh-sìp bàht dâi mái?
(c) pairng bpai nòy krúp (kâ) hòk-sìp bàht dâi mái?
(d) pairng bpai nòy krúp (kâ) yêe-sìp bàht dâi mái?
(e) pairng bpai nòy krúp (kâ) săhm-sìp bàht dâi mái?

Exercise 2

(a) nêe tâo-rài krúp (kâ)?
(b) pairng bpai nòy
(c) lót nòy dâi mái krúp (ká)?
(d) hâh-sìp bàht dâi mái krúp (ká)?
(e) sěe dairng mâi sŏo-ay
(f) sěe kěe-o mee mái?

Exercise 3

(a) sùp-bpa-rót bai la tâo-rài?
(b) sôm loh la tâo-rài?
(c) glôo-ay wěe la tâo-rài?
(d) ma-la-gor bai la tâo-rài?
(e) ma-môo-ung bai la tâo-rài?
(f) nóy-nàh loh la tâo-rài?
(g) dtairng moh bai la tâo-rài?

Exercise 4

(a) a-ròy mái?/ a-ròy châi mái?
(b) pairng mái?/ pairng châi mái?
(c) sŏo-ay mái?/ sŏo-ay châi mái?
(d) sěe dairng mee mái?/ sěe dairng mee châi mái?

Exercise 5

(a) nêe (rêe-uk wâh) a-rai?
(b) a-rai ná?
(c) ma-môo-ung châi mái krúp?
(d) bai la tâo-rài?
(e) lót nòy dâi mái?

Reading practice

2 Words

gin	gun	jai	doo	dee
dtah	dtee	bin	bai	bpai
bpee	mohng	bpoo	rohng	yOOng
un	mee	gun	lorng	loh

3 Sentences

bin mah	bin bpai bin mah	yOOng bin bpai bin mah
mah doo	yin dee mah doo	lOOng yin dee mah doo
bpoo dum	mee bpoo dum	nai nah mee bpoo dum
ngoo dtai	dtee ngoo dtai	yahm lao dtee ngoo dtai
nahng ngahm dung	doo nahng ngahm dung	ror doo nahng ngahm dung

4 Dates

(i)–(c) (ii)–(d) (iii)–(a) (iv)–(e) (v)–(b)

Unit 3

Exercise 1

(a) bpai sa-yăhm sa-kwair mái?
(b) bpai rohng-rairm ree-noh mái?
(c) bpai ta-nŏn sOO-kŎOm-wít soy săhm-sìp gâo mái?
(d) bpai sa-năhm bin dorn meu-ung mái?

Exercise 2

(a) tĕung sèe-yâirk láir-o lée-o kwăh
(b) lée-o sái láir-o kâo soy
(c) lée-o kwăh láir-o jòrt têe-nôhn
(d) bpai sÒOt soy láir-o jòrt glâi glâi rót sĕe dairng

Exercise 3

(a)–(v)–(B) (b)–(iii)–(E) (c)–(iv)–(A) (d)–(i)–(C) (e)–(ii)–(D)

Exercise 4

(a) bpai ta-nŏn sOO-kŎOm-wít soy hâh-sìp săhm mái?
(b) kâo krúp. bpai sÒOt soy
(c) châi krúp. bpai tâo-rài?
(d) pairng bpai nòy krúp
(e) jèt-sìp bàht dâi mái?

Exercise 5

(a) jòrt glâi glâi sèe-yâirk krúp (kâ)
(b) bpai sÒOt soy krúp (kâ)
(c) tĕung sèe-yâirk láir-o lée-o sái krúp (kâ)
(d) jòrt têe-nôhn glâi glâi rót sĕe dairng dairng krúp (kâ)

Reading practice

1 Syllables (live syllables marked in bold)

bpai	jòrt	mâhk	**gun**
dee	**ree-noh**	dtìt	**rohng**

2 Tones

bèep	nahng	gùt	jÒOt	nút
bpee	dàhp	jahn	jàhk	dtai
lâhp	rao	mêet	rôrp	bpàhk

3 Words

yâhk	mee	nút	gùp	ngahn
yOOng	gùt	mâhk	jàhk	rêep
ai	norn	yorm	lôok	jòrt

Unit 4

Exercise 1

(a) kŏr may-noo nòy
(b) kŏr kâo pùt gài săhm jahn
(c) kŏr bee-a sĭng sŏrng kòo-ut
(d) kŏr núm kăirng bplào gâir-o nèung
(e) chék bin krúp (kâ)

Exercise 2

(a) kŏr doo nòy (b) kŏr chim nòy (c) kŏr jòrt rót têe-nôhn nòy

Exercise 3

(a) (iii) (b) (i) (c) (ii) (d) (iv)

Exercise 4

(a) sa-yăhm sa-kwair yòo têe-năi?
(b) rohng rairm ree-noh yòo têe-năi?
(c) hôrng náhm yòo têe-năi?
(d) ta-nŏn sOO-kŎOm-wít soy săhm-sìp săhm yòo têe-năi?
(e) kOOn mah-lee yòo têe-năi?

Exercise 5

(a) Peter/Sue/Tom yòo kûng nai
(b) Nikki/Eddie/Nuan yòo kûng nôrk
(c) Sue/Tom yòo kûng bon
(d) Peter yòo kûng lâhng
(e) Nikki/Eddie yòo kûng nâh
(f) Nuan yòo kûng lŭng/kûng kâhng

Reading practice

1 Words

chai	chahm	soy	bàht	kum
chôrp	tahng	pah	púk	tum
tÓOk	keun	deung	dtèuk	keu
ker-ee	ler-ee	pairng	dairng	bpàirt
yen	lék	bpen	jèt	gèp
bpèt	gôr	may-noo	kon	long

2 Sentences

bpàirt	bpàirt bàht	bpàirt bàht pairng	bpàirt bàht pairng bpai
jeen	kon jeen	bpen kon jeen	lOOng bpen kon jeen
bpai	mâhk bpai	jèt jahn mâhk bpai	gin jèt jahn mâhk bpai

3 Public signs

(i) (a) (ii) (c)

Unit 5

Exercise 1

(a) tăir-o née mee bprai-sa-nee mái?
(b) tăir-o née mee ta-nah-kahn mái?
(c) tăir-o née mee hôrng náhm mái?
(d) tăir-o née mee toh-ra-sùp mái?

Exercise 2

(a) sòng bpóht-gáht bpai a-may-ri-gah tâo-rài?
(b) sòng bpai tahng ah-gàht tâo-rài?
(c) kŏr sa-dtairm sìp-sŏrng bàht hâh doo-ung
(d) kŏr jòt-măi ah-gàht pàirn nèung
(e) túng mòt tâo-rài?

Exercise 3

(a) doo-ung	(b) pàirn	(c) tôo-ay
(d) jahn	(e) hôrng	(f) kon

Exercise 4

(a) yàhk ja jòrt rót têe-nôhn
(b) yàhk ja bpai sa-yăhm sa-kwair
(c) dtôrng-gahn jòt-măi ah-gàht pàirn nèung
(d) ao kâo pùt

Reading practice

1 Words

kăi	kŏr	kùp	chèet	tăhm
tòok	pìt	fàhk	sĕe	sÒOt
sŏrn	săo	sùk	sìp	hùk
hăh	lŭng	wùt	lăi	nŏo

2 Words

kŏr-tôht	tăir-o	mee	mái	lĕr/rĕu
soy	ròrk	bpai	tahng	sùk
sŏrng	săhm	nah-tee	mâhk	bpen rai
sìp-sŏrng	bàht	tahng	ah-gàht	jòt-măi
a-may-ri-gah	long	jèt-sìp	mòt	

3 Numbers

(i) (f) (ii) (d) (iii) (b) (iv) (e) (v) (a) (vi) (c)

4 Sentences

tai	kon tai	bpen kon tai	lOOng bpen kon tai
dtàhk	jung-wùt dtàhk	jàhk jung-wùt dtàhk	mah jàhk jung-wùt dtàhk
mâhk	lăhn mâhk	mee lăhn mâhk	yai mee lăhn mâhk
kon	sìp kon	lôok sìp kon	mee lôok sìp kon
kon	săhm kon	săo săhm kon	lôok săo săhm kon

Unit 6

Exercise 1

(a) kŏr pôot gùp kOOn mah-lee nòy dâi mái?
(b) chôo-ay pôot dung dung nòy dâi mái?
(c) ror sùk krôo ná krúp (ká)
(d) krai pôot krúp (ká)
(e) kOOn mah-lee ja glùp mah mêu-rài?

Exercise 2

(a) pŏm/chún kít wâh ja òrk bpai kûng nôrk
(b) pŏm/chún kít wâh ja bpai bprai-sa-nee dtorn cháo
(c) pŏm/chún kít wâh ja bpai bâhn kOOn sŏm-chai dtorn bài
(d) pŏm/chún kít wâh ja glùp mah dtorn yen

Exercise 3

(a) kOOn sŏm-chai bòrk wâh (káo) ja bpai ta-nah-kahn dtorn cháo
(b) kOOn sŏm-chai bòrk wâh (káo) ja bpai bâhn pêu-un dtorn bài
(c) kOOn sŏm-chai bòrk wâh (káo) ja jòrt rót têe soy săhm-sìp săhm
(d) kOOn sŏm-chai bòrk wâh (káo) ja glùp bâhn dtorn yen

Exercise 4

(a) kOOn sŏm-chai ja glùp mêu-rài?
(b) kOOn sŏm-chai ja yòo mêu-rài?
(c) kOOn sŏm-chai ja róo mêu-rài?
(d) kOOn sŏm-chai ja toh mah mêu-rài?
(e) kOOn sŏm-chai ja bòrk pŏm/chún mêu-rài?
(f) kOOn sŏm-chai ja toh mah bòrk pŏm/chún mêu-rài?

Reading practice

Yupha is Thai. She comes from Loei. Damrong is Yupha's husband. Damrong comes from Tak. Yupha and Damrong have five children. They have two sons and three daughters

Unit 7

Exercise 1

(a) bpen nít-nòy (b) (mâi) nahn
(c) bpen nít-nòy (d) bpen nít-nòy
(e) (mâi) yâhk krúp. prór wâh mee sĕe-ung sŏong sĕe-ung dtùm.

Exercise 2

(a) ker-ee bpai (têe-o) ung-grìt mái?
(b) ker-ee ree-un pah-săh ung-grìt mái?
(c) ker-ee gin fish and chips mái?
(d) ker-ee bpai (têe-o) poo-gèt mái?
(e) ker-ee tum ngahn têe grOOng-tâyp mái?

Exercise 3

(a) mâi kôy pairng tâo-rài
(b) mâi kôy glai tâo-rài
(c) mâi kôy a-ròy tâo-rài
(d) mâi kôy dee tâo-rài
(e) mâi kôy chút tâo-rài
(f) mâi kôy yâhk tâo-rài

Exercise 4

(a) pairng gwàh
(b) glai gwàh
(c) a-ròy gwàh
(d) dee gwàh
(e) chút gwàh
(f) yâhk gwàh

Exercise 5

(a) yâhk gwàh
(b) ngâi gwàh
(c) ngâi gwàh
(d) yâhk gwàh

Reading practice

1 Words

mâi	nêe	pôr	mâir	nèung	kôo
yòo	gài	dtàir	sùng	nòy	dtòr
chêu	châi	pêe	têe	àhn	wâh

2 Phrases

châi mái?	mâi châi	nêe tâo-rài?	yêe-sìp bàht
pairng bpai nòy	jòrt têe-nêe	mâi pairng ròrk	yòo têe-nôhn
mâi bpen rai	yòo têe-nǎi?	àhn mâi yâhk	kít wâh mâi mah

3 Dialogue

Peter How much is it to Soi 33?
Tuk-tuk Soi 33? That'll be 80 baht.
Peter 80 baht? That's a bit too expensive.
Tuk-tuk No it isn't. The traffic is very congested.

Unit 8

Exercise 1

(a) jòrt rót (láir-o) réu yung?
(b) gin kâo (láir-o) réu yung?
(c) pôot gùp kOOn sǒm-chai (láir-o) réu yung?
(d) bòrk kOOn mah-lee (láir-o) réu yung?
(e) òrk bpai kûng nôrk (láir-o) réu yung?

Exercise 2

(a) mee pêe nórng gèe kon?
(b) mee pêe sǎo gèe kon?
(c) mee nórng chai gèe kon?
(d) mee lôok gèe kon?
(e) mee lôok chai gèe kon?
(f) mee lôok sǎo gèe kon?

Exercise 3

(a) sa-bai dee krúp (kâ)
(b) bpen nít-nòy krúp (kâ)
(c) (mâi) nahn krúp (kâ)
(d) mâi gèng (ròrk) krúp (kâ)
(e) kòrp-kOOn krúp (kâ)
(f) (mâi) mee krúp (kâ)
(g) dtàirng láir-o krúp (kâ)/ yung krúp (kâ)

Exercise 4

(a) gin gah-fair gèe tôo-ay?
(b) gin kâo pùt gÔOng gèe jahn?
(c) gin bee-a gèe kòo-ut?
(d) ao sa-dtairm gèe doo-ung?
(e) gin ma-môo-ung gèe bai?

Exercise 5

(a) kOOn chêu a-rai ká?
(b) ah-yÓO tâo-rài ká?
(c) yòo meu-ung tai nahn mái ká?
(d) kǒr-tôht kâ dtàirng ngahn láir-o réu yung?
(e) mee lôok láir-o réu yung ká?
(f) (lôok) ah-yÓO tâo-rài ká?

Reading practice

1 Words

dtôrng tíng bâhn hâi róo
sôm née tâh gâo náhm
láir-o gÔOng rórn hôrng séu
kâo nóhn gâir-o nâh dâi

2 Phrases

dâi mái? mâi dâi sǎhm-sìp hâh
róo-jùk mái? gôr láir-o gun kâo pùt gÔOng
gâir-o nèung tǎir-o née sǒrng róy bàht

3 Dialogue

Somchai Could I have two plates of shrimp fried rice and a plate of duck rice?
Waiter There's no duck rice. We have chicken and rice and red pork and rice.
Somchai We'll have red pork rice then and three glasses of orange juice.
Waiter There's no orange juice. We only have Pepsi.

Unit 9

Exercise 1

(a) (mâi) bpen (b) (mâi) pèt (c) (mâi) bpen
(d) (mâi) a-ròy (e) (mâi) sòop

Exercise 2

(a) mêu-rài gôr dâi (b) a-rai gôr dâi
(c) krai gôr dâi (d) têe-năi gôr dâi

Exercise 3

(a) rao dern bpai mâi dâi. glai gern bpai
(b) ka-nŏm tai mâi a-ròy. wăhn gern bpai
(c) pŏm (chún) mâi ao. pairng gern bpai
(d) káo mâi chôrp ah-hăhn tai. pèt gern bpai
(e) pŏm (chún) pôot pah-săh tai mâi dâi. yâhk gern bpai

Exercise 4

(a) tâh glai bpai gôr mâi dtôrng dern
(b) tâh mâi a-ròy gôr mâi dtôrng gin
(c) tâh mâi yàhk bpai gôr mâi dtôrng
(d) tâh mâi pèt mâhk gôr kít wâh gin dâi

Exercise 5

(a) hâi kOOn sŏm-chai jòrt rót dee gwàh
(b) hâi kOOn sŏm-chai sùng ah-hăhn dee gwàh
(c) hâi kOOn sŏm-chai pôot gùp kOOn mah-lee dee gwàh
(d) hâi kOOn sŏm-chai toh-ra-sùp dee gwàh

Reading practice

1 Words

pâhk pah-săh yài yĭng kOOn kâh
rao káo* ao kâo tâo-rài? tâo-nún
ree-un kĕe-un lée-o mêu-a mĕu-un pêu-un
dtoo-a hŏo-a woo-a sŏo-ay chôo-ay dôo-ay
gern gèrt chern dern jer ter
ja ká kâ ná a-rai? ba-mèe

(* pronounced with a high tone)

2 Phrases

kOOn chêu a-rai ká?
loh la tâo-rài?
láir-o lée-o sái
ao ba-mèe náhm chahm nèung
dern bpai sŏrng nah-tee tâo-nún
bpen pêu-un kOOn mah-lee
rêe-uk wâh nóy-nàh
láir-o kOOn cha-ní-dah lâ krúp
lôok chai ah-yÓO săhm kòo-up
sĕe dairng sŏo-ay mâhk ná ká
gâo-sìp-èt bàht kâ
ao náhm a-rai ká?
ao bpép-sêe kòo-ut yài
yàhk ja long ta-bee-un dôo-ay
ja bpai mêu-rài ká?
yòo meu-ung tai nahn mái?
pôot pah-săh tai bpen mái?

Unit 10

Exercise 1

(a) mâi kâo jai
(b) pôot èek tee dâi mái?
(c) bplair wâh a-rai?
(d) pôot cháh cháh nòy dâi mái?
(e) kĕe-un yung-ngai?

Exercise 2

(a) bplair wâh meu-ung
(b) bplair wâh gin
(c) bplair wâh róo
(d) bplair wâh mâi kâo jai

Exercise 3

(a) chee-ung mài bpai yung-ngai?
(b) ma-môo-ung gin yung-ngai?
(c) toh-ra-sùp chái yung-ngai?
(d) 'sa-bai' kĕe-un yung-ngai?

Exercise 4

(a) mâi chôrp ler-ee
(b) mâi dee ler-ee
(c) mâi ao ler-ce
(d) mâi kâo jai ler-ee
(e) (fung) mâi róo rêu-ung ler-ee

Exercise 5

(a) a-rai ná?
(b) pôot cháh cháh nòy dâi mái?
(c) 'nŭng' bplair wâh a-rai?
(d) kâo jai (láir-o)

Reading practice

1 Words

gwàh	kwăh	grOOng	bpra-dtoo	bplah
bplào	dtrong	glai	glâi	glùp
krai	klái	krúp	kwahm	bpra-dtâyt
ta-nŏn	dta-lòk	ka-yŭn	sa-yăhm	sa-pâhp
ka-nàht	sa-nÒOk	sa-tăhn	sa-bai	bor-ri-sùt
cha-lŏrng	cha-làht	fa-rùng	ka-yà	bor-ri-gahn

2 Conversation

Interviewer Have you lived in Thailand a long time?
Businessman No. Only about 6 months.
Interviewer You speak Thai very well. Like a native speaker.
Businessman Not at all! When Thais speak, sometimes I don't understand at all. And if I speak Thai, Thais don't understand (me) either.
Interviewer Where did you learn Thai?
Businessman I studied at a school in the Sukhumwit Road area and I used a textbook and tapes at home.
Interviewer Is Thai difficult?
Businessman Yes. But if I hadn't had tapes to listen to, it would have been more difficult.
Interviewer And can you read and write Thai?
Businessman I can read a little, if they are easy words. But I can't really write.

Unit 11

Exercise 1

(a) chôrp mâhk jing jing/jung ler-ee
(b) dee mâhk jing jing/jung ler-ee
(c) nâh bèu-a mâhk jing jing/jung ler-ee
(d) pèt mâhk jing jing/jung ler-ee
(e) pairng mâhk jing jing/jung ler-ee

Exercise 2

(a)–(ii), (iii), (iv), (vi), (viii)
(b)–(i), (v), (vii), (ix), (x)

Reading practice

1 Words

yé	lé té	dtè	gè gà
láir	gàir	páir	dtàir
dtó	lér tér	yér	yér yáir
prór	gòr	mòr	hŏo-a rór

2 Passage

I'm from the Northeast. I live in a small village in Nongkhai. Before, I used to do rice farming, but I didn't like it because it's hard work. So I thought it would be better to come and work here. Now I'm working in a nooodle shop in the Sukhumwit area. I wash up all day long. Sometimes I think it's boring. But I don't want to go back home because I don't want to do rice farming and the salary here is alright. It's better than up country.

3 Passage

Khun Chanida is from the South. She was born in Phuket. Her father is a policeman and her mother a housewife. They have three children. Chanida's parents and her brothers and sisters moved here when Chanida was five years old. Now Chanida's younger brother is studying at Mahidol University. He wants to be a doctor. Chanida's father wants her younger brother to go and continue his studies in America.

4 Passage

Peter You're from the North, aren't you?

Somchai Yes, I was born in Chiangmai. My parents moved here 30 years ago when I was still small. My father wanted me to study here because he thought that the schools here were better.

Peter Do you like living here?

Somchai Not very much. The traffic is really congested here. In Chiangmai the air is cleaner and the traffic isn't as congested as here.

Unit 12

Exercise 1

(a)–(iii) (b)–(iv) (c)–(ii) (d)–(i)

Exercise 2

(a) gâo mohng krêung
(b) bài sŏrng mohng yêe-sìp
(c) hâh mohng yen
(d) èek sìp-hâh nah-tee sèe tÔOm

Exercise 3

(a) bpai chee-ung mài jorng dtŏo-a têe-năi?
(b) rót (may) bpai chee-ung mài òrk gèe mohng?
(c) chee-ung mài yòo hàhng jàhk grOOng-tâyp gèe gi-loh?
(d) chái way-lah dern tahng gèe chôo-a mohng?
(e) kêun rót (may) têe-năi?

Reading practice

1

bpóht-gáht
bpee-dter
ber toh-ra-sùp
sa-dtairm
gèp sa-dtahng
soy ga-săym-săn
bee-a sĭng
bprai-sa-nee

2

(i)–(g) (ii)–(f) (iii)–(e) (iv)–(a) (v)–(b) (vi)–(c) (vii)–(d)

3

Nongkhai is 614 kilometres from Bangkok. VIP Co. Ltd has first-class air-conditioned coaches leaving Bangkok twice a day at 08.00 hrs and 21.30 hrs. The journey takes approximately 11 hours. The fare is 380 baht per person.

Unit 13

Exercise 1

(a) chôo-ay jòrt rót hâi nòy dâi mái?
(b) chôo-ay séu bOO-rèe hâi nòy dâi mái?
(c) chôo-ay sùng kâo pùt gài jahn nèung hâi nòy dâi mái?
(d) chôo-ay jorng dtŏo-a rót fai hâi nòy dâi mái?

Exercise 2

(b) chôo-ay séu bOO-rèe hâi kOOn mah-lee nòy dâi mái?
(c) chôo-ay sùng kâo pùt gài jahn nèung hâi kOOn mah-lee nòy dâi mái?
(d) chôo-ay jorng dtŏo-a rót fai hâi kOOn mah-lee nòy dâi mái?

Exercise 3

(a) bplào, mâi dâi bpai
(b) bplào, mâi dâi sùng
(c) bplào, mâi dâi séu
(d) bplào, mâi dâi bòrk

Exercise 4

(a) bplào krúp (kâ), mâi pairng
(b) bplào krúp (kâ), mâi bèu-a
(c) bplào krúp (kâ), mâi pèt
(d) bplào krúp (kâ), mâi glai

Exercise 5

(a) kŏr fàhk gOOn-jair wái nai dtôo sáyf dâi mái?
(b) kŏr fàhk glôrng tài rôop wái nai dtôo sáyf dâi mái?
(c) kŏr fàhk (toh-ra-sùp) meu tĕu wái nai dtôo sáyf dâi mái?
(d) kŏr fàhk dtŏo-a krêu-ung bin wái nai dtôo sáyf dâi mái?

Reading practice

1

Clerk Have you been to Wat That Phanom yet?
Sue Where?
Clerk Wat That Phanom.
Sue No, not yet. We'd like to go tomorrow, but we don't know how to get there.
Clerk You can go with a tour. There's an air-conditioned coach that goes every morning and returns in the evening.
Sue Really? How much does the tour cost?
Clerk 470 baht each.
Sue What time does the bus leave?
Clerk 8 o'clock in the morning. It leaves from right in front of this hotel and returns at 5 o'clock in the evening.
Sue And where do you book?
Clerk I can book for you. Are you going?
Sue Hang on a minute. We'll think about it first.

2

Sue Excuse me. Is it forbidden to take photos here?
Thai I don't think it is. But I'll go and ask an official for you. Hang on a minute . . . Excuse me, you can take photos here, can't you?
Official Here, you can. But inside photography is forbidden. Please tell the farangs they have to take their shoes off inside, too.

3

(a)–(v) (b)–(i) (c)–(iv) (d)–(iii) (e)–(ii)

4

Ladies and gentlemen, we've arrived in Nakhorn Ratchasima and we're going to stop for a break and eat rice porridge for about half an hour. It's half past midnight now. The bus will leave at 1.00 a.m. sharp. Please come back to the coach before that. When you get off the bus, please take your bus ticket with you. Don't forget it because you must show it in the restaurant. If you don't have your ticket on you, you'll have to pay for the food yourself.

Unit 14

Exercise 1

(a) gum-lung ja sùng ah-hăhn
(b) gum-lung ja glùp bâhn
(c) gum-lung ja òrk bpai kûng nôrk
(d) gum-lung ja séu rót mài
(e) gum-lung ja jorng dtŏo-a rót fai bpai chee-ung mài

Exercise 2

(a) wun têe gâo mók-ga-rah
(b) wun têe sìp-gâo mí-tOO-nah
(c) wun têe săhm-sìp-èt sĭng-hăh
(d) wun têe hâh préut-sa-jìk-gah
(e) wun têe săhm may-săh

Exercise 3

(a) bâhn têe pŏm (chún) púk yòo mâi kôy yài tâo-rài
(b) ah-hăhn têe rao gin mâi kôy pèt tâo-rài
(c) kon tai têe pŏm (chún) róo-jùk pôot pah-săh ung-grìt gèng
(d) rohng ree-un têe pŏm (chún) ree-un yòo glai
(e) ah-jahn têe sŏrn pah-săh tai mah jàhk chee-ung mài
(f) sêu-a têe pŏm (chún) chôrp pairng gern bpai
(g) núng-sĕu têe pŏm (chún) hâi kOOn yòo têe-năi?
(h) bpee têe pŏm ree-un pah-săh tai mee núk ree-un mâi mâhk
(i) wun têe rao bpai têe-o nakhorn phanom mâi kôy rórn tâo-rài

Reading practice

1

I've worked here nearly 20 years. It's alright working here. I clean the rooms and do the laundry. I come to work at 8 a.m. and go home at 4 p.m. Most of the guests here are foreigners. There are farangs, Chinese and Japanese too. Some are very kind. They give tips of over 100 baht. But it's the rainy season now. There aren't many guests. There's not much work either. So I sit chatting with my friends all day.

2

Malee Have you ever been to the seaside in Thailand, Sue?
Sue Yes. I've been to Pattaya once, two or three months ago.
Malee Was it fun?
Sue Well . . . it wasn't much. There were lots of people. I didn't like it. I prefer it quiet.
Malee If you're going to the seaside, I think it's better to go to Hua Hin. It's a lot quieter than Pattaya. There are fewer tourists. Otherwise, you should go to Koh Samet. It's fun renting a bungalow.
Sue What's a bungalow like?
Malee Most have just a bedroom and a bathroom. There's no air conditioning and no kitchen. But you can stay there quite comfortably, because there are sure to be good seafood restaurants nearby.

3

John Can I change my room?
Clerk Why is that, then?
John The air conditioner is broken.
Clerk Hang on a minute and I'll go up and take a look.
John There's no need. The toilet doesn't work either. There's no water. It would be better to change rooms.
Clerk You can't.
John Why is that, then?
Clerk There aren't any other rooms.

4

I got married in Bangkok. My husband is English. He worked at a large company in the Sukhumwit area. We came back to England three years ago. To tell you the truth, I really didn't want to come and live in England because I could hardly speak English. I had studied it at school but I wasn't very good. When English people spoke I couldn't understand a thing. So my husband had me study English at a school near home. At the school there were students of every nationality – Japanese, Chinese, German, African and Arabs, too. I had to study four days a week – Monday, Tuesday, Wednesday and Friday. I studied 2–3 hours a day from 9 o'clock until mid-day. After studying for about six months I think my English really improved a lot.

Consonant classes

The following chart lists all the Thai consonants according to class and gives the pronunciation for each consonant both at the beginning of a word and at the end. Perhaps the easiest way to remember the class of a consonant is to memorize the shorter lists of mid-class and high-class consonants so that everything not on those lists can be assumed to be low class.

Low class

	น	ม	ง	ร	ล	ย	ว
initial	**n**	**m**	**ng**	**r**	**l**	**y**	**w**
final	**n**	**m**	**ng**	**n**	**n**	**y**	**w**

	ค	ช	ซ	ท	พ	ฟ
initial	**k**	**ch**	**s**	**t**	**p**	**f**
final	**k**	**t**	**t**	**t**	**p**	**p**

	ฆ	ธ	ภ	ญ	ณ
initial	**k**	**t**	**p**	**y**	**n**
final	**k**	**t**	**p**	**n**	**n**

	ฌ	ฑ	ฒ	ฬ	ฮ
initial	**ch**	**t**	**t**	**l**	**h**
final	**—**	**t**	**t**	**n**	**—**

Mid class									
	ก	จ	ด	ต	บ	ป	อ	ฎ	ฏ
initial	**g**	**j**	**d**	**dt**	**b**	**bp**	zero	**d**	**dt**
final	**k**	**t**	**t**	**t**	**p**	**p**	—	**t**	**t**
High class									
	ข	ฉ	ถ	ผ	ฝ	ศ,ส,ษ	ห	ฐ	
initial	**k**	**ch**	**t**	**p**	**f**	**s**	**h**	**t**	
final	**k**	**t**	**t**	**p**	**p**	**t**	—	**t**	

Vowels

Long vowels											
-า	-อ	โ-	-ี	-ู	-ื	เ-	แ-	เ-ีย	เ-ือ	-ัว	เ-ิ
-ah	**-or**	**-oh**	**-ee**	**-oo**	**-eu**	**-ay**	**-air**	**-ee-a**	**-eu-a**	**-oo-a**	**-er**

Short vowels									
-ั-	ไ-	ใ-	-ิ	-ุ	-ึ	เ-็	แ-็	เ-า	-ะ
-u	**-ai**	**-ai**	**-i**	**-OO**	**-eu**	**-e**	**-air**	**-ao**	**-a**

Summary of tone rules

Words without tone marks

Initial consonant class	Live syllable	Dead syllable	
		Short vowel	Long vowel
Low class	**Mid tone**	**High tone**	**Falling tone**
Mid class	**Mid tone**	**Low tone**	**Low tone**
High class	**Rising tone**	**Low tone**	**Low tone**

Words with tone marks

Initial consonant class	mái àyk ่ (-)	mái toh ้ (-)	mái dtree ๊ (-)	mái jùt-dta-wah ๋ (-)
Low class	**Falling**	**High**	**High**	**Rising**
Mid class	**Low**	**Falling**	**High**	**Rising**
High class	**Low**	**Falling**	**High**	**Rising**

Taking it further

The following books will be useful if you wish to further your knowledge of Thai.

Dictionaries

Thai–English Dictionary by Domnern Garden and Sathienpong Wannapok, Bangkok: Amarin Printing and Publishing, 1994.

Thai English Student's Dictionary by Mary Haas, Stanford: Stanford University Press, 1964. This is the best dictionary for the serious beginner, with a romanized pronunciation guide to each Thai script entry and numerous examples of usage.

A New Thai Dictionary with Bilingual Explanation by Thianchai Iamwaramet, Bangkok: Ruam San, 1993.

Robertson's Practical English–Thai Dictionary by Richard Robertson, Rutland, Vermont and Tokyo: Charles E. Tuttle, 1969. A small, but invaluable dictionary for the beginner, which provides Thai script and romanized Thai equivalents to approximately 2,500 English words.

Grammar

Thai: An Essential Grammar by David Smyth, London: Routledge, 2002.

Reader

Thai for Advanced Readers by Benjawan Poomsan Becker, Berkeley, CA: Paiboon Publishing, 2000.

General

Linguistic Diversity and National Unity: Language Ecology in Thailand by William A. Smalley, Chicago and London: University of Chicago Press, 1994.

This volume offers an invaluable insight into the relationship between the national language, regional dialects and minority languages in Thailand.

Thai–English vocabulary

(*n*)**noun** (*v*)**verb**

a-may-ri-gah *America* อเมริกา

a-may-ri-gun *American* อเมริกัน

a-páht-mén *apartment* อพาร์ทเม้นท์

a-rai? *what?* อะไร

a-rai gôr dâi *anything* อะไรก็ได้

a-rai ná? *pardon?* อะไรนะ

a-ròy *tasty* อร่อย

ah-gàht *weather, climate* อากาศ

ah-jahn *teacher, lecturer* อาจารย์

ah-tít *week* อาทิตย์

ah-yÓO *age* อายุ

àhn *read* อ่าน

àht (ja) *may* อาจ(จะ)

ai dtim *ice cream* ไอศครีม

air *air conditioned* แอร์

ao *want (v)* เอา

ao . . . bpai *take* เอา . . . ไป

ba-mèe	*egg noodles*	บะหมี่
ba-mèe náhm	*egg noodle soup*	บะหมี่น้ำ
bâhn	*house, home*	บ้าน
bahng	*some*	บาง
bahng krúng	*sometimes*	บางครั้ง
bàht	*baht (unit of currency)*	บาท
bai	(classifier)	ใบ
bài	*afternoon*	บ่าย
bàirp	*style*	แบบ
bee-a sǐng	*Singha beer*	เบียร์สิงห์
ber	*number*	เบอร์
bon	*on*	บน
bOO-rèe	*cigarette*	บุหรี่
bòrk (wâh)	*say (that); tell*	บอก (ว่า)
bor-ri-sùt	*company*	บริษัท
bor-ri-wayn bâhn	*house compound*	บริเวณบ้าน
bung-ga-loh	*bungalow*	บังกาโล
bpai	*go*	ไป
. . . bpai nòy	*a little too . . .*	. . .ไปหน่อย
bpen	*to be; able to*	เป็น
bpen yung-ngai?	*how is it?*	เป็นอย่างไร
bpép-sêe	*Pepsi*	เป๊ปซี่
bper sen	*per cent*	เปอร์เซ็นต์
bpèt	*duck*	เป็ด
bplah	*fish*	ปลา
bplair	*translate*	แปล
. . . bplair wâh a-rai?	*what does . . . mean?*	แปลว่าอะไร

bplào	*no*	เปล่า
bplèe-un	*change (v)*	เปลี่ยน
bplòrt-pai	*safe (adj)*	ปลอดภัย
bpóht-gáht	*postcard*	โปสการ์ด
bpra-mahn	*about*	ประมาณ
bpra-tâyt	*country*	ประเทศ
bprai-sa-nee	*post office*	ไปรษณีย์
bprùp ah-gàht	*air conditioned*	ปรับอากาศ
bpun-hăa	*problem*	ปัญหา
cháh	*slow*	ช้า
chahm	*bowl*	ชาม
châht	*nation*	ชาติ
chái	*to use*	ใช้
chái dâi	*reasonable, acceptable*	ใช้ได้
chái way-lah	*to take time*	ใช้เวลา
châi mái?	(question particle)	ใช่ไหม
chai ta-lay	*seaside*	ชายทะเล
cháo	*morning*	เช้า
chao dtàhng bpra-tâyt	*foreigners*	ชาวต่างประเทศ
chèet	*spray (v)*	ฉีด
chék bin	*can I have the bill?*	เช็คบิล
chern	*please; to invite*	เชิญ
chêu	*first name,*	ชื่อ
chêu-a	*believe*	เชื่อ
chim	*taste (v)*	ชิม
chôhk dee	*good luck*	โชคดี
chôo-a-mohng	*hour*	ชั่วโมง

chôo-ay . . .	*please . . . ; to help*	ช่วย . . .
chôrp	*like*	ชอบ
chún	*I (female)*	ฉัน
chún	*floor, level; class*	ชั้น
chún nèung	*first class*	ชั้นหนึ่ง
chút	*clear*	ชัด
dâi	*can*	ได้
dee	*good*	ดี
dee kêun	*improve*	ดีขึ้น
děe-o . . .	*wait a moment*	เดี๋ยว . . .
dèk	*child*	เด็ก
dern	*walk (v)*	เดิน
dern tahng	*travel (v)*	เดินทาง
deu-un	*month*	เดือน
dèuk	*late at night, dark*	ดึก
di-chún	*I (female)*	ดิฉัน
doo	*look at*	ดู
dôo-ay	*too, also*	ด้วย
doo-ung	(classifier)	ดวง
dung	*loud*	ดัง
dtàhng jung-wùt	*up country*	ต่างจังหวัด
dtàir (wâh)	*but*	แต่ (ว่า)
(dtàir) cháo	*(from) early morning*	(แต่)เช้า
dtairng moh	*water melon*	แตงโม
dtàirng ngahn	*marry; married*	แต่งงาน
dtem (láir-o)	*full*	เต็ม(แล้ว)
dtèuk	*concrete building*	ตึก
dtèun	*to wake up*	ตื่น

dtìt	*to stick, be stuck*	ติด
dtìt air	*to be air conditioned*	ติดแอร์
dtìt dtoo-a	*on you, with you*	ติดตัว
dtòk long	*agree(d)*	ตกลง
dtôm yum gÔOng	*shrimp 'tom yam'*	ต้มยำกุ้ง
dtôn-mái	*tree*	ต้นไม้
dtôo sáyf	*safe (n)*	ตู้เซฟ
dtoo-a	*body*	ตัว
dtoo-a	(classifier)	ตัว
dtǒo-a	*ticket*	ตั๋ว
dtòr	*continue*	ต่อ
dtorn	*period of time*	ตอน
dtorn bài	*afternoon*	ตอนบ่าย
dtorn cháo	*morning*	ตอนเช้า
dtorn glahng keun	*night time*	ตอนกลางคืน
dtorn glahng wun	*daytime*	ตอนกลางวัน
dtorn née	*now*	ตอนนี้
dtorn yen	*evening*	ตอนเย็น
dtôrng	*have to, must*	ต้อง
dtrong	*straight, exact*	ตรง
dtrong née	*right here*	ตรงนี้
dtùm	*low*	ต่ำ
dtum-rah	*textbook*	ตำรา
dtum-ròo-ut	*policeman*	ตำรวจ
dtung	*money, satang*	สตางค์
èek	*again; further*	อีก
èek tee	*again*	อีกที
eng	*self*	เอง
èun	*other*	อื่น

fa-rùng	*westerner*	ฝรั่ง
fa-rùng-sàyt	*French*	ฝรั่งเศส
fàhk	*deposit (v)*	ฝาก
fairn	*spouse, partner*	แฟน
fung	*listen*	ฟัง
gài	*chicken*	ไก่
gâir	*repair (v)*	แก้
gâir-o	*glass*	แก้ว
gairng	*curry*	แกง
gairng gài	*chicken curry*	แกงไก่
gèe?	*how many?*	กี่
gèe mohng?	*what time?*	กี่โมง
gèng	*good at*	เก่ง
gèp	*collect, keep*	เก็บ
gèp wái	*keep*	เก็บไว้
. . . gern bpai	*too . . .*	. . . เกินไป
gèrt	*to be born*	เกิด
gèu-up	*almost*	เกือบ
gi-loh	*kilometre*	กิโล
glai	*far*	ไกล
glâi	*near*	ใกล้
gloo-a	*afraid*	กลัว
glôo-ay	*banana*	กล้วย
glôrng tài rôop	*camera*	กล้องถ่ายรูป
glôrng tài wee-dee-oh	*video camera*	กล้องถ่ายวีดีโอ
glùp	*return*	กลับ
gOOn-jair	*key*	กุญแจ
gÔOng	*shrimp*	กุ้ง

gôr . . .	*well . . .*	ก็ . . .
. . . gôr láir-o gun	*let's settle for . . .*	. . . ก็แล้วกัน
gòrn	*before, first*	ก่อน
grOOng-tâyp	*Bangkok*	กรุงเทพ ฯ
gum-lung . . . yòo	*in the process of . . .*	กำลัง . . . อยู่
gum-lung ja	*about to . . .*	กำลังจะ . . .
gùp	*with*	กับ
. . . gwàh	*more than . . .*	กว่า
gwâhng	*wide*	กว้าง
hâhm	*forbid; forbidden*	ห้าม
hàhng jàhk	*at a distance from*	ห่างจาก
hâi	*to get someone to do something; for; give*	ให้
hàirng	(classifier)	แห่ง
hôrng	*room*	ห้อง
hôrng kroo-a	*kitchen*	ห้องครัว
hôrng náhm	*toilet, bathroom*	ห้องน้ำ
hôrng norn	*bedroom*	ห้องนอน
hôrng rúp kàirk	*living room*	ห้องรับแขก
hôrng sôo-um	*toilet*	ห้องส้วม
hun-loh	*hello (on telephone)*	ฮันโล
ìm	*full (with food)*	อิ่ม
ja	(future time marker)	จะ
jàhk	*from*	จาก
jahn	*plate*	จาน
jai dee	*kind hearted*	ใจดี
jâo kŏrng	*owner*	เจ้าของ
jâo kŏrng pah-săh	*native speaker*	เจ้าของภาษา

jâo nâh-têe	*official*	เจ้าหน้าที่
jing	*true, truly*	จริง
jon těung	*until*	จนถึง
jorng	*book (v)*	จอง
jòrt	*park (v)*	จอด
jòt-măi ah-gàht	*aerogramme*	จดหมายอากาศ
jum-gùt	*Ltd*	จำกัด
jung ler-ee	*really, very*	จังเลย
jung-wùt	*province*	จังหวัด
kâ, ká	(polite particles)	ค่ะ, คะ
ka-moy	*burglar*	ขโมย
ka-nŏm	*cake, dessert*	ขนม
kâh	*cost*	ค่า
kâh châo	*rent*	ค่าเช่า
kâh doy-ee săhn	*fare*	ค่าโดยสาร
kâh mút-jum	*deposit*	ค่ามัดจำ
kâhng	*side*	ข้าง
kàirk	*guest; Indian*	แขก
kâo	*enter*	เข้า
kâo jai	*understand*	เข้าใจ
káo	*he, she, they*	เขา
kâo	*rice*	ข้าว
kâo dtôm	*rice porridge*	ข้าวต้ม
kâo nâh bpèt	*duck rice*	ข้าวหน้าเป็ด
kěe-un	*write*	เขียน
kem	*salty*	เค็ม
ker-ee	*used to (do); once (did)*	เคย
kêun	*get on (a bus); go up*	ขึ้น

keun	*night*	คืน
kít	*think; charge*	คิด
kít doo	*consider*	คิดดู
klorng	*canal*	คลอง
klôrng	*fluent*	คล่อง
koh-lâh	Coca-Cola	โคล่า
kon	*person*	คน
kong	*bound to be, sure to be*	คง
koo-ee	*chat (v)*	คุย
koo-un (ja)	*should, ought to*	ควร(จะ)
kòo-up	*year(s old)*	ขวบ
kòo-ut	*bottle*	ขวด
kOOn	*you* (polite title)	คุณ
kŏr . . . nòy	*I'd like . . .*	ขอ . . . หน่อย
kŏr-tôht	*excuse me*	ขอโทษ
kŏrng	*of; things*	ของ
kŏrng wăhn	*sweet, dessert*	ของหวาน
kòrp-kOOn	*thank you*	ขอบคุณ
koy	*to wait*	คอย
krai?	*who?*	ใคร
krêe-ut	*stressed, tense*	เครียด
krêu-ung bprùp ah-gàht	*air conditioner*	เครื่องปรับอากาศ
krêung	*half*	ครึ่ง
krêung chôo-a mohng	*half an hour*	ครึ่งชั่วโมง
kroo	*teacher*	ครู
krôo	*a moment*	ครู่
krúng	*time(s)*	ครั้ง

krúp, krúp pŏm	(polite particles)	ครับ, ครับผม
kum	*word*	คำ
kun	(classifier)	คัน
kûng bon	*upstairs*	ข้างบน
kûng lâhng	*downstairs*	ข้างล่าง
kûng nai	*inside*	ข้างใน
kûng nôrk	*outside*	ข้างนอก
kùp	*drive (v)*	ขับ
kwăh	*right*	ขวา
kwahm	(abstract noun prefix)	ความ
kwahm jing	*(in) truth; actually*	ความจริง
kwahm kít	*idea*	ความคิด
kwahm rúk	*love*	ความรัก
kwahm sa-àht	*cleaning*	ความสะอาด
kwahm sÒOk	*happiness*	ความสุข
la	*per*	ละ
láhng	*wash (plates)*	ล้าง
lâhng	*under*	ล่าง
láir	*and*	และ
láir-o	*and then; already*	แล้ว
láir-o . . . lâ?	*and how about . . . ?*	แล้ว . . . ล่ะ
lâir-o gôr . . .	*and*	แล้วก็
. . . láir-o réu yung?	*. . . yet (or not)?*	แล้วหรือยัง
lée-o	*turn (v)*	เลี้ยว
lék	*small*	เล็ก
lêm	(classifier)	เล่ม
lên	*play (v)*	เล่น
lĕr?	(question particle)	หรือ

ler-ee bpai	*carry on, go on*	เลยไป
lêrk	*cease; give up*	เลิก
leum	*forget*	ลืม
loh	*kilo*	โล
long	*get off (a bus)*	ลง
long ta-bee-un	*register*	ลงทะเบียน
lôo-ung nâh	*in advance*	ล่วงหน้า
lôok	(classifier)	ลูก
lôok	*child/children*	ลูก
lôok chai	*son*	ลูกชาย
lôok săo	*daughter*	ลูกสาว
lòr	*handsome*	หล่อ
lorng	*try out*	ลอง
lót	*reduce*	ลด
lŭng	*behind*	หลัง
ma-hăh-wít-ta-yah-lai	*university*	มหาวิทยาลัย
mah	*come*	มา
mah tĕung	*reach*	มาถึง
mâhk	*very, much*	มาก
. . . mái?	(question particle)	ไหม
mái	*wood*	ไม้
mài	*again; new*	ใหม่
mâi	*not*	ไม่
mâi bpen rai	*never mind*	ไม่เป็นไร
mâi dee	*bad*	ไม่ดี
mâi dtôrng	*there's no need*	ไม่ต้อง
mâi kôy . . . (tâo-rài)	*not very . . .*	ไม่ค่อย . . . (เท่าไร)

mâi . . . ler-ee	*not at all*	ไม่ . . . เลย
mâi . . . ròrk	*not . . . at all*	ไม่ . . . หรอก
mǎi-kwahm wâh a-rai?	*what does it mean?*	หมายความว่าอะไร
mâir	*mother*	แม่
mâir bâhn	*housewife*	แม่บ้าน
mâir náhm	*river*	แม่น้ำ
ma-la-gor	*papaya*	มะละกอ
ma-môo-ung	*mango*	มะม่วง
may-noo	*menu*	เมนู
mee	*have*	มี
mêu-a	*when*	เมื่อ
mêu-a gòrn	*formerly*	เมื่อก่อน
mêu-rài?	*when?*	เมื่อไร
mĕu-un	*like, similar, as*	เหมือน
mĕu-un gun	*likewise; fairly*	เหมือนกัน
meu-ung tai	*Thailand*	เมืองไทย
mèun	*10,000*	หมื่น
mòo bâhn	*village*	หมู่บ้าน
mÓOng lôo-ut	*mosquito screen*	มุ้งลวด
mŏr	*doctor*	หมอ
mun	*it*	มัน
ná	(question particle)	นะ
nâh	*in front (of)*	หน้า
nâh	*next; season*	หน้า
nâh fŏn	*rainy season*	หน้าฝน
nâh bèu-a	*boring*	น่าเบื่อ
nâh rúk	*lovable, cute*	น่ารัก

nâh sŏn jai	*interesting*	น่าสนใจ
nâh yòo	*nice to live in/at*	น่าอยู่
nah-tee	*minute*	นาที
náhm	*water*	น้ำ
náhm tôo-um	*flood*	น้ำท่วม
nahm sa-gOOn	*surname*	นามสกุล
nahn	*a long time*	นาน
nai	*in*	ใน
nâir	*certain*	แน่
nâirn	*crowded*	แน่น
nêe	*this*	นี่
nêe eng	*this very . . .*	นี่เอง
nêe kâ/krúp	*here you are*	นี่ค่ะ/ครับ
néu-a	*beef*	เนื้อ
nèung	*one, a*	หนึ่ง
nin-tah	*gossip (v)*	นินทา
nít nèung	*a little bit*	นิดหนึ่ง
nít-nòy	*a little bit*	นิดหน่อย
nórng chai	*younger brother*	น้องชาย
nórng săo	*younger sister*	น้องสาว
nòy	*a bit*	หน่อย
nóy-nàh	*custard apple*	น้อยหน่า
nùk	*heavy; hard (work)*	หนัก
núk ree-un	*pupil (school)*	นักเรียน
núk sèuk-săh	*student*	นักศึกษา
núk tÓO-rá-gìt	*businessman*	นักธุรกิจ
núm bplah	*fish sauce*	น้ำปลา
núm kăirng	*ice*	น้ำแข็ง

núm kăirng bplào	*iced water*	น้ำแข็งเปล่า
núm ma-nao	*lemonade*	น้ำมะนาว
núm mun hŏy	*oyster sauce*	น้ำมันหอย
núm sôm	*orange juice*	น้ำส้ม
núm sôm kún	*fresh orange juice*	น้ำส้มคั้น
nûng	*sit; travel by*	นั่ง
nŭng	*movie*	หนัง
ngahn	*work (n)*	งาน
ngâi	*easy*	ง่าย
ngêe-up	*quiet, calm*	เงียบ
ngern deu-un	*salary*	เงินเดือน
ngong	*dazed, confused*	งง
oh kay	*OK*	โอ เค
ôr	*exclamation of realization*	อ้อ
òrk	*go out; leave*	ออก
pah-săh	*language*	ภาษา
pâhk dtâi	*the South*	ภาคใต้
pâhk ee-săhn	*the Northeast*	ภาคอีสาน
pâhk glahng	*the Central Region*	ภาคกลาง
pâhk nĕu-a	*the North*	ภาคเหนือ
pàirn	(classifier)	แผ่น
pairng	*expensive*	แพง
pêe-chai	*older brother*	พี่ชาย
pêe-nórng	*brothers and sisters*	พี่น้อง
pêe-săo	*older sister*	พี่สาว
pèt	*spicy*	เผ็ด
pêu-un	*friend*	เพื่อน

pìt	*wrong*	ผิด
pŏm	*I (male)*	ผม
pŏn-la-mái	*fruit*	ผลไม้
pôo-chai	*man/boy*	ผู้ชาย
pôo-doy-ee săhn	*passenger*	ผู้โดยสาร
pôo-jùt-gahn	*manager*	ผู้จัดการ
pôo-rái	*criminal*	ผู้ร้าย
pôo-yài	*adult*	ผู้ใหญ่
pôo-yĭng	*woman/girl*	ผู้หญิง
pôot	*speak*	พูด
pôot lên	*joke (v)*	พูดเล่น
por	*enough*	พอ
pôr	*father*	พ่อ
prÔOng née	*tomorrow*	พรุ่งนี้
prór wâh	*because*	เพราะว่า
púk	*stay; rest (v)*	พัก
pùt	*stir fry, fried*	ผัด
pút lom	*fan (n)*	พัดลม
ráhn-ah-hăhn	*restaurant*	ร้านอาหาร
ray-o	*quick*	เร็ว
rêe-uk wâh . . .	*(it's) called . . .*	เรียกว่า . . .
ree-un	*study, learn*	เรียน
rêet	*iron (v)*	รีด
réu	*or*	หรือ
. . . réu bplào?	*. . . or not?*	. . . หรือเปล่า
rohng rairm	*hotel*	โรงแรม
rohng ree-un	*school*	โรงเรียน

róo	*know (facts)*	รู้
róo rêu-ung	*understand*	รู้เรื่อง
róo-jùk	*know (people, places)*	รู้จัก
róo-sèuk	*feel*	รู้สึก
rôop	*shape, form*	รูป
ror	*wait*	รอ
rorng táo	*shoes*	รองเท้า
rót	*car*	รถ
rót dtìt	*traffic jam*	รถติด
rót fai	*train*	รถไฟ
rót may	*bus*	รถเมล์
rót too-a	tour bus	รถทัวร์
rúp	*receive*	รับ
sa-àht	*clean*	สะอาด
sa-bai	*to be well, comfortable*	สบาย
sa-dairng	*show (v)*	แสดง
sa-dtáirm	*stamp*	แสตมป์
sa-gòt	*spell (v)*	สะกด
sa-mĕr	*always*	เสมอ
sa-năhm bin	*airport*	สนามบิน
sa-tăhn tôot	*embassy*	สถานทูต
sa-wùt dee	*hello*	สวัสดี
săh-mee	*husband*	สามี
sâhp	*know (facts)*	ทราบ
sái	*left*	ซ้าย
săi	*(telephone) line*	สาย
see	(mood particle)	ซี
sĕe	*colour*	สี

sěe dairng	*red*	สีแดง
sěe dum	*black*	สีดำ
sěe kǎo	*white*	สีขาว
sěe kěe-o	*green*	สีเขียว
sěe lěu-ung	*yellow*	สีเหลือง
sěe núm dtahn	*brown*	สีน้ำตาล
sěe núm ngern	*blue*	สีน้ำเงิน
sěe-a	*spend; waste; broken*	เสีย
sěe-ung	*sound; tone*	เสียง
sèe-yâirk	*crossroads*	สี่แยก
séu	*buy*	ซื้อ
sêu-a pâh	*clothes*	เสื้อผ้า
sí	(mood particle)	ซิ
sôm	*orange (n)*	ส้ม
sòng	*send*	ส่ง
sŏo-ay	*beautiful, pretty*	สวย
sŏo-un	*garden*	สวน
sòo-un mâhk	*mostly*	ส่วนมาก
sŏon	*zero*	ศูนย์
sŏong	*high*	สูง
sòop bOO-rèe	*smoke (v)*	สูบบุหรี่
sÒOt soy	*end of the soi*	สุดซอย
sôrm	*repair, mend*	ซ่อม
sŏrn	*teach*	สอน
soy	*soi, lane*	ซอย
súk	*wash (clothes)*	ซัก
sùng	*to order*	สั่ง
sùp-bpa-rót	*pineapple*	สับปะรด

ta-lay	*sea*	ทะเล
ta-na-kahn	*bank*	ธนาคาร
ta-nŏn	*road*	ถนน
tâh	*if*	ถ้า
tâh yàhng nún	*in that case*	ถ้าอย่างนั้น
tăhm	*ask*	ถาม
tahn	*eat*	ทาน
tahng	*way*	ทาง
tahng ah-gàht/reu-a	*by air/sea*	ทางอากาศ/เรือ
tahng kwăh/sái	*on the right/left*	ทางขวา/ซ้าย
tai	*Thai*	ไทย
tài rôop	*take a photograph*	ถ่ายรูป
tăir-o née	*this vicinity*	แถวนี้
tâo-nún	*only*	เท่านั้น
tâo-rài?	*how much?*	เท่าไร
táyp	*tape*	เทป
tee	*time*	ที
têe	*at*; (relative pronoun)	ที่
têe-kèe-a bOO-rèe	*ashtray*	ที่เขี่ยบุหรี่
têe-năi?	*where*	ที่ไหน
têe-nêe	*here*	ที่นี่
têe-nôhn	*over there*	ที่โน่น
têe-o	*visit, go out*	เที่ยว
tĕung	*reach (v)*	ถึง
toh	*telephone (v)*	โทร
toh-ra-sùp	*telephone (n)*	โทรศัพท์
toh-ra-sùp meu tĕu	*mobile phone*	โทรศัพท์มือถือ
too-a	*tour*	ทัวร์

tòok	*correct; cheap*	ถูก
tÓOk	*every*	ทุก
tòrt	*take off (clothes)*	ถอด
tum	*do, make*	ทำ
tum nah	*do rice farming*	ทำนา
tum ngahn	*work (v)*	ทำงาน
tum-mai	*why?*	ทำไม
tûn	*you (polite)*	ท่าน
túng . . . láir . . .	*both . . . and . . .*	ทั้ง . . . และ . . .
túng mòt	*altogether*	ทั้งหมด
túng wun	*all day*	ทั้งวัน
un	(classifier)	อัน
ung-grìt	*English*	อังกฤษ
wâh	*think, say; that*	ว่า
wăhn	*sweet*	หวาน
wâhng	*free, vacant*	ว่าง
way-lah	*time*	เวลา
wěe	*bunch (of bananas); comb*	หวี
wun	*day*	วัน
wun née	*today*	วันนี้
wun săo wun ah-tít	*weekend*	วันเสาร์วันอาทิตย์
yàh	*don't*	อย่า
yah gun yOOng	*insecticide*	ยากันยุง
yâhk	*difficult*	ยาก
yàhk (ja)	*want to*	อยาก(จะ)
yài	*large*	ใหญ่
yái	*move (home)*	ย้าย

yâir	*to be a nuisance, hassle*	แย่
yêe-bpÒOn	*Japanese*	ญี่ปุ่น
yér-yáir	*lots*	เยอะแยะ
yòo	*situated at; live at*	อยู่
yÒOt	*to stop*	หยุด
yung	*still*	ยัง
yung-ngai?	*how?*	อย่างไร

English–Thai vocabulary

about, approximately	**bpra-mahn**	ประมาณ
about to . . .	**gum-lung ja**	กำลังจะ . . .
acceptable	**chái dâi**	ใช้ได้
actually	**kwahm jing**	ความจริง
administrator	**pôo-bor-ri-hăhn**	ผู้บริหาร
adult	**pôo-yài**	ผู้ใหญ่
(in) advance	**lôo-ung nâh**	ล่วงหน้า
aerogramme	**jòt-măi ah-gàht**	จดหมายอากาศ
afraid	**gloo-a**	กลัว
afternoon	**(dtorn) bài**	ตอนบ่าย
again	**èek; èek tee; mài**	อีก; อีกที; ใหม่
age	**ah-yÓO**	อายุ
agree(d)	**dtòk long**	ตกลง
air; by air	**ah-gàht; tahng ah-gàht**	อากาศ; ทางอากาศ
air conditioned	**dtìt air; bprùp ah-gàht**	ติดแอร์; ปรับอากาศ
air conditioner	**krêu-ung bprùp ah-gàht**	เครื่องปรับอากาศ
airport	**sa-năhm bin**	สนามบิน
all day	**túng wun**	ทั้งวัน
almost	**gèu-up**	เกือบ

already	láir-o	แล้ว
also	dôo-ay	ด้วย
altogether	túng mòt	ทั้งหมด
always	sa-měr	เสมอ
America	a-may-ri-gah	อเมริกา
American	a-may-ri-gun	อเมริกัน
and	láir; láir-o gôr	และ; แล้วก็
anything	a-rai gôr dâi	อะไรก็ได้
apartment	a-páht-mén	อพาร์ทเม้นท์
arrive	mah tĕung	มาถึง
ashtray	têe-kìe-a bOO-rèe	ที่เขี่ยบุหรี่
ask	tăhm	ถาม
bad	mâi dee	ไม่ดี
baht	bàht	บาท
banana	glôo-ay	กล้วย
Bangkok	grOOng-tâyp	กรุงเทพ ฯ
bank	ta-na-kahn	ธนาคาร
bathroom	hôrng náhm	ห้องน้ำ
beautiful	sŏo-ay	สวย
because	prór wâh	เพราะว่า
bedroom	hôrng norn	ห้องนอน
beef	néu-a	เนื้อ
beer	bee-a	เบียร์
before	gòrn	ก่อน
behind	kûng lŭng	ข้างหลัง
believe	chêu-a	เชื่อ
big	yài	ใหญ่
black	sĕe dum	สีดำ

blue	**sěe núm ngern**	สีน้ำเงิน
book (n)	**núng-sěu**	หนังสือ
book (v)	**jorng**	จอง
boring	**nâh bèu-a**	น่าเบื่อ
born	**gèrt**	เกิด
both . . . and . . .	**túng . . . láir . . .**	ทั้ง . . . และ . . .
bottle	**kòo-ut**	ขวด
bound to	**kong**	คง
bowl	**chahm**	ชาม
boy	**pôo-chai**	ผู้ชาย
boyfriend	**fairn**	แฟน
broken	**sěe-a**	เสีย
brother (older)	**pêe-chai**	พี่ชาย
brother (younger)	**nórng chai**	น้องชาย
brothers and sisters	**pêe-nórng**	พี่น้อง
brown	**sěe núm dtahn**	สีน้ำตาล
building (concrete)	**dtèuk**	ตึก
bungalow	**bung-ga-loh**	บังกาโล
burglar	**ka-moy**	ขโมย
bus; tour bus	**rót may; rót too-a**	รถเมล์; รถทัวร์
businessman	**núk tÓO-rá-gìt**	นักธุรกิจ
but	**dtàir (wâh)**	แต่(ว่า)
buy	**séu**	ซื้อ
(it's) called . . .	**rêe-uk wâh . . .**	เรียกว่า . . .
camera;	**glôrng tài rôop;**	กล้องถ่ายรูป;
video camera	**glôrng tài wee-dee-oh**	กล้องถ่ายวีดีโอ
can	**dâi; bpen**	ได้; เป็น
canal	**klorng**	คลอง

car	**rót**	รถ
Central Region	**pâhk glahng**	ภาคกลาง
certain	**nâir**	แน่
change (v)	**bplèe-un**	เปลี่ยน
chat (v)	**koo-ee**	คุย
cheap	**tòok**	ถูก
chicken	**gài**	ไก่
chicken curry	**gairng gài**	แกงไก่
child	**dèk**	เด็ก
child (one's own)	**lôok**	ลูก
cigarette	**bOO-rèe**	บุหรี่
class; first class	**chún; chún nèung**	ชั้น; ชั้นหนึ่ง
clean	**sa-àht**	สะอาด
clear	**chút**	ชัด
clothes	**sêu-a pâh**	เสื้อผ้า
collect	**gèp**	เก็บ
colour	**sěe**	สี
come	**mah**	มา
company	**bor-rí-sùt**	บริษัท
confused	**ngong**	งง
continue	**dtòr**	ต่อ
correct	**tòok**	ถูก
cost	**kâh**	ค่า
country	**bpra-tâyt**	ประเทศ
criminal	**pôo-rái**	ผู้ร้าย
crossroads	**sèe-yâirk**	สี่แยก
crowded	**nâirn**	แน่น

curry	**gairng**	แกง
custard apple	**nóy-nàh**	น้อยหน่า
cute	**nâh rúk**	น่ารัก
daughter	**lôok săo**	ลูกสาว
day	**wun**	วัน
daytime	**(dtorn) glahng wun**	(ตอน)กลางวัน
deposit (n)	**kâh mút-jum**	ค่ามัดจำ
deposit (v)	**fàhk**	ฝาก
difficult	**yâhk**	ยาก
distant from	**hàhng jàhk**	ห่างจาก
do	**tum**	ทำ
doctor	**mŏr**	หมอ
don't	**yàh**	อย่า
drive	**kùp**	ขับ
duck	**bpèt**	เป็ด
easy	**ngâi**	ง่าย
eat	**gin; tahn**	กิน; ทาน
egg noodles	**ba-mèe**	บะหมี่
egg noodle soup	**ba-mèe náhm**	บะหมี่น้ำ
embassy	**sa-tăhn tôot**	สถานทูต
English	**ung-grìt**	อังกฤษ
enough	**por**	พอ
enter	**kâo**	เข้า
evening, in the evening	**(dtorn) yen**	ตอนเย็น
every	**tÓOk**	ทุก
excuse me	**kŏr-tôht**	ขอโทษ
expensive	**pairng**	แพง

fairly . . .	**. . . mĕu-un gun**	. . . เหมือนกัน
fan (n; cooling device)	**pút lom**	พัดลม
far	**glai**	ไกล
fare	**kâh doy-ee săhn**	ค่าโดยสาร
father	**pôr**	พ่อ
feel	**róo-sèuk**	รู้สึก
fish	**bplah**	ปลา
fish sauce	**núm bplah**	น้ำปลา
flood	**náhm tôo-um**	น้ำท่วม
floor, level	**chún**	ชั้น
fluent	**klôrng**	คล่อง
for	**hâi**	ให้
forbid	**hâhm**	ห้าม
foreigner	**chao dtàhng bpra-tâyt**	ชาวต่างประเทศ
forget	**leum**	ลืม
formerly	**mêu-a gòrn**	เมื่อก่อน
free (vacant)	**wâhng**	ว่าง
French	**fa-rùng-sàyt**	ฝรั่งเศส
friend	**pêu-un**	เพื่อน
from	**jàhk**	จาก
fruit	**pŏn-la-mái**	ผลไม้
fry (stir fry)	**pùt**	ผัด
full	**dtem (láir-o)**	เต็ม(แล้ว)
full (stomach)	**ìm**	อิ่ม
garden	**sŏo-un**	สวน
German	**yer-ra-mun**	เยอรมัน
get off (e.g. a bus)	**long**	ลง

get on (e.g. a bus)	kêun	ขึ้น
get someone to do something	hâi	ให้
girlfriend	fairn	แฟน
give	hâi	ให้
give up; cease	lêrk	เลิก
glass	gâir-o	แก้ว
go	bpai	ไป
go out	òrk	ออก
go up	kêun	ขึ้น
good	dee	ดี
good at	gèng	เก่ง
gossip (v)	nin-tah	นินทา
green	sěe kěe-o	สีเขียว
half	krêung	ครึ่ง
half an hour	krêung chôo-a mohng	ครึ่งชั่วโมง
handsome	lòr	หล่อ
happiness	kwahm sÒOk	ความสุข
hard (work)	nùk	หนัก
have	mee	มี
he	káo	เขา
heavy	nùk	หนัก
hello	sa-wùt dee	สวัสดี
hello (on telephone)	hun-loh	ฮันโล
help (v)	chôo-ay	ช่วย
here	têe-nêe	ที่นี่
high	sǒong	สูง
hotel	rohng rairm	โรงแรม

hour	**chôo-a-mohng**	ชั่วโมง
house, home	**bâhn**	บ้าน
housewife	**mâir bâhn**	แม่บ้าน
how?	**yung-ngai**	อย่างไร
how are you?	**sa-bai dee lĕr?**	สบายดีหรือ
how many?	**gèe**	กี่
how much?	**tâo-rài**	เท่าไร
husband	**săh-mee**	สามี
I (female)	**chún/di-chún**	ฉัน/ดิฉัน
I (male)	**pŏm**	ผม
ice	**núm kăirng**	น้ำแข็ง
ice cream	**ai dtim**	ไอศครีม
iced water	**núm kăirng bplào**	น้ำแข็ง เปล่า
if	**tâh**	ถ้า
improve	**dee kêun**	ดีขึ้น
in	**nai**	ใน
in front (of)	**nâh**	หน้า
insecticide	**yah gun yOOng**	ยากันยุง
inside	**kûng nai**	ข้างใน
interesting	**nâh sŏn jai**	น่าสนใจ
iron (v)	**rêet**	รีด
is	**bpen**	เป็น
it	**mun**	มัน
Japanese	**yêe-bpÒOn**	ญี่ปุ่น
joke (v)	**pôot lên**	พูดเล่น
keep	**gèp wái**	เก็บไว้
key	**gOOn-jair**	กุญแจ

kilo	**loh**	โล
kilometre	**gi-loh**	กิโล
kind (adj)	**jai dee**	ใจดี
kitchen	**hôrng kroo-a**	ห้องครัว
know (facts)	**róo; sâhp**	รู้; ทราบ
know (people, places)	**róo-jùk**	รู้จัก
language	**pah-săh**	ภาษา
large	**yài**	ใหญ่
lecturer	**ah-jahn**	อาจารย์
left (side)	**sái**	ซ้าย
like (v)	**chôrp**	ชอบ
like (similar)	**mĕu-un**	เหมือน
likewise	**mĕu-un gun**	เหมือนกัน
listen	**fung**	ฟัง
live (in, at)	**yòo**	อยู่
living room	**hôrng rúp kàirk**	ห้องรับแขก
long (time)	**nahn**	นาน
look at	**doo**	ดู
lots	**yér-yáir**	เยอะแยะ
loud	**dung**	ดัง
love	**rúk**	รัก
low	**dtùm**	ต่ำ
Ltd	**jum-gùt**	จำกัด
luck: good luck	**chôhk dee**	โชคดี
man	**pôo-chai**	ผู้ชาย
manager	**pôo-jùt-gahn**	ผู้จัดการ
mango	**ma-môo-ung**	มะม่วง
married	**dtàirng ngahn**	แต่งงาน

may	**àht (ja)**	อาจ(จะ)
mean: what does ... mean?	**... bplair wâh a-rai?**	... แปลว่าอะไร
	... măi-kwahm wâh a-rai?	... หมายความว่าอะไร
menu	**may-noo**	เมนู
minute	**nah-tee**	นาที
moment	**krôo**	ครู่
money	**ngern; dtung**	เงิน; สตางค์
month	**deu-un**	เดือน
morning	**cháo**	เช้า
mosquito screen	**mÓOng lôo-ut**	มุ้งลวด
mostly	**sòo-un mâhk**	ส่วนมาก
mother	**mâir**	แม่
move (home)	**yái (bâhn)**	ย้าย(บ้าน)
movie	**nŭng**	หนัง
must	**dtôrng**	ต้อง
name (n; v)	**chêu**	ชื่อ
nation	**châht**	ชาติ
native speaker	**jâo kŏrng pah-săh**	เจ้าของภาษา
near	**glâi**	ใกล้
never mind	**mâi bpen rai**	ไม่เป็นไร
new	**mài**	ใหม่
next	**nâh**	หน้า
night	**keun**	คืน
night time, at night	**(dtorn) glahng keun**	(ตอน)กลางคืน
noodle shop	**ráhn gŏo-ay dtĕe-o**	ร้านก๋วยเตี๋ยว
Northeastern Region	**pâhk ee-săhn**	ภาคอีสาน
Northern Region	**pâhk nĕu-a**	ภาคเหนือ

not	**mâi**	ไม่
not . . . at all	**mâi . . . ròrk**	ไม่ . . . หรอก
not at all . . .	**mâi . . . ler-ee**	ไม . . . เลย
not very . . .	**mâi kôy . . . tâo-rài**	ไม่ค่อย . . . เท่าไร
now	**dtorn née**	ตอนนี้
number	**ber**	เบอร์
of	**kŏrng**	ของ
official (n)	**jâo-nâh-tee**	เจ้าหน้าที่
only	**tâo-nún**	เท่านั้น
or	**réu**	หรือ
. . . or not?	**. . . réu bplào?**	. . . หรือเปล่า
orange	**sôm**	ส้ม
orange juice	**núm sôm**	น้ำส้ม
order	**sùng**	สั่ง
other	**èun**	อื่น
outside	**kûng nôrk**	ข้างนอก
owner	**jâo kŏrng**	เจ้าของ
papaya	**ma-la-gor**	มะละกอ
pardon?	**a-rai ná?**	อะไรนะ
park (v)	**jòrt**	จอด
passenger	**pôo-doy-ee săhn**	ผู้โดยสาร
Pepsi	**bpép-sêe**	เป๊ปซี่
per	**la**	ละ
per cent	**bper sen**	เปอร์เซ็นต์
person	**kon**	คน
photograph (v)	**tài rôop**	ถ่ายรูป
pineapple	**sùp-bpa-rót**	สับปะรด

plate	**jahn**	จาน
play (v)	**lên**	เล่น
please	**chôo-ay . . .**	ช่วย . . .
policeman	**dtum-ròo-ut**	ตำรวจ
post office	**bprai-sa-nee**	ไปรษณีย์
postcard	**bpóht-gáht**	โปสการ์ด
problem	**bpun-hăh**	ปัญหา
province	**jung-wùt**	จังหวัด
pupil (school)	**núk ree-un**	นักเรียน
quick	**ray-o**	เร็ว
quiet	**ngêe-up**	เงียบ
rainy season	**nâh fŏn**	หน้าฝน
reach (v)	**tĕung**	ถึง
read	**àhn**	อ่าน
red	**sĕe dairng**	สีแดง
reduce	**lót**	ลด
register (v)	**long ta-bee-un**	ลงทะเบียน
rent (n)	**kâh châo**	ค่าเช่า
repair (v)	**sôrm; gâir**	ซ่อม; แก้
rest (v)	**púk**	พัก
restaurant	**ráhn-ah-hăhn**	ร้านอาหาร
return (v)	**glùp**	กลับ
rice	**kâo**	ข้าว
rice farming	**tum nah**	ทำนา
rice porridge	**kao dtôm**	ข้าวต้ม
right (side); on the right	**kwăh; tahng kwăh**	ขวา; ทางขวา
river	**mâir náhm**	แม่น้ำ
road	**ta-nŏn**	ถนน
room	**hôrng**	ห้อง

safe (adj)	**bplòrt-pai**	ปลอดภัย
safe (n)	**dtôo sáyf**	ตู้เซฟ
salary	**ngern deu-un**	เงินเดือน
salty	**kem**	เค็ม
Saturday	**wun săo**	วันเสาร์
say (that); tell	**bòrk (wâh)**	บอก(ว่า)
school	**rohng ree-un**	โรงเรียน
sea	**ta-lay**	ทะเล
seaside	**chai ta-lay**	ชายทะเล
self	**eng**	เอง
send	**sòng**	ส่ง
she	**káo**	เขา
shoes	**rorng táo**	รองเท้า
should, ought to	**koo-un (ja)**	ควร(จะ)
show (v)	**sa-dairng**	แสดง
shrimp	**gÔOng**	กุ้ง
sister (older)	**pêe-săo**	พี่สาว
sister (younger)	**nórng săo**	น้องสาว
sit	**nûng**	นั่ง
situated at	**yòo**	อยู่
slow	**cháh**	ช้า
small	**lék**	เล็ก
smoke (v)	**sòop bOO-rèe**	สูบบุหรี่
some	**bahng**	บาง
sometimes	**bahng krúng**	บางครั้ง
soi, lane	**soy**	ซอย
son	**lôok chai**	ลูกชาย
sound (n)	**sěe-ung**	เสียง

speak	**pôot**	พูด
spell	**sa-gòt**	สะกด
spend	**sěe-a**	เสีย
spicy	**pèt**	เผ็ด
spray (v)	**chèet**	ฉีด
stamp	**sa-dtáirm**	แสตมป์
stay	**púk**	พัก
still	**yung**	ยัง
stir fried	**pùt**	ผัด
stop (v)	**yÒOt**	หยุด
stressed, tense	**krêe-ut**	เครียด
stuck	**dtìt**	ติด
student	**núk sèuk-săh**	นักศึกษา
study (v)	**ree-un**	เรียน
style	**bàirp**	แบบ
Sunday	**wun ah-tít**	วันอาทิตย์
surname	**nahm sa-gOOn**	นามสกุล
sweet (adj)	**wăhn**	หวาน
sweet (n) (dessert)	**kŏrng wăhn**	ของหวาน
take	**ao . . . bpai**	เอา . . . ไป
take off (clothes)	**tòrt**	ถอด
tape (cassette)	**táyp**	เทป
taste (v) (something)	**chim**	ชิม
tasty	**a-ròy**	อร่อย
teach	**sŏrn**	สอน
teacher	**kroo; ah-jahn**	ครู; อาจารย์
telephone (v)	**toh**	โทร

telephone (n)	**toh-ra-sùp**	โทรศัพท์
telephone (mobile)	**toh-ra-sùp meu tĕu**	โทรศัพท์มือถือ
telephone line	**săi**	สาย
textbook	**dtum-rah**	ตำรา
Thai	**tai**	ไทย
Thailand	**meu-ung tai**	เมืองไทย
thank you	**kòrp-kOOn**	ขอบคุณ
they	**káo**	เขา
thing	**kŏrng**	ของ
think	**kít**	คิด
this	**nêe**	นี่
ticket	**dtŏo-a**	ตั๋ว
time	**way-lah; tee**	เวลา; ที
time(s)	**krúng**	ครั้ง
today	**wun née**	วันนี้
toilet	**hôrng náhm**	ห้องน้ำ
tomorrow	**prÔOng née**	พรุ่งนี้
too, also	**dôo-ay**	ด้วย
too . . .	**. . . (gern) bpai**	. . . (เกิน)ไป
tour	**too-a**	ทัวร์
traffic jam	**rót dtìt**	รถติด
train	**rót fai**	รถไฟ
translate	**bplair**	แปล
travel (v)	**dern tahng**	เดินทาง
tree	**dtôn-mái**	ต้นไม้
true, truly	**jing**	จริง
try out	**lorng**	ลอง
turn	**lée-o**	เลี้ยว

understand	kâo jai; róo rêu-ung	เข้าใจ; รู้เรื่อง
university	ma-hăh-wít-tá-yah-lai	มหาวิทยาลัย
until	jon tĕung	จนถึง
up country	dtàhng jung-wùt	ต่างจังหวัด
upstairs	kûng bon	ข้างบน
use (v)	chái	ใช้
very	mâhk	มาก
visit (v)	têe-o	เที่ยว
wait	ror; koy	รอ; คอย
wake up (oneself)	dtèun	ตื่น
walk (v)	dern	เดิน
want (something)	ao	เอา
want to	yàhk (ja)	อยาก(จะ)
wash (clothes)	súk	ซัก
wash (dishes)	láhng	ล้าง
waste (v)	sĕe-a	เสีย
water	náhm	น้ำ
water melon	tairng moh	แตงโม
weather, climate	ah-gàht	อากาศ
week	ah-tít	อาทิตย์
weekend	wun săo wun ah-tít	วันเสาร์วันอาทิตย์
well (be well)	sa-bai	สบาย
well . . . (hesitation)	gôr . . .	ก็ . . .
westerner	fa-rùng	ฝรั่ง
what?	a-rai	อะไร
when?	mêu-rài	เมื่อไร
when	mêu-a	เมื่อ

where?	**têe-năi**	ที่ไหน
white	**sěe kăo**	สีขาว
who?	**krai**	ใคร
why?	**tum-mai**	ทำไม
wide	**gwâhng**	กว้าง
with	**gùp**	กับ
wood	**mái**	ไม้
word	**kum**	คำ
work (n)	**ngahn**	งาน
work (v)	**tum ngahn**	ทำงาน
write	**kěe-un**	เขียน
wrong	**pìt**	ผิด
yellow	**sěe lěu-ung**	สีเหลือง
... yet (or not)?	**... láir-o (réu yung)?**	... แล้ว(หรือยัง)
you	**kOOn; tûn**	คุณ; ท่าน
zero	**sŏon**	ศูนย์

grammar index

Numbers in brackets refer to the unit in which each grammar point is first covered.